BATTLING WALL STREET

BATTLING WALL STREET

The Kennedy Presidency

Donald Gibson

Sheridan Square Press

New York

Copyright © 1994 by Donald Gibson

LIBRARY OF CONGRESS CATALOGING-IN-PUBLICATION DATA

Gibson, Donald, 1945-
    Battling Wall Street : The Kennedy presidency / Donald Gibson
        p. cm.
    Includes bibliographical references and index.
    ISBN 1-879823-09-8 (hc.) : $24.95 -- ISBN 1-879823-10-1 (pbk.) :
$16.95
    1. United States--Economic policy--1961-1971. 2. United States--
Economic policy--1971-1981. United States--Economic
policy--1981- 4. Wall Street. I. Title.
    HC106.6G53 1994
    338.973--dc20   94-23305
                                                           CIP

HC
106.6
653
1994

Published in the United States by
Sheridan Square Press, Inc.
145 West 4th Street
New York, NY 10012

Distributed to the trade by
National Book Network
4720-A Boston Way
Lanham, MD 20706

10 9 8 7 6 5 4 3 2 1

Dedication

John Kennedy once offered the following meaning of the word "courage": "A man does what he must—in spite of personal consequences, in spite of obstacles and dangers and pressures—and that is the basis of all human morality." This book is dedicated to everyone who tries to live in this way.

Acknowledgments

In 1992 I had two chapters of this book completed, and I had finished the research for all but one of the other chapters. I began looking for a publisher by making up a very short list of publishers who had recently produced books that challenged the power structure and displayed an independent commitment to the truth. Sheridan Square Press was on that short list, and I was very happy when I heard from them.

Over the next year, I worked with Sheridan's editors to complete the initial draft of this book. On the rare occasions when disagreements arose, they were always willing to consider the facts and my reasoning; no writer can ask for more than that. The initial editing was done by Ellen Ray, who improved the book but never altered its meaning. She also boosted my morale with her generous and encouraging comments. The final editing and preparation of the book was handled by William Schaap. Always reasonable and considerate, Bill brought the book to completion while dealing patiently with my impatience.

Three people were extremely important to me in writing this book. Their contributions were personal and intellectual. In different ways, all three quickly appreciated what this book meant in terms of the significance of John Kennedy's short time as President of the United States. I am deeply indebted to my wife Peg Gibson and to Robert Burtt and Ed Mulready.

The initial typing of the manuscript was done by Cathy Schmidt. Cathy was kind, patient, and extremely competent. She also helped in overcoming a variety of computer problems.

Numerous other people made direct or indirect contributions to the completion of this book. I want to thank Dr. Cyril Wecht for early interest and encouragement. I also want to thank the following people: Ellen Davidson, Kerry Manning, Margie Vinkler, and Blanche and Malvern Thomas.

Finally, I have relied in several chapters on massive amounts of work done by other people. These debts are acknowledged in footnotes and references.

Contents

INTRODUCTION

Finding Kennedy

There are too many John F. Kennedys. There is the aimless Kennedy and the ambitious Kennedy. There is Kennedy the liberal and Kennedy the conservative. There is Kennedy the hawk and Kennedy the dove. There is the Kennedy who was a friend and servant of the East Coast big business interests and the Kennedy who was anathema to the power brokers.

There are other images, some of which are closer to the truth than others. Though the complete truth about any person is unattainable, that does not mean that there is no real persona to be understood, nor does it mean that all opinions are equal. In the attempt to understand anything, a man, a president, an economic crisis, it is possible to move from a state of ignorance to a state of partial, even substantial, knowledge. In the process, total truth may remain forever elusive, but one can get closer to it.

The various judgments about John F. Kennedy cannot all be accurate unless he was a political chameleon who would make even the most flexible of lizards green with envy. John Kennedy's political colors did not shift and change. As president, and before, he had a very definite and coherent set of goals and a consistent overall strategy to achieve them. He was a practical politician and leader. In the pursuit of his objectives, he was aware of what was immediately possible and what was necessary. If compromise was unavoidable, he took what he could get. We shall see, however, that he was frequently willing to confront or circumvent forces that other political leaders would rarely challenge. It is by examining Kennedy's basic goals and the most important actions taken to achieve them that we will get closer to the truth about him and his time as president. This will prove to be simpler than one might think, because not only

1

was Kennedy clear and consistent, but he also ran into an opposition that publicly and emphatically rejected his methods and purposes. His actions and the reaction to him not only fit together as pieces of a puzzle, but, as with a puzzle, the proper arrangement of pieces yields a coherent picture. The end result will be an image that is closer to the truth, an image that will show that many of the existing ideas about Kennedy are wrong.

The Various Images of John Kennedy

John Kennedy has often been portrayed as a rather empty man, someone without deeply held values who was driven by ambition to seek high office. Lewis J. Paper suggests[1] that Kennedy had little in the way of long-term goals, plans, or strategies. Paper claims that Kennedy had no "structured view of the world" and no commitment to any particular "philosophy or creed of government." In Paper's view, his only developed concerns were with helping the poor and winning a crusade against communism. In general, Paper says, Kennedy was reluctant to involve himself too deeply in domestic affairs.[2]

In a conclusion that flows from an analysis of JFK's father, Joseph Kennedy, Richard J. Whalen says:[3]

> Like his father, he [JFK] was intent on the pursuit of power, and left it to the intellectuals to rationalize his deeds. He was in politics, not to advance an ideology, but to derive personal satisfaction. His politics was as self-centered as his father's fortune-building; the one was the natural successor to the other.

This picture of Kennedy as nothing more than a narcissistic power seeker is offered in a softer version by Chester Bowles, who served in the Kennedy administration and did have some good things to say about Kennedy. Bowles says[4] that Kennedy had no basic moral reference point and that seeking the presidency was essentially a matter of personal achievement.

In a recent restatement of some of the same views, Robert M. Solow and James Tobin say[5] that Kennedy entered the White House with no defined economic program and no organized views on the economy. According to them, Kennedy didn't even have a particularly good understanding of economic issues. Others have portrayed Kennedy not so much as someone without a policy agenda, but as someone who had extremely modest goals matched by extreme caution in the pursuit of those goals.

Hobart Rowen, in a stream of broad generalizations, presents Kennedy as a young version of Eisenhower. Rowen describes Kennedy as conservative, middle-of-the-road, traditional, and conventional. While loosely associating Kennedy with liberal economic policy, he also says the essence of Kennedy's policy was free-market economics. Rowen's Kennedy is cautious, if not downright timid.[6] Similarly, Herbert S. Parmet[7] characterizes Kennedy as cautious and hesitant, a president whose policies were only slightly different from those of the Eisenhower administration. He was, says Parmet, a fiscal conservative.

Others have also emphasized Kennedy's commitment to free-market or free-enterprise economics. In the context of a discussion of the Kennedy administration's willingness to run deficits in the federal budget, Hugh Sidey says[8] the following:

> Reduced to its simplest terms, the Kennedy plan was to unleash the economy by removing burdensome taxes and letting the fresh money flow into industry for plant modernization and into consumer hands for spending on new products. If the economy responded to the transfusion properly, it would mean such boom times that tax collections would swell and erase the temporary deficits.

. This is an image of a president who gets more money into people's pockets, but otherwise sits idly by hoping for a good result. This particular image might be quite accurate if the president's name were Ronald Reagan. But, as we will see, Kennedy was not nearly so passive.

In addition to the descriptions of Kennedy as a fairly passive president without well defined or deeply held values, there are images of him as someone who avoided any conflicts with powerful interests or as a president who was simply a servant of such interests. Paper[9] says that Kennedy was very reluctant to do anything that offended important groups and that he put off decisions that produced conflict.

Bruce Miroff[10] points to economic growth as Kennedy's primary goal, but argues that this made Kennedy extremely sensitive to and responsive to big business. Summarizing Kennedy's overall performance, Miroff says:[11]

> Kennedy's presidential record cannot, in sum, sustain his reputation as a progressive. Behind the image of the popular hero lies the reality of service to established power and established values.

This idea that Kennedy was essentially a servant of established power is also asserted by Jim F. Heath. Within the nation's overall business community, according to Heath,[12] Kennedy was appreciated most by its "eastern establishment wing." Heath went on to say that even though Kennedy was to the left of the average businessman, he never ventured "far from easy hailing distance of the business leaders whose help he needed most—the influential titans of the major corporations." A somewhat similar image is presented by James N. Giglio,[13] who finds President Kennedy's alleged sexual adventures to be more impressive than his leadership, which he describes as cautious and very supportive of corporate interests.

From these accounts we get the Kennedy who was ambitious, self-centered, and without basic principles. He is a man with limited understanding of economic issues, generally conservative, and either timid and unwilling to challenge powerful interests or a virtual servant of such interests. These are images of Kennedy. But, as is the case with many words in our language, the word "image" can mean either of two very different things. One meaning of the word image is "exact likeness." Another is "illusory form," a deception, an apparition. It will be shown that these are of the second type, that they are based on either very biased or very incomplete readings of the record.

Not all of the images that have been constructed of Kennedy are so wrong; some in fact do lead in the right direction and will serve as departure points for a new and extended understanding of President Kennedy and of the forces with which he struggled. Some accounts point to Kennedy's deeply progressive commitments. Others avoid the negative and wildly incorrect descriptions noted above, but give us a kind of wishy-washy notion of Kennedy which calls forth a shrug of the shoulders instead of the intense interest which his actions and efforts actually demand.

The most dominant and frequently repeated image of a wishy-washy Kennedy is that of a liberal or moderate president who at some point adopted what is called a Keynesian approach to government economic policy. In general, this means a fairly limited attempt to use government powers to create money and credit and government spending to affect overall demand in the economy. Keynesian policy would not typically include any other significant interventions in the economy and, in the view of many Keynesians, even the government's power to affect spending, or demand, should only be used to stop or reverse an ongoing recession. Kennedy has often been described as a Keynesian, sometimes a reluctant or hesitant Keynesian.[14]

We will see that Kennedy was quite willing to adopt policies that are correctly called Keynesian. We will also see that the term Keynesian is too limiting to describe accurately Kennedy's program. One of the feeblest images of Kennedy and his economic policies is presented in the supposedly authoritative account by Arthur Schlesinger, Jr. In *A Thousand Days* Schlesinger frequently describes Kennedy as a Keynesian, but at one point he recognizes two additional aspects of Kennedy's approach. He says that Kennedy was interested in raising the minimum wage, creating programs to retrain workers, and finding ways to deal with regional economic difficulties, all of which are in the economist's category of structural problems. The other factor shaping Kennedy's policies, according to Schlesinger, was the influence of his father's "deep mistrust of those who sought to tamper" with the economic system.[15]

Schlesinger's account leads to a conclusion that Kennedy was a free-market Keynesian looking for government solutions for a few specific problems. Actually, Schlesinger adds some confusion to this portrayal of Kennedy by mentioning[16] Kennedy's interest in economic planning and by indicating that Kennedy was looking for an overall strategy to generate growth and opportunity. Indeed, Kennedy was developing that strategy and attempting to implement it throughout his time in office. This attempt was the source of an increasingly intense disagreement over policy between Kennedy and a network of important private interests. Schlesinger does refer[17] to a mistrust between Kennedy and Establishment interests based in the New York financial community. He claims, however, that this disappeared as Kennedy and the Establishment embraced each other in order to further the national interests. This is not true; not only did they not embrace each other, but in fact the Establishment's rejection of Kennedy became increasingly intense during his time in office.

Schlesinger ends up creating a fundamentally misleading image of Kennedy and of Kennedy's opposition. He does that by overlooking much of JFK's domestic policy, by downplaying the severity of the conflicts over Kennedy's domestic and international policies, and by completely ignoring the attacks on Kennedy, which were public and extreme. This allows Schlesinger to suggest[18] that Kennedy could be described accurately as a Tory Democrat, as an aristocrat concerned with "commoners" but committed to preserving the status quo. Kennedy was interested in improving the conditions of life, but his interest was not of the type expressed in ceremonial settings by members of the British royal family and aristocracy. Kennedy was committed to economic, political, and social progress, not to preservation of the status quo.*

Schlesinger's account, while not consistent, generally gives us a Kennedy who is, in domestic affairs, a rather mild-mannered Keynesian, reluctant to disrupt the established order. This view is not that different from the more explicitly negative images reviewed above, although unlike some of those accounts, Schlesinger's does acknowledge Kennedy's insight in economic matters.[19] He doesn't go far enough, however. As was noted earlier, Kennedy has been portrayed as a person with little understanding of economic policy, with no real defined commitments, and even with little interest in this area. There is another Kennedy.

Theodore C. Sorensen quotes economist Seymour Harris's assessment of Kennedy in 1962:[20]

> His major responsibility is our security. What astonishes me is how much time the President nevertheless devotes to economic problems, how interested he is in them and how much he has learned in the last two years. He is now by far the most knowledgeable President of all time in the general area of economics.

Sorensen adds that "Kennedy, long after graduating from Harvard, had learned far more economics than most men in either public or academic life."

Senator Paul Douglas of Illinois had been a professor of economics at the University of Chicago, president of the American Economic Association, and chairman of Congress's Joint Economic Committee. He was viewed by many as the nation's top labor economist. Douglas said that in 1960, even before Kennedy reportedly learned so much, he posed very profound questions to him about monetary and banking policy.[21]

---

* Kenneth P. O'Donnell and David F. Powers indicate that Kennedy did not view Schlesinger as a trustworthy recorder of events (O'Donnell and Powers, pp. 314-15 [references in the footnotes are all to works cited in the bibliography; see the note preceding the endnotes]).

Is this the same man who had little knowledge of and little interest in economic policy? What of the president without convictions or purposes? Was the idea of getting the country moving again, which became a constant theme in the 1960 campaign,[22] merely an election gimmick? Walter W. Heller described President Kennedy as deeply committed to higher rates of economic growth.[23] According to O'Donnell and Powers,[24] Kennedy and Heller went against prevailing economic doctrine with the definite purpose of increasing the nation's productive powers. According to Sorensen,[25] Kennedy was deeply committed to basic goals and showed "unusual determination" in his efforts to achieve those goals. His convictions, says Sorensen, were the results of "his own reasoning and learning."

The economic program was not simply or even primarily the kind of passive, free-market policy attributed to Kennedy. It was also something more than even an aggressive Keynesian program of government spending. This is suggested by Sorensen's brief summary[26] of some of the Kennedy administration economic initiatives. That summary, although pointing in the right direction, is far from complete, and Sorensen never deals with the intense reaction that greeted Kennedy's policies. The same is true of Heller's account[27] of Kennedy's economic policy. While it is informative and much closer to the truth than the stories told by Paper, Parmet, Rowen, and Sidey, Heller's account is less than the whole story and misses entirely the political conflict surrounding Kennedy's actions, as well as the ways in which Kennedy's economic policies were related to other major issues of the time.

The accounts of Kennedy's purposes and actions presented by O'Donnell and Powers, Sorensen, and Heller are useful, but only partial, rebuttals to what is an impressive quantity of nonsense about Kennedy. Kennedy's convictions and commitments were still not sufficiently explained, the relationship between his domestic and foreign policy still not adequately described. If JFK did pursue some new policies and did so with great determination, surely he encountered more serious opposition than the Southern congressmen and the American Medical Association mentioned by Paper,[28] or the assortment of rightwing extremists identified by Schlesinger.[29] In short, there is a lot more that needs to be explored.

JFK and U.S. Steel

There is one conflict in which Kennedy became enmeshed that has been given fairly extensive analysis. It did involve opponents more formidable than doctors worried about loss of autonomy or status, or small-town conservatives who feared all big government as a direct threat to freedom. That conflict involved Kennedy's brief but intense confrontation with U.S. Steel in 1962.

This encounter has been treated as the only, or the last, or the most significant conflict between Kennedy and America's entrenched economic powers. It was none of these. Instead, it was just one of many instances in which President Kennedy clashed with the core of the U.S. Establishment. In the discussion that follows, this event will serve as a departure point for a bigger and more important story.

ONE

The Steel Crisis as a Telltale Event

The April 1962 face-off between President Kennedy and U.S. Steel has been described as "the most dramatic confrontation in history between a President and a corporate management."[1] This and other similar descriptions[2] reflect the significance of this confrontation accurately, but various interpretations of this conflict either contain inconsistencies or generate conclusions at odds with acknowledged facts. Also, something more was involved than the management of one corporation or even a group of corporations. President Kennedy was forced into a confrontation with a segment of the U.S. economic establishment that was far more influential than merely a group of big business executives.

Part of Kennedy's overall economic strategy was to prevent or limit price increases that would have a negative impact on the whole economy. Steel was one of those items which played an important role in the cost and price of a wide variety of other products. When JFK took office in 1961, steel prices had been stable for a couple of years, but in the view of some experts rising steel prices had been the largest contributor to industrial price increases between 1947 and 1958.[3] Because steel was so important to the economy as a whole, Kennedy decided to involve himself and his administration in an effort to help the steel companies and the union arrive at an agreement that would maintain the very recent price stability in steel.

President Kennedy also wanted the U.S. steel industry to be efficient and successful, so while he was asking for their cooperation in holding prices down, he was attempting to help the companies in three ways. First, the discussions with the steel union were aimed at getting a very modest agreement that would keep labor costs from pushing prices up. Second, the president was recommending measures to Congress that would promise tens of millions of dollars of additional capital to the steel industry.[4] Third, Kennedy's overall economic plan was intended to stimulate growth in the economy generally, and this would particularly benefit the steel industry, which at that time was operating at only 65 percent of capacity.* In addition, Kennedy said he was willing to consider any other option that would help the companies and keep prices stable.[5]

The president, Secretary of Labor Arthur Goldberg, and others in the administration participated in three-party negotiations lasting about one year, in order to produce a settlement between labor and the steel companies that preserved price stability. This work seemingly paid off when an agreement was reached on March 31, 1962, and new contracts were signed by U.S. Steel and Bethlehem Steel on April 6, followed by other companies in the next few days. The union had agreed to take much less than it wanted and less than had been achieved in most settlements since World War II. The workers received no general increase in wages and received a 2.5 percent benefits increase, a cost for the companies that was, in the view of the Kennedy administration, offset by rising productivity in the industry.[6]

President Kennedy congratulated both the union and the steel companies on March 31 for reaching an agreement that preserved existing prices. He, Goldberg, and Secretary of Commerce Luther Hodges, as well as union leaders, were absolutely certain that everyone involved in the negotiations understood fully that the year-long effort was aimed at producing this kind of agreement so that prices in steel would not have to be increased.[7]

President Kennedy was surprised to learn on April 10, four days after U.S. Steel signed the new labor contract, that the Chairman of U.S. Steel, Roger Blough, was coming to Washington and wanted to talk. Blough was given an appointment, and at about 5:45 he handed the president a memo that informed him that U.S. Steel was going to announce a general 3.5 percent price increase, effective at midnight. This information was being provided to the media and would become public within about thirty minutes of the meeting.[8]

Kennedy was outraged. At any time during the many months leading up to the settlement, Blough could have notified him that U.S. Steel would not or could not conform to the president's goals. Instead, he and the board of U.S. Steel waited until an agreement was reached and then perfunctorily informed Kennedy that U.S. Steel was not going to live up to its part of the deal. Kennedy was acutely aware that if he allowed this to happen, his capacity to achieve anything in domestic and international policy would be seriously undermined, if not destroyed. He must have recognized this almost immediately, because within 24 hours his public statements showed such a perception, and he was mobilizing all available resources in order to force the executives of U.S. Steel and the companies following its lead to change their minds.

---

* As things turned out, growth and rising demand would lead to an increase in steel output from 98 million tons in 1962 to 127 million tons in 1964.

Within one day Kennedy set in motion a series of actions intended to raise the political and economic costs to U.S. Steel and to those companies that had followed it (including Bethlehem Steel, Republic, Jones & Laughlin, and Youngstown Sheet and Tube) and to deter remaining companies from joining in. Investigations into the issue of collusion and price fixing were begun by the Federal Trade Commission and by Robert Kennedy's Justice Department. The Defense Department was instructed to review quickly its purchasing practices and to let it be known that the government would favor companies that did not join with U.S. Steel.*[9] Kennedy also delivered a blistering attack on the steel companies in his news conference on April 11. On April 12, Attorney General Robert Kennedy announced that he had started a grand jury probe into the price-setting actions and that subpoenas were being issued for documents held by U.S. Steel.[10]

On the same day, April 12, the board of Inland Steel, one of the smaller but still significant companies,** announced that it would not raise its prices. Apparently this action prompted Bethlehem Steel, which competed directly with Inland, to announce on the following day that it was rescinding its price increase. U.S. Steel then announced that it too was withdrawing its price increase, and at that point, the afternoon of April 13, the three-day confrontation was over, and Kennedy had avoided a huge defeat.[11]

Joseph Block, Chairman of Inland Steel, reportedly made the decision not to go along with U.S. Steel and the others because of the actions taken by Kennedy.***[12] Kennedy's statements in the news conferences held the day after the announced price increase, April 11, and on the first Wednesday after U.S. Steel capitulated, April 18, provide his viewpoint on what happened and why. The facts support Kennedy's assessment of the events, but he left unsaid some things that still need to be clarified.

---

* It appears that Douglas Dillon, secretary of the treasury, suggested that Kennedy consider withdrawing a proposal for an investment tax credit that would benefit business, including the steel companies, if they invested in new plants and equipment. There are indications that U.S. Steel may have wanted to kill this proposal, or, at least, was willing to sacrifice its possible benefits in order to undermine Kennedy's overall program. Kennedy rejected Dillon's suggestion. (Belair; Sorensen, p. 511.)

** According to an April 15 *New York Times* report, Inland Steel represented only 5.3 percent of total production in 1961. Bethlehem Steel accounted for 14.9 percent of the total and U.S. Steel, not as dominant as it once had been, produced 25.2 percent of the total. Kaiser Steel, even smaller than Inland, also contributed to the outcome by refusing to go along with the increase.

*** In his account, McConnell (1963, pp. 94, 105, 114-15) refers to Block's explanation and then ignores it in favor of an arbitrary conclusion that it was market forces and competition that explain the events. Kennedy's judgment that both government action and market forces played a role fits with the known facts and with Block's explanation. Competition was cited during and after the events as a relevant factor, but its alleged role changed with the commentator and timing of the remarks. For example, some explained the price increase as a response to competition in that more money was needed for investments in more competitive facilities. Others said that the same competition was a cause of the companies' failure to sustain higher prices. (McConnell, 1963, p. 106; Pomfret, p. 19; Sorensen, p. 503.) Blair (1972, p. 637) concludes that Kennedy's actions were a major factor in the steel companies' decisions to back away from the price increase.

It was Kennedy's view that the steel companies had engaged in an illegal activity, that their action was not economically justifiable, that they were reneging on an implicit but very definite commitment, and that their action threatened the success of his whole economic program and was in conflict with the nation's interests.

Most of these issues were raised by Kennedy in the April 11 news conference, the day after Blough's surprise visit to the White House.[13] He pointed to obvious indications of price fixing, noting

> the suddenness by which every company in the last few hours, one by one, as the morning went by came in with their almost identical, if not identical, price increases, which isn't really the way we expect the competitive private enterprise system to always work.

He then referred to the particular method being used by the companies by describing the rapid announcements from the companies as a "parade." He was referring to what is known as "price leadership," whereby the need for repeated meetings or communications is avoided by having one company serve as price leader. U.S. Steel was apparently playing that role.

He then pointed to the fact that the companies involved had very different economic situations, *i.e.*, since their market and profit situations differed, it was not to every company's advantage to join in the price setting.

The price increase itself, even if not an illegally orchestrated one, was, in Kennedy's view, unjustifiable. He pointed out that

> Steel output per man is rising so fast that labor costs per ton of steel can actually be expected to decline in the next twelve months. And, in fact, the Acting Commissioner of the Bureau of Labor Statistics informed me this morning that, and I quote, "employment costs per unit of steel output in 1961 were essentially the same as they were in 1958." The cost of major raw materials—steel scrap and coal—has also been declining.

He also said that steel profits in the first quarter of 1962 had been among the best in history, and that expectations for the coming year were for higher profits as demand increased. Kennedy noted that the steel industry had paid out over $600 million in dividends in each of the preceding five years.*

President Kennedy viewed the company actions as unjustifiable and probably illegal; he also viewed U.S. Steel's behavior on the prior day as a stunning violation of the trust that had been the foundation for the negotiations of the past year. Kennedy pointed out that in every discussion he or his secretary of labor

---

* Even an observer as sympathetic to business as Grant McConnell (1963, pp. 16, 30-31) thought the steel companies were doing fairly well given that they were operating at 65 percent capacity. Kennedy, as noted earlier, was offering legislation that would help industry and was taking actions which would raise the demand for steel, hence increasing their profits.

had had with the steel companies, it was emphasized that the whole purpose of the effort and the reason for labor's concessions was to achieve continued price stability.* Kennedy pointed out that "at no time did anyone suggest that if such an agreement was gained that it would be still necessary to put up prices. That word did not come until last night."

As Kennedy indicated, there had been a multitude of opportunities for U.S. Steel or other companies to advise the president they would need to raise prices. Blough's ability to call the White House and get an appointment with the president on the same day was an example of how accessible to them he was, and how easy it would have been for them to warn or caution Kennedy about the outcome of this serious administration effort.

According to McConnell,[14] the decision to raise prices was made by U.S. Steel weeks before Kennedy was told. That meant the company executives also waited for the new labor agreement to be announced and for Kennedy to be given credit for his involvement before they notified him. It is not surprising, then, that Kennedy emphasized his surprise, saying that U.S. Steel's decision "came to me after the decision [labor settlement] was made. There was no prior consultation or information given to the Administration."

Kennedy accused the steel companies of damaging the nation, a charge he believed to be true and that he used as one of his weapons against the companies. Summing up several of his criticisms, he said that the "simultaneous and identical actions of United States Steel and other leading steel corporations increasing steel prices by some $6 a ton constitute a wholly unjustifiable and irresponsible defiance of the public interest."

President Kennedy pointed to the effect of steel prices on the cost of consumer goods, machinery for businesses and farms, and items purchased for the national defense. He said he found it hard to accept, and the American people would find it hard to accept, "a situation in which a tiny handful of steel executives whose pursuit of private power and profit exceeds their sense of public responsibility, can show such utter contempt for the interest of 185,000,000 Americans."**

* On September 6, 1961, about seven months before the confrontation, Kennedy had written to the heads of the steel companies about the need to avoid a "price-wage spiral in steel." In his letter to Roger Blough he reviewed the recent history of steel prices, listed some facts showing that the steel industry's profit picture was good, and pointed to the negative consequences of any new price increases. Kennedy requested that prices be kept stable for the rest of 1961, saying, "It would clearly then be the turn of the labor representatives to limit wage demands to a level consistent with continued price stability." In the 1962 settlement, labor had, in Kennedy's view, limited its demands, and he, of course, expected the continued price stability. Kennedy concluded his letter saying, "I am sure that the owners and managers of our nation's major steel companies share my conviction that the clear call of national interest must be heeded." A copy of this letter was provided by the Kennedy Library in Boston. The author also requested a copy of Roger Blough's response to Kennedy; I was informed that Blough's letter could not be located. It is clear from Kennedy's letter and the subsequent events that Blough must have known that U.S. Steel's price increase would be viewed by Kennedy as a strategic challenge.

** Quoting this statement, *Fortune* magazine (1962a, p. 97) accused Kennedy of being "immoderate" and using "the rhetoric of the Garrison State." *Time-Life-Fortune* were, along with the *Wall Street Journal*, among the few publications to support U.S. Steel. As we shall see later, *Time* was hardly a

He also said that "the last twenty-four hours indicates that those with great power are not always concerned about the national interests."

Kennedy noted that price and wage decisions in the U.S. are and should be generally "freely and privately" arrived at, but "the American people have a right to expect in return for that freedom, a higher sense of business responsibility for the welfare of their country than has been shown in the last two days."

The president did believe that he had a responsibility for promoting the general welfare of the nation. Also, this was but one of many instances in which his commitment to that responsibility brought him into conflict with "those with great power."

In his next news conference, one week later and four days after U.S. Steel withdrew the price increase, Kennedy[15] made some conciliatory remarks* and indicated what he thought had been at stake in this confrontation. His comments were in response to one of the questions put to him.

Q: Mr. President, there has been considerable speculation that the victory you have won in the steel situation will be of great assistance for the passage of your legislative program in Congress. Would you care to comment on that, sir?

Kennedy: Well, I hope it's of assistance in passing the tax credit** which is intended to provide, combined with price stability, a means for our industry to modernize itself, and in fact to encourage it. I hope—in my opinion if the rise in prices had been permitted to stand it would have been extremely difficult to secure the passage of this legislation.

I think that the line that has been held provides a much better atmosphere, and I think that if this legislation is passed, it will materially help the steel companies and industry in general. And I'm very strongly in support of it.

As far as the rest of the program, I think that that part of the program which is involved with economy, I think will be helped by the fact that we've been able to maintain at this time a stable price level.

---

disinterested observer, as it was indirectly tied to U.S. Steel through numerous connections to Morgan banking interests.

* These remarks and Kennedy's decision to end some of the initiatives against the steel industry did not mean, as is implied by Schlesinger (p. 639), that the conflict was over. About 18 months later, October of 1963, new actions were initiated against U.S. Steel and other steel companies by Robert Kennedy's Justice Department. Based in part on information gathered during the grand jury investigation begun during the earlier confrontation, the Justice Department was again pursuing the issue of price fixing. *Business Week* (1963) observed that this investigation must have had at least "a tacit go-ahead" from the president. About one year after the 1962 confrontation Kennedy was giving a speech in the same hotel in which Eisenhower was receiving the steel industry's public service award. Kennedy joked to the audience that he had been the steel industry's "man of the year last year. They wanted to come down to the White House to give me their award, but the Secret Service wouldn't let them do it" (O'Donnell and Powers, p. 472).

** The tax credit to which Kennedy is referring would allow corporations to deduct from their tax obligations a percentage of the cost of investments in new plant and equipment. See Chapter Two.

Kennedy was pointing out that if he had been defeated in this confrontation, his entire economic program would have been jeopardized. This raises an important question. Was the defeat of Kennedy's overall economic program the real purpose of U.S. Steel's actions? Kennedy was probably the first person to imply such a possibility; he wasn't the last.

The larger significance of these events was raised at that time and later by media commentators and analysts, as well as by members of Kennedy's administration. In some cases, observers suggested that leaders of U.S. Steel in particular had grand strategic objectives in mind when they challenged the president.

Analyzing the events a few years later, Theodore Sorensen drew on his experience as an aide to Kennedy. He quoted Kennedy[16] as having said that if he "had failed to get a rescission, that would have been an awful setback to the office of the Presidency." Sorensen went on to say[17] that Kennedy had prevented "a serious blow to his program, his prestige and his office." He then noted that some in the steel industry may have wanted to show Kennedy who was boss, but he concluded[18] that the conflict was essentially the result of thoughtlessness and shortsightedness, and not part of a more basic political division.* By attributing U.S. Steel's and the other companies' actions to a narrow profit motive and to blundering, Sorensen was in effect saying that there was not any broader significance to this conflict. Arthur Schlesinger came to the same conclusion,[19] explaining the behavior of Blough and U.S. Steel as merely a result of their belief that government had no legitimate role in price decisions.

Many people noted specific results of Kennedy's victory and directly or indirectly suggested what the cost of a defeat would have been. For example, Labor Secretary Goldberg said that Kennedy's victory would allow union leaders to cooperate with the administration in keeping prices down.[20] Sen. Hubert Humphrey remarked that Kennedy's victory saved his investment tax credit proposal. On a more general level the *New York Times* observed that "Steel's surrender to President Kennedy appeared today to have bolstered the Administration's stock in and out of Congress."[21] By implication, a defeat of Kennedy might have caused the administration's stock to plunge.

Fortune magazine went so far as to suggest that U.S. Steel Chairman Roger Blough was acting on behalf of other businessmen in a calculated effort to undermine Kennedy's attempt to create cooperation between government and business. *Fortune* observed:[22]

There is a theory—unsupported by any direct evidence—that Blough was acting as "business statesman" rather than as a businessman judging his market. According to this theory, Kennedy's letter of last September 6 poised over the industry a threat of

* Sorensen (pp. 519-20) mentions that in the summer of 1962 there was strong criticism of Kennedy from some business executives, even accusations that Kennedy opposed free enterprise and favored socialism. But his comments fail to point out that such attacks were not restricted to the summer of 1962, that the source of the attacks was more significant and organized than just many "executives," and that the attacks on Kennedy were related to a wide range of issues and to his entire economic program.

"jawbone control" of prices. For the sake of his company, the industry, and the nation, Blough sought a way to break through the bland "harmony" that has recently prevailed between government and business.

This theory could account for the otherwise inexplicable timing and manner of U.S. Steel's announcement. If Blough wanted to create the greatest possible uproar and provoke maximum presidential reaction, his procedure was beautifully calculated.*

This explanation suggests that Kennedy was being put in a no-win situation. He could be humiliated by a successful move to raise prices or he could retaliate and lose the cooperation of business. Kennedy, if he viewed it this way, decided that humiliation would be the bigger loss.

Grant McConnell picked up on *Fortune*'s comments and suggested[23] that this was a "political struggle" in which U.S. Steel's actions were "designed to alienate the President from labor and to curtail the President's power to act with effectiveness in economic affairs." Although McConnell described U.S. Steel's behavior as "mysterious" and at times was baffled by the motives of U.S. Steel, he essentially portrayed this as a conflict instigated by the manufacturing giant to destroy Kennedy's effectiveness.

About U.S. Steel's methods McConnell said:[24]

> ...the timing and manner of the price increase gave it the quality of an affront to the presidency. Whatever the intentions had been on either side, this was a challenge which could only diminish the dignity and influence of the office if it remained unmet.**

Adding some mystery to this story, he made this additional observation:[25]

> To accept [U.S. Steel's] action, then, would vastly increase the determination of everyone in conflict with the administration in any way and would harden all opposition. Acceptance would have had the result of forcing the administration to abandon any hope of dealing actively with economic issues, which was, of course, one of the chief desires of many business leaders.

Why would business leaders want to destroy Kennedy's ability to deal with economic issues? What "business leaders"?

The steel crisis has often been viewed as essentially an isolated event or, at most, as an important conflict reflecting normal tension between a Democratic president and "business." But it is only a departure point for a bigger story. It

---

* *Fortune* (1962a) chose to title their editorial "Steel: The Ides of April." What they intended by this play on the famous warning from Shakespeare's *Julius Caesar* is not clear.

** Writing several years later on the general topic of the presidency, McConnell (1967, p. 72) said that Kennedy had by his reactions to the price increase "subjected his office, and the country, to grave peril." It is clear in all accounts, including McConnell's, that President Kennedy was placed in this difficult situation by U.S. Steel's leaders and it was they who were subjecting Kennedy and the country to peril.

was only one event in an ongoing struggle over the country's direction, both at home and abroad. When Blough delivered his challenge to Kennedy on April 10, 1962, he was representing more that just a corporation. When President Kennedy described his opposition in this conflict as "those with great power," he was referring to more than just a corporation or even a group of corporations. U.S. Steel, like a number of major banks and a few other large industrial corporations, was directed by a group of men who were leaders of America's financial and corporate system.

In his analysis of the steel crisis, Roy Hoopes says[26] that the corporate decision to raise prices was approved by an executive committee that included company executives and members of U.S. Steel's board of directors. Among those directors were Henry Heald, John Myers, Jr., Alexander Nagle, Charles Ingersoll, Amory Houghton, and Joseph Spang. All of these men were not only directors of U.S. Steel, but also held important positions in other institutions. For example, Myers was a senior vice-president at the Morgan Guaranty Trust Company. Heald was president of the Ford Foundation and a director of American Telephone and Telegraph and of the Equitable Life Assurance Society. Nagle was a director of First National City Bank, Prudential Insurance Company, National Biscuit Co., and American Sugar Refining Company. The remaining members of the executive committee and of the U.S. Steel board represented a large number of other major banks and corporations as well as a variety of important non-corporate organizations.*

When Kennedy referred to "those with great power" he was talking about a group of men representing a multitude of important institutions; they were something more than just businessmen. Why did they want to undermine Kennedy? The answer to that question will appear if we look carefully at what the president was attempting to do. We will also see that Kennedy was not timid, nor aimless, nor submissive. Writing about the immediate consequences of the steel crisis, Joseph A. Loftus of the *New York Times* observed:[27]

By his decisive action and swift triumph over the giant steel industry, 44-year-old John F. Kennedy bid for a place in the pantheon of "strong" Presidents.

---

* Among the other directors, there were connections to General Mills, International Nickel Co., Lever Brothers, Bank of Montreal, Bell Telephone, Royal Bank of Canada, British-American Oil Co., Metropolitan Life, Corning Glass, Schlumberger, Gilette, Hanover Bank, Atlantic Refining Co., and Johns-Manville Corporation. There was also a second connection to the Morgan Guaranty Bank, a relationship that probably reflected the history of U.S. Steel, which had been organized at the beginning of the century by J.P. Morgan, Sr. In addition to two directors with connections to Morgan, the chairman of U.S. Steel, Roger Blough, was, according to unnamed sources cited by the *New York Times* (1962), installed in the company's hierarchy by "powerful Wall Street interests." Those interests were most likely associated with Morgan Banking. The connection between Morgan and U.S. Steel is potentially very important in light of the other events discussed later. The U.S. Steel board also included directors who were members of some of America's most influential private organizations, including the Council on Foreign Relations, the Committee for Economic Development, the Conference Board, and the Business Council (Marquis *Who's Who*, 1962-63).

This was the first historic domestic issue in which President Kennedy swiftly summoned all the power and prestige of his office and triumphed. History will decide whether the story is a profile in courage.

As we shall see, Kennedy's overall national program and his international policies brought him into conflict with much more than "the giant steel industry."

TWO

The National Program

Kennedy assumed the presidency of the United States with a program which had as its central purpose the advancement of the productive powers of the nation. This progress was to be achieved through an intense effort to expand and improve both the human and technological capabilities of the country.

During the two years and ten months that he held office, Kennedy attempted to use the power of his office and of the federal government to achieve this goal through tax measures, government programs, government spending, and monetary and credit policy. He tried to shape investment processes, educational policy, and scientific and technological developments in order to realize the country's immediate potential and to qualitatively enhance that potential in the future. Few stones were left unturned in this effort.

Kennedy's aggressiveness in pursuit of economic progress was consistent with his view of the obligations of and the potential power of a president. In an interview given during the presidential campaign, Kennedy observed:[1]

> The responsibility of the President, therefore, is especially great. He must serve as a catalyst, an energizer, the defender of the public good and the public interest against all the narrow private interests which operate in our society. Only the President can do this, and only a President who recognizes the true nature of this hard challenge can fulfill this historic function.

Having said that he thought the president should be very active in defending the general interests of the nation, Kennedy shortly thereafter gave his views on the power of the presidency:[2]

I believe that our system of checks and balances, our whole constitutional system, can only operate under a strong President. The Constitution is a very wise document. It permits the President to assume just about as much power as he is capable of handling. If he fails, it is his fault, not the system's. I believe that the President should use whatever power is necessary to do the job unless it is expressly forbidden by the Constitution.

Immediately after his inauguration Kennedy defined his job as one of reversing the recent "downtrend in our economy,"[3] and he proposed "to expand the Nation's investment in physical and human resources, and in science and technology."[4]

This focus on scientific and technological progress and economic growth was present in the 1960 campaign,[5] and Kennedy's views on this were clearly reflected in the work of his economic advisers during the months leading up to the inauguration. They noted that Kennedy sought the optimum development of natural and human resources and of the productive capacity of the free world.[6]

Kennedy's concern was primarily, though not exclusively, with long-term changes in the economy, meaning from several years to decades. When he spoke on this issue and when he proposed actions, he looked to both the past and the future. In one of his early messages to Congress he observed:[7]

> The history of our economy has been one of rising productivity, based on improvement in skills, advances in technology, and a growing supply of more efficient tools and equipment. This rise has been reflected in rising wages and standard of living for our workers, as well as a healthy rate of growth for the economy as a whole. It has also been the foundation of our leadership in world markets, even as we enjoyed the highest wage rates in the world.

When he looked to the future well-being of the nation in general and to the common long-term interests of business and labor, Kennedy again emphasized the critical role to be played by technological progress:[8]

> Among both businessmen and workers, there is growing recognition that the road to higher real profits and higher real wages is the road of increased productivity. When better plant and equipment enable the labor force to produce more in the same number of hours, there is more to share among all of the contributors to the productive process—and this can happen with no increase in prices. Gains achieved in this manner endure, while gains achieved in one turn of the price-wage spiral vanish on the next.

In this 1962 Economic Report to Congress Kennedy is appealing to labor and business to recognize that a harmony of interests can be created around the goal of rising productivity and prosperity. He carried this same message to the United Auto Workers convention in May of 1962.[9]

Kennedy was seeking much more than just a recovery from the recession that existed when he took office. In his 1963 State of the Union Address, after 22 months of recovery from that recession, he emphasized that the country needed a higher rate of growth.[10] In a tax reform proposal also in 1963 he similarly argued that the growth rate was still not high enough and that productive investment, while rising, was still not adequate.[11] Throughout his presidency, Kennedy was committed, in words and action, to higher levels of sustained economic progress. He stated in 1961[12] his support for "long range planning for national economic growth."* Kennedy consistently used his office in an attempt to inject growth-oriented planning into government policy. In the process he tried to change or strengthen the direction of government policies through a multitude of proposals, all of which were part of a coherent strategy to drive the economy forward.

Tax Policy

In his 1966 book, *New Dimensions of Political Economy*, Walter Heller reviewed many of the policy initiatives undertaken by the Kennedy administration. Heller, who was the chairman of the Council of Economic Advisers under Kennedy, briefly recounted[13] proposals such as the investment tax credit, liberalization of depreciation, and tax reduction.** He also accurately reflected Kennedy's emphasis on modernization, mechanization, automation, and overall scientific and technological progress.[14] He did not, however, provide a complete review of Kennedy's proposals, particularly those of a more controversial nature. Those proposals have generally been ignored in other works on the Kennedy administration or given perfunctory treatment.[15]

Kennedy's tax reforms were tactical measures, a part of the overall strategy of using government to further economic progress. The specific proposals were never meant to be his final word, but were steps in what he viewed as a continuing process. Tax reform was intended to increase investment in plant and equipment and to stimulate economic growth.[16] This amounted to an aggressive effort to channel the flow of money and credit away from short-term, speculative, and nonproductive investments.

Three months after taking office, Kennedy submitted a tax reform program to Congress. Part of this program was the investment tax credit, which would allow companies to deduct from their taxes part of the value of investment in plant and equipment. This tax break would be available only on new plant and equipment which was located in the United States and had an expected life of

---

* The interest in growth-oriented planning was not new. Shortly after being elected to the Senate in 1953, Kennedy made a series of speeches outlining a regional development and growth program for New England (Burns, p. 124).
** Heller made a strong case for the success of those policies the Kennedy administration did get implemented. He observed that from early 1961 to early 1966 real compensation of all employees grew by 30 percent, corporate after-tax profits doubled, and real GNP grew by about 33 percent (Heller, p. 77).

six years or more.*[17] In January of 1962 Kennedy again pressed Congress for this reform, noting:[18]

> The tax credit increases the profitability of productive investment by reducing the net cost of acquiring new equipment. It will stimulate investment in capacity expansion and modernization, contribute to the growth of our productivity and output, and increase the competitiveness of American exports in world markets.

Even though Kennedy later also sought general tax reductions, most of his tax proposals were like the investment tax credit, that is, they were intended to mold the economy by channeling the decisions of those who controlled money and credit.

Part of the tax reform was aimed at foreign investments by large corporations and by private and institutional investors. Many big companies were in the process of increasing their foreign investments, a process which gave birth to new terminology—the multinational, global, or transnational corporation—and a host of new conflicts over tax revenues, the U.S. trade position, and job creation and production.[19] Most of this would occur after Kennedy's time. In 1961 Kennedy critically assessed several tax-related aspects of foreign investments. Existing law actually encouraged U.S. companies operating abroad to keep income in those foreign countries in order to avoid paying taxes to the U.S. government. Referring to this as a tax deferral privilege, Kennedy proposed to eliminate this by taxing those foreign profits each year even if they were kept outside the U.S. (Companies would still be allowed credit for taxes paid to foreign governments.) Kennedy proposed, however, that the deferral privilege be continued for investments in developing countries. In other words, investment would to some extent be redirected from Europe and Canada to the United States and to underdeveloped areas.[20]

Corporations operating in low-tax countries or in tax havens such as Switzerland would lose those tax advantages. Also, Kennedy pointed out, this would recover the taxes lost to the U.S. in cases where corporations were using accounting and organizational techniques to shift profits artificially to tax havens.[21] Tax deferral privileges were to be eliminated for all profits made from non-productive foreign investments (trading, licensing, insurance, etc.), regardless of location.

Kennedy went on to propose the elimination of all tax breaks for companies set up by U.S. interests in the form of foreign investment companies. He also specifically targeted wealthy individuals who were transferring wealth abroad to avoid paying estate taxes; he proposed the elimination of the laws permitting this.[22] In 1962 he restated his support for all of the reforms described above.[23]

---

* This version of the investment tax credit was different from the one eventually passed. The original version, as described in Kennedy's message (1961d, pp. 4-5), appears to have contained an even greater emphasis than the final version on stimulating investment that would not have taken place without tax change.

When Kennedy proposed a general tax cut* in 1963,[24] he also focused on "large oil and gas producers" who were manipulating a 1954 law to avoid taxes and gain an advantage over smaller producers. He also proposed changes in foreign tax credits which allowed U.S.-based oil, gas, and mineral companies to avoid paying U.S. taxes.[25]

In his tax reform proposals Kennedy was willing to give breaks to businesses if they were making productive investments. He was also willing to withdraw all provisions that discouraged investment in the U.S., gave special privileges to certain companies, or simply allowed big companies to escape tax payment. His tax policy was not anti-business; it was pro-production, equitable, and nationally oriented. Changes were intended to benefit the United States as a whole, as well as small business, underdeveloped countries, and the poor. The special rights and privileges of large corporations, investors, and others were to be curtailed.

Kennedy's willingness to infringe on the prerogatives of international investors and multinational corporations carried over to other recommendations involving the wealthy and powerful. Kennedy was convinced that billions of dollars in income from interest and dividends was going unreported and untaxed each year. He proposed to use a withholding tax, as with wages, to secure those tax revenues.[26] He suggested the elimination of a provision which allowed wealthy people to write off up to 100 percent of their charitable contributions while a 20- to 30-percent deduction was normal for the non-wealthy. He wanted a change in taxes on dividends so that those families with income over $180,000 would pay a higher rate, more like those with lower income levels. He proposed changes to prevent "high-bracket taxpayers" from concealing income gained through the use of personal holding companies. Other proposals and recommendations included the following: a modest anti-speculation provision that would require that properties be held for one year rather than the existing six months in order to benefit from capital gains tax rates; elimination of special tax preferences for wealthy individuals transferring properties as gifts; and repeal of the $50 dividend exclusion and the 4 percent dividend credit.[27]

Although most of these measures did not survive the compromises made with congressional committees,[28] they provided additional indicators of Kennedy's overall economic and social goals. How much of this would have been passed, given five more years in the White House, is impossible to say.The evaluation of Kennedy's policies should not rest on their success or failure alone. If they are judged to be progressive initiatives, the blame for their failure should be placed on those members of Congress who rejected them and on the business interests that felt threatened by the changes. What they indicate about Kennedy is that he felt wealth should be acquired through productive and generally

---

* As proposed in his 1963 message to Congress, the tax cuts for individuals and businesses were, in percentage terms, intended to give the largest reductions to the poorest third of the population and to small businesses. The tax cut was somewhat unusual in that it came in the midst of recovery and not as a counter-cyclable measure. (Kennedy, 1963a, pp. 2-3; 1963b, pp. 2-7.)

beneficial investments and that he took a dim view of profits accruing from speculation, purely financial transactions, and inheritance. He never opposed in any general way the right to own property, earn profits, or expand wealth. What he did try to do with everything from global investment patterns to tax breaks for individuals was to reshape laws and policies so that the power of property and the search for profit would not end up destroying rather than creating economic prosperity for the country. In this he was very clear, consistent, and coherent.

His ideology was neither that of free enterprise nor of socialism, but rather one based on the idea that economic and social progress were the goals and that the power and policies of government were important parts of the means to achieve those goals.

Technology and Economic Progress

Consistent with the emphasis in his tax policies on growth and prosperity, Kennedy repeatedly focused on technological progress and industrial modernization as necessary components in a program of economic progress. In the area of electric power, Kennedy asserted in 1961 that the country needed to triple its power capacity by 1980 and that government policy and the cooperation of private industry would be needed to achieve this goal. He proposed specifically that the Atomic Energy Commission assume an important role in this by achieving the rapid development of nuclear power, in part, through the construction of various types of reactors.[29]

When Kennedy addressed the issue of energy in his 1962 message on conservation,[30] he emphasized again the necessity of increasing energy production and the need for low-cost energy:

> One of the major challenges in resource conservation lies in the orderly development and efficient utilization of energy resources to meet the nation's electric power needs—needs which double every decade. The goal of this administration is to insure an abundance of low-cost power for all consumers—urban and rural, industrial and domestic. To achieve this, we must use more effectively all sources of fuel, find cheaper ways to harness nuclear energy, develop our hydroelectric potential, utilize presently unused heat produced by nature or as a byproduct of industrial processes, and even capture the energy of the tides where feasible.

This was followed immediately by a statement that Kennedy was directing the Federal Power Commission to undertake a study that would allow long-range planning "for the expansion of our nation's electric power supply." He went on to say:[31]

> Under existing authority contained in the Federal Power Act, the Commission will project our national power needs for the 1960's and 1970's and suggest the broad outline of a fully interconnected system of power supply for the entire country.

Approximately ten years later much of the discussion of energy would be redirected away from the development and creation of new energy sources to an emphasis on energy scarcity. Even when discussing the general topic of "conservation," Kennedy consistently emphasized resource development and technological progress.

When Kennedy said in 1961[32] that the country needed an economic growth program that "goes well beyond antirecession measures," he emphasized that his administration was making a new commitment to advances in technology. He proposed that price stability should be achieved through technological progress rather than through "a slack economy." This last comment seemed to be a criticism of those who were, in Kennedy's view, inclined to check inflation by severely limiting the growth of the money supply. Specifically, he recommended the maximum development and use of water resources through the expansion of hydroelectric power and through the discovery of economically practical methods of desalinating ocean and brackish waters. He promised a redoubling of efforts to do this, and he promised to share advances in this area with any and every nation in the world.[33] He also proposed[34] a new commitment to the development of fusion energy.

In this 1962 message to Congress concerning conservation, Kennedy addressed the issue of mineral resources in much the same way he spoke of energy, that is, he argued for a development and expansion of such resources, based in part on technological progress:[35]

> Conservation of mineral resources benefits from the fact that, for practical purposes, they are not fixed in quantity—the usable volume and variety of minerals increase as technology advances. We have learned to use a host of materials which had no previous value or had value only in limited uses.
>
> Technical research is obviously the critical element in a program of conserving and strengthening both our mineral resources and our minerals industries. To assure us of adequate quantities of minerals in the future, and to enable our minerals industries to compete in world markets, we must find more effective means of discovering and extracting mineral deposits, learn to refine materials of lower quality, and find both new uses for minerals which are relatively abundant, and substitutes for those which are scarce or difficult to procure.

The emphasis Kennedy placed on technological progress, even in the context of a message to Congress concerning "conservation," is completely consistent with his determination to use tax policy to channel money and credit into productive investment.

The two concerns converged in his 1963 tax proposal, which suggested that the law be changed to allow businesses to deduct immediately from their taxes any expenditures made for machinery and equipment used in research and development.[36] At the time, tax writeoffs were allowed, but only if spread over the life of the equipment.

Although the U.S. economy was clearly the leading economy in the world in the early 1960s, Kennedy emphasized the need for modernization, growth, and the acceleration of advances in productivity. If the economy were going to advance and grow in this fashion it would be necessary to upgrade and expand education to provide the technicians, engineers, and scientists who would both create and operate new and growing systems of production. Logically, Kennedy recommended[37] increased investment in education to match rising private and public investments in physical capital.

Education

Relating the need for expansion of and improvement in education to the "new age of science and space" and to the goals of technological progress and economic growth, Kennedy observed that "this country reserves its highest honors for only one kind of aristocracy—that which the Founding Fathers called 'an aristocracy of achievement arising out of a democracy of opportunity.'"[38]

In his recommendations for new educational goals and programs Kennedy advocated expanding educational opportunities:[39]

> The President's Science Advisory Committee has predicted that the dramatically increasing demand for engineers, mathematicians, and physical scientists will require that the output of Ph.D.s in these fields alone be increased two and a half times, to a total of 7,500 annually by 1970, and that the number of masters degrees awarded annually be substantially increased.... It is clearly contrary to the national interests to have the number of graduate students limited by the financial ability of those able and interested in pursuing advanced degrees.

Consistent with these concerns, Kennedy recommended[40] raising the number of grants and fellowships awarded through the National Science Foundation from 2,800 in 1963 to 8,700 in 1964. He also sought expanded education and training of technicians and a general increase in funds for student loans, scholarships, financial assistance, and work-study programs.

He recommended a more generous program of loans and repayment for those studying to be teachers and suggested new federal insurance for private banks lending money to students for educational purposes. Finally, he recommended new programs of federal assistance to create a national system of public community junior colleges and to aid local schools to build new classrooms, raise teacher salaries in disadvantaged areas, and generate new programs in depressed rural and urban areas. Some of these proposals would be part of the Higher Education Facilities Act that was signed into law December 16, 1963.[41]

A number of these recommendations were intended to increase equality in and improve opportunities for education. Many of the others were aimed at educating the scientists, engineers, and technicians who would both expand the productive system and provide the educated labor force that this expansion would demand. The overall thrust of this was consistent with Kennedy's other initiatives to intensify the investment in and development of an increasingly modern technological and industrial system of production.

While Kennedy's policy initiatives were concentrated on national economic progress, as with his educational proposals, he was also committed to reducing inequality and assisting those at the bottom. By 1962 he had succeeded in temporarily extending unemployment benefits, increasing the minimum wage, raising social security benefits, providing federal aid for dependent children of the unemployed, and increasing federal aid to depressed areas.[42] He also suggested a review of the existing policy that required that fathers must be absent in order for children to qualify for federal assistance under the Aid to Families With Dependent Children program. These efforts were supplementary to his primary goal of raising income, reducing poverty, and reducing unemployment through generalized economic prosperity and progress. In the pursuit of those core goals he treated government spending and the size and shape of the budget as a means to an end.

The Federal Budget, Deficit Spending, and Money

Kennedy's view of the budget and deficits was consistent with his overall orientation toward government's role in the economy. Government spending, tax policy, and budgetary policy were evaluated in light of his primary commitment to promoting growth and technological progress. The questions of deficits, borrowing, and debt were important, but secondary. He was clear about this and appears to have been uninterested in any debate about whether or not he was a Keynesian. In a speech at Yale in June of 1962 he stated that[43]

> debts, public and private, are neither good nor bad, in and of themselves. Borrowing can lead to overextension and collapse, but it can also lead to expansion and strength. There is no single, simple slogan in this field that we can trust.

In a message to Congress the following year he defended deficits if they were useful to stimulate investment and growth.[44] Heller[45] described Kennedy as extremely cautious in 1961 concerning deficit spending, while Schlesinger[46] described Kennedy's willingness in 1962 to favor budget deficits while the economy was still growing as "radical." What seems to make sense, given Kennedy's determination to stimulate investment and growth, is that he had a natural concern with the potential problems of growing deficits that induced the alleged caution during the early months in office, but was more than willing to incur those deficits if they contributed to his primary objectives.*

As we have seen, Kennedy approached the major policy choices with well defined and quite specific aims, that is, increasing investment and raising real

---

* There is no reason to doubt Heller's addendum (p. 113) that Kennedy had political considerations in mind when he chose to create the deficits through tax reduction more than by spending increases. The tax cut could be more easily sold to both liberals and conservatives.

income. Both inflation and recession could undermine his central policy goals. He observed in his Economic Report of 1962:[47]

> The task of economic stabilization does not end with the achievement of full recovery. There remains the problem of keeping the economy from straying too far above or below the path of steady high employment. One way lies inflation, and the other way lies recession. Flexible and vigilant fiscal and monetary policies will allow us to hold the narrow middle course.

Whatever caution Kennedy felt in 1961, he quickly committed to tax cuts and deficit spending in 1962 and 1963 as a useful adjunct to his other measures. Even in that supposedly cautious year of 1961,* there were hints of this when, in his tax message, he noted that, "High capital formation can be sustained only by a high and rising level of demand for goods and services."[48] Both deficits and the appropriate monetary policy could contribute to that rising level of demand.

Kennedy wanted to expand the capacity of the president to prevent recessions. Early in 1961, he took a number of actions to stimulate recovery. Included were the acceleration of federal purchases and procurement, distribution of highway funds, the return of tax refunds, and payments of veterans' life insurance dividends. Later in 1961[49] Kennedy accelerated spending for the space program and for national security without asking for any tax increases. In this effort he got the cooperation of the Federal Reserve and the Treasury in expanding the money supply and the supply of credit and in making money available specifically for small business and home mortgages.[50]

In 1962 Kennedy made an attempt to formalize presidential powers to prevent economic downturns.[51]

> To combat future recessions—to keep them short and shallow if they occur—I urge adoption of a three-part program for sustained prosperity, which will (1) provide stand-by power, subject to congressional veto, for temporary income tax reductions, (2) set up a stand-by program of public capital improvements, and (3) strengthen the unemployment insurance system.
>
> These three measures will enable the Government to counter swings in business activity more promptly and more powerfully than ever before. They will give new and concrete meaning to the declaration of policy made in the Employment Act.**

---

* If we were trying to find the origins of Kennedy's views on government spending and deficits we could go all the way back to *Why England Slept*, published in 1940. It is clear there that even as a young man Kennedy was critical of policies that placed balanced budgets ahead of all else. Kennedy observed (p. 44) that prior to World War II England risked its national security for fear of the "risk of financial disaster." He noted (pp. 45-46, 55) that defense forces were reduced to keep spending down and (pp. 83, 116) he criticized business interests for placing budget considerations ahead of military preparedness. The book is not a great work, but it does have more in it of interest than some have said (*e.g.*, Paper, pp. 36-41).

** Kennedy was referring to a 1946 act, discussed briefly at the end of this chapter.

They will constitute the greatest step forward in public policy for economic stability since the Act itself.

The tax reduction authority Kennedy wanted[52] would have allowed the president to initiate up to a five percent cut in income taxes unless it was rejected by a joint resolution of Congress within 30 days of its proposal. It would then remain in effect for six months subject to modification or renewal by either the president or a joint resolution of Congress.

The second part of that program dealing with capital improvements was described as follows:[53]

Stand-by capital improvements authority. Second, I recommend that the Congress provide stand-by authority to the President to accelerate and initiate up to $2 billion of appropriately timed capital improvements when unemployment is rising, as follows:

(1) The President would be authorized to initiate the program within two months after the seasonally adjusted unemployment rate

(a) had risen in at least three out of four months (or in four out of six months) and

(b) had risen to a level at least one percentage point higher than its level four months (or six months) earlier.

(2) Before invoking this authority, the President must make a finding that current and prospective economic developments require such action to achieve the objectives of the Employment Act.

(3) Upon such finding, the President would be authorized to commit

(a) up to $750 million in the acceleration of direct Federal expenditures previously authorized by the Congress,

(b) up to $750 million for grants-in-aid to State and local governments,

(c) up to $250 million in loans to States and localities which would otherwise be unable to meet their share of project costs, and

(d) up to $250 million additional to be distributed among the above three categories as he might deem appropriate.

(4) The authority to initiate new projects under the capital improvements program would terminate automatically within 12 months unless extended by the Congress— but the program could be terminated at any time by the President.

The third part of his program[54] included a series of recommendations to increase and liberalize unemployment benefits.

These proposals are of interest on several counts. Kennedy was trying to augment the presidential powers that he had already assessed prior to election as sufficient. He clearly had decided that more power was necessary. The attempt here was to shift some decision-making power away from the marketplace and, perhaps, from the Federal Reserve, to the president. He obviously felt that cyclical downturns, or recessions, were not acceptable, and he thought the economy could be made to expand continuously, or with only very minor interruptions. These optimistic views and the accompanying actions are entirely consistent with his other initiatives discussed in this chapter.

A continuous expansion of the economy, and most certainly an expansion based on real growth in production, would require an adequate growth in the money supply and a growing availability of credit at low interest rates. Kennedy observed in 1961[55] that ways must be found and can be found to increase the flow of credit, at declining rates of interest,* for long-term loans for productive investment. In that context he referred, without explanation, to measures already being taken in 1961 to achieve this. This may have been a reference to the accelerated expenditures and increased funds for small businesses and mortgages which were discussed earlier.

While Kennedy actively solicited, and perhaps temporarily gained, the cooperation of the Federal Reserve Board, he was alert to any chance of increasing his own influence over the money supply and interest rates.** The Commission on Money and Credit, sponsored by the private Committee for Economic Development, made a multitude of recommendations in its 1961 report entitled *Money and Credit*. While Kennedy was not very receptive to this study, he did quickly accept one of its recommendations, which would allow the incoming president to designate a chairman who served the same four years as the president.[56] The existing policy, then and now, is that the chairman is picked by the president from the Board members, but the timing of the selection is not coordinated with the presidential term of office.

Kennedy's concerns with growth and investment shaped his policies in the areas of spending, deficits, and money. He was committed in principle to economic progress, not to either balanced budgets or deficits. He enthusiastically embraced deficits, however, in order to prevent an interruption of the increasing rates of investment and growth. He sought to increase the capacity of the president to take action to counter economic downturns. He wanted the Federal Reserve's cooperation in making sure there was enough low-interest credit available and he looked for other means to achieve this.

The Program as a Whole

What has been reviewed here are the many pieces of an overall strategy to drive the U.S. economy forward. The whole would be greater than the sum of the parts, as each specific policy would reinforce and intensify the other initiatives. The tax credit for investment and the numerous changes designed to shift capital

---

* Kennedy (1962/1988, pp. 91-92) was concerned with an emerging problem of increasing deficits for the U.S. in international transactions and with a resulting loss of gold reserves. In light of this, Kennedy reached an agreement with Federal Reserve Chairman William McC. Martin to attempt to keep long-term rates low to encourage investment while short-term rates would be high enough to keep money in the U.S. (Rowen, p. 212).

** In 1963 Kennedy seems to have made an effort to increase the money and credit supply by injecting money into the economy through the Treasury in a way that bypassed the Federal Reserve (Marrs, p. 275).

from non-productive to productive investments would contribute to and be reinforced by the programs to develop and expand various forms of energy production. The educational policy would generate the creators and operators of a growing and more productive economy. Taking tax privileges away from the very wealthy and from large oil and mineral companies would not only express the democratic intentions of the administration, but would also make productive investment in the nation more likely. Deficits were not sought so that Kennedy could claim to be a Keynesian, but rather as a way to facilitate and intensify the effects of his other policies and to prevent recession from wiping out the gains made during recovery. Maintaining an adequate growth in money and credit and keeping interest rates down would allow for improvements in and expansion of the productive base of the economy. Budget and monetary policy would enhance the effects of the tax policy and other initiatives. In short, the combined effects of all these initiatives would be synergistic, having a greater impact than would be expected based on an evaluation of each part simply added together.

As noted in the Introduction, Kennedy has been described as cautious, hesitant, and fiscally conservative.[57] It has been said that the essence of his philosophy was the "free-market economy"[58] and that he was uninterested in and had no plans or goals for the nation.[59] As this chapter should suggest, these remarks are nowhere near the truth.

In one of the most recent assessments of the Kennedy administration, James N. Giglio suggests[60] that Kennedy was extremely cautious in public policy and that his tax proposals served corporate interests. In a summary he says:[61]

> Most of Kennedy's legislative proposals had evolved from Roosevelt's Economic Bill of Rights address of 11 January 1944. Subsequent party platforms and policy papers had honed Roosevelt's ideas, becoming linked to Kennedy through his Senate sponsorship, the 1960 party platform, and his campaign promise to get America moving again. Kennedy merely reflected the latest Democratic effort to promote the Roosevelt legacy. In many ways his liberalism was terribly traditional; it sought to consolidate and extend the great Democratic gains of the past.

This is a rather inconsistent statement, suggesting the consolidation of "great Democratic gains" on one hand, but using the phrases "merely reflected" and "terribly traditional" on the other hand. It is also misleading and incomplete, as is the book as a whole, since it fails to mention much of what has been reviewed here. There is also no discussion of what was in that 1960 party platform.

Certainly, Kennedy's economic strategy could be compared to Roosevelt's Economic Bill of Rights, but Kennedy's program went beyond Roosevelt's statement of goals to an actual program to achieve those goals. Roosevelt's Bill of Rights read as follows:

> The right to a useful and remunerative job in the industries or shops or farms or mines of the nation;

The right to earn enough to provide adequate food and clothing and recreation;

The right of every farmer to raise and sell his products at a return which will give him and his family a decent living;

The right of every businessman, large and small, to trade in an atmosphere of freedom from unfair competition and domination by monopolies at home or abroad;

The right of every family to a decent home;

The right to adequate medical care and the opportunity to achieve and enjoy good health;

The right to adequate protection from the economic fears of old age, sickness, accident and unemployment;

The right to a good education.

These rights were meant as goals and were apparently Roosevelt's statement in 1944 of more general ideas discussed within his administration as early as 1941.[62] Much of Kennedy's program was aimed at achieving these goals, but his program was focused to a much greater degree on generating the economic progress that would be necessary, and it included an aggressive set of policies to produce that progress.

The Democratic platform in 1960 did more than just hone Roosevelt's ideas although it did not give full expression to what would be Kennedy's policies. What role Kennedy played in shaping that platform is difficult to determine.[63] Two points are fairly clear. Much of Kennedy's policy was included (or the platform became his policy), and he went beyond this ambitious statement of policy.

In the process of elaborating on and adding to Roosevelt's Economic Bill of Rights, the 1960 party platform included many of the initiatives later taken by Kennedy. There was a strong general commitment to economic growth, greater productivity, and full employment.[64] There were recommendations to expand loans to small businesses, to provide loans in depressed areas, and to make efforts to keep interest rates down and expand credit.[65] Proposals were made for energy development, resource development, and an effort to achieve desalinization of ocean water.[66] There was also a general policy of closing tax loopholes that favored privileged groups.[67]

Roosevelt's ideas apparently inspired this platform, which went beyond those basic statements. Perhaps this platform inspired Kennedy's program for economic progress. A great deal of it was there in specific or general terms, but Kennedy went beyond the platform. There was one obvious difference. The platform strongly emphasized the necessity of balanced budgets with surpluses in good times offsetting deficits during recession.[68] Kennedy would wind up proposing deficits in the midst of recovery. There were also other ways in which Kennedy would move beyond the platform while being faithful to its spirit.

On a general level, Kennedy's speeches and messages to Congress contained an even stronger focus on scientific, technological, and industrial progress than was present in the platform. His educational policy had a greater emphasis on natural sciences and technical areas than did the platform. Specifically, he went beyond the platform in the following: tax proposals to redirect the foreign investments of U.S. companies; distinctions in tax reform between productive and non-productive investment; eliminating tax privileges of U.S.-based global investment companies; cracking down on foreign tax havens and other proposals to eliminate tax privileges enjoyed by the wealthy; his tax proposals concerning large oil and mineral companies; his version of the investment tax credit; and expanding the powers of the president to deal with recession. In these areas, Kennedy took what was already an active and growth-oriented party position and extended and deepened it.

He treated the platform proposals in the same way he treated his proposals to Congress and his actions as president, as part of an ongoing, open-ended process of change to achieve economic and social progress. This orientation was also reflected in Kennedy's references to the Employment Act of 1946. In a 1962 message to Congress he said that his proposal to expand presidential powers to reverse recessions would give "new and concrete meaning" to that act. Even before taking office he expressed his intention to "return to the spirit as well as the letter of the Employment Act of 1946."[69] By emphasizing the spirit of that act rather than the letter, Kennedy may have been referring to the fact that while the act suggested goals of full employment and expanding national wealth (the "spirit"), the language of the act was weak and perhaps contradictory (the "letter"). By "spirit" he may also have had in mind the stronger and more ambitious wording of earlier versions of the act. One draft version, December 18, 1944, had stated that every American has a "right to useful and remunerative" work, that the government has a "responsibility" to "guarantee that right," and that the government shall undertake programs "to contribute to the national wealth."[70]

In office, Kennedy moved beyond the specific proposals of the Democratic platform, which already provided dynamic and growth-oriented prescriptions for the next Democratic president. His proposals would be consistent with the goals of Roosevelt's Economic Bill of Rights and the spirit of the Employment Act of 1946. His separate policies formed a coherent whole that included aspects of Keynesian economic theory but also provided much greater focus on expanding and improving the productive base of the economy and included many specific actions not derived from Keynes. This is clearly true if Keynesian policy is defined as an attempt to increase employment and prevent or end economic downturns through deficit spending by government.[71] The Keynesian goal of maintaining adequate demand in the economy is very general and nonspecific in terms of substantive economic goals. Kennedy's proposals were focused on scientific and technological progress, increased productivity, and expanding production. The program as a whole and in its specifics was both different from and more than standard Keynesian policies.

Kennedy was intensely committed to the national interests of the United States. His policies were intended to preserve and enhance the economic position of the U.S. in the world economy. He did not, however, view the progress of the United States as in any way at odds with the progress of other nations, nor did he seek such progress for the purpose of world domination. His goals for other nations and other peoples were completely consistent with his goals for the United States, even if his capacity to affect global trends was more limited. In the next chapter we see that Kennedy's foreign policy was an extension of his domestic policy, even though the ambiguities of particular situations rendered clear and consistent action difficult.

THREE

The International Policy

President Kennedy was attempting to shape government policy and private decision making in order to accelerate economic progress in the United States. That progress meant not just an expansion of and improvement in the scientific and technological components of the economy, but also rising levels of education, expanding opportunities, a rising standard of living, and declining poverty. This determination to reach a new and greater level of economic progress and democracy through government action was as much a part of Kennedy's international policy as it was of his national program. The difficulties he faced at the global level were even more daunting than those he confronted domestically, and in some ways his powers to effect change were more limited. In any event, Kennedy set out to achieve the same kinds of goals in foreign policy that he pursued in his domestic policy.

Kennedy confronted situations that made simple choices and consistent action very difficult. He did have, however, a coherent set of goals and clear preferences. The major problem for most nations and for the majority of people in the world was, and still is, the debilitating effects of economic backwardness and grinding poverty. In response to this, Kennedy made economic development the centerpiece of his global policy. He viewed economic progress as something that had to be achieved if any of the other important goals were to be accomplished. This paralleled his domestic orientation. The other goals, which Kennedy apparently respected, were the independence and autonomy of other nations, basic democratic rights in the political sense, and the economic democracy created by rising standards of living and expanded opportunities. Consistent with his regard for the independence of other nations and his own inclination to employ government powers to shape economic trends, he favored economic planning, at home and abroad, and had a tolerance for socialism if it were based on popular support and preserved basic rights. Given these views, Kennedy was opposed to arrangements or policies that perpetuated economic backwardness, that meant domination by one nation over others, or that preserved the power of people who had no commitment to economic and social progress. This entailed opposition to colonialist or neo-colonialist policy, to domination of nations by foreign interests of whatever political nature, and to entrenched interests opposed to political or economic progress. Kennedy's policies in this regard, both domestic and foreign, would in turn be opposed by an impressive array of individuals and groups.

Economic Development

In his inaugural address on January 20, 1961, Kennedy expressed in general terms the direction he wished the foreign policy of the United States to take. In part, he said:[1]

> Let both sides [the West and the communist bloc] seek to invoke the wonders of science instead of its terrors. Together let us explore the stars, conquer the deserts, eradicate disease, tap the ocean depths and encourage the arts and commerce.
> Let both sides unite to heed in all corners of the earth the command of Isaiah to "undo the heavy burdens...[and] let the oppressed go free."...
> Now the trumpet summons us again—not as a call to bear arms, though arms we need; not as a call to battle, though embattled we are; but a call to bear the burden of a long twilight struggle, year in and year out, "rejoicing in hope, patient in tribulation," a struggle against the common enemies of man: tyranny, poverty, disease and war itself.

In this first speech as president, Kennedy called for cooperation in achieving economic progress and for both sides to end the oppression of people wherever they are. He noted the need for strength of arms, but went on to emphasize that the common enemies of man are tyranny, poverty, disease, and war.

In a message sent to Congress just two months later,[2] Kennedy said that the "1960s can be—and must be—the crucial 'decade of development'" for Latin America, Africa, the Middle East, and Asia. This focus on economic development had been prominent in speeches made by Kennedy while still a Senator.

In a 1957 speech concerning the problems of the Middle East, Kennedy proposed[3] a variety of development projects for the region as a strategy to defuse tensions by promoting common action. In a 1958 speech given in Puerto Rico he proposed a development program which included, among other things, the formation of an inter-American capital development bank and a program of technical assistance for Latin America.[4] Also in 1958, in a speech to the Senate,[5] Kennedy recommended long-term multinational development assistance for India.

It would appear that Kennedy was giving these issues more than just casual attention and that he had identified what he thought to be specific problems well before his election as president. In a speech to the Senate in February of 1959,[6] Kennedy discussed the need to make better use of the Development Loan Fund to assist economic development. In that context he criticized what he viewed as "overreliance on inflexible, hard loans through the Export-Import and World Banks, with fixed-dollar repayment schedules that retard instead of stimulating economic development." Kennedy would later try as president to create new loan policies and credit conditions to facilitate development. Before examining those attempts, there are several other early expressions of his views worth noting.

Kennedy ended that February 1959, speech saying:[7]

> We can give a convincing demonstration that we have not a propaganda or crisis interest but an enduring long-term interest in the productive economic growth of the less developed nations. We can finally make it clear to ourselves that international economic development is not, somehow, a nagging responsibility, to be faced each year in the context of giveaways and taxes—but a vast international effort, an enterprise of positive association, which lies close to the heart of our relations with the whole Free World and which requires active American leadership.
>
> As a nation, we think not of war but of peace; not of crusades of conflict but of covenants of co-operation; not of the pageantry of imperialism but of the pride of new states freshly risen to independence. We like to look, with Mr. Justice Holmes, beyond the vision of battling races and an impoverished earth to catch a dreaming glimpse of peace. In the words of Edmund Burke, we sit on a "conspicuous stage," and the whole world marks our demeanor. In this year and in this Congress we have an opportunity to be worthy of that role.

This was not only a call for a greater commitment to development, but also a rejection of the idea that the world should be an arena for a contest between races. In this remark and in his rejection of the "pageantry of imperialism," Kennedy was disassociating himself from groups in the United States and Europe that wished to pursue the colonial or imperial domination of backward countries. In fact, his emphasis on development was itself a clear rejection of the imperial or colonial policy of actively suppressing economic development.

As noted above, in 1959 Kennedy expressed a dissatisfaction with the loan policies of the Export-Import and World Banks. In 1960 he criticized the policies of private banks in a presentation to the Senate which focused in part on the development needs of Latin America, Asia, Africa, and the Middle East. Kennedy argued[8] that the United States must assist development "in a spirit of generosity motivated by a desire to help our fellow citizens of the world—not as narrow bankers or self-seeking politicians."

In his 1961 message to Congress on foreign aid, in which he declared the 1960s the decade of development, President Kennedy proposed[9] a coordinated development effort which would be planned and financed on a long-term basis and would involve cooperation between the underdeveloped and the industrialized nations. Kennedy went on to propose[10] a new program of U.S. government loans provided on a long-term basis (up to 50 years) with low or no interest charges and geared specifically to the promotion of growth and development. He then noted[11] that such a loan program was "not normal banking practice." Whatever he meant by that comment, it is clear that Kennedy intended to put much greater emphasis than had his predecessor on long-term government loans, industrial development, government planning, and government-to-government coordination and negotiation.

Kennedy also set out to expand economic aid to poorer nations and to shift the purpose of such aid from military support to economic development. Although opposition in Congress prevented Kennedy from getting all he wanted, he was partially successful and he did manage to reverse the pattern of the 1950s by making economic development aid larger in dollar terms than military aid.[12]

Kennedy's development efforts in this hemisphere were naturally aimed at Latin America, and the phrase "alliance for progress," which he used in his inaugural address, was formalized to identify this program.[13] In Colombia in late 1961, he restated his commitment to economic development and promised,[14] as part of the Alliance for Progress, U.S. cooperation in "an intensive effort to develop and industrialize the economies of Latin America, reducing dependence on raw materials and steadily narrowing the relative gap between the wealthy industrialized countries and the republics of Latin America."

As noted above, Kennedy did not get everything he wanted from Congress, but two years later he still felt that much had been accomplished, and he defended the effectiveness of loans and aid in general and of the Alliance for Progress in particular. In April of 1963 he observed:[15]

> Despite noisy opposition from the very first days, despite dire predictions that foreign aid would "bankrupt" the Republic, despite warnings that the Marshall Plan and successor programs were "throwing our money down a rathole," despite great practical difficulties and some mistakes and disappointments, the fact is that our aid programs generally and consistently have done what they were expected to do.

Kennedy's defense of and commitment to development assistance was connected with his perception that underdevelopment was in part due to past colonial policies and to the neo-colonial, or imperialist, policies which were supported by powerful interests in the U.S. and Europe.* Kennedy also believed

---

* Colonialism refers to the direct and formal control of other territories for the purpose of extracting wealth. The policy of colonialism was also one of suppressing economic development in the captured territories in order to keep them weak and dependent on the production and export of agricultural products and raw materials. Neo-colonialism, or imperialism, refers to the same policy of suppressing economic development and extracting wealth, but the process is carried out without direct and formal control of other societies. Instead, neo-colonialist forces use trade policy, foreign aid, influence, bribery and corruption, intelligence operations, military assistance, and ultimately military force to sustain

that it was underdevelopment and poverty that provided the conditions that made communism attractive to many in the underdeveloped world. He opposed neo-colonialism and wanted to offer an economic development program that would give progressive forces in the Third World an alternative to communism.

John Kennedy's opposition to colonialist policies may have originated in an identification with Ireland's long subjugation to England. JFK's actions and comments during his 1963 trip to Ireland suggest this, including his decision to honor publicly the Irish resistance fighters who died in the 1916 Easter Rebellion. He called his visit to Ireland one of the greatest emotional experiences of his life and promised to return in 1964.[16]

When Robert Kennedy decided to give his first speech before a large audience following his brother's assassination, he addressed these issues and noted that his views had also been his brother's views. Speaking to the Sons of St. Patrick in Scranton, Pennsylvania, in March of 1964, Robert Kennedy directly connected Ireland's painful history to the issue of U.S. policy toward colonies and the underdeveloped nations. He specifically linked an appreciation for Ireland's historical difficulties to America's obligation to foster economic and political independence. He also reminded his audience that there was a great deal to be done to help other nations "to free themselves from economic domination." Robert Kennedy also indicated his views about the British Establishment by noting that Queen Victoria's response to mass starvation in Ireland in 1847 had been to offer five pounds to the Society for Irish Relief.[17]

Communism and Colonialism

Kennedy was asked during an interview in 1959 if he were as disturbed by other nations taking a neutralist position as had been Eisenhower's Secretary of State John Foster Dulles.

Kennedy gave the following response:[18]

Oh, I think it's inevitable. That's the great trend. During the immediate years ahead this is likely to be an increasing trend in Africa and probably also in Latin America. In Asia, however, there may be some movement away from a wholly uncommitted neutralism as a result of the growing awareness of the Chinese threat. The desire to be independent and free carries with it the desire not to become engaged as a satellite of the Soviet Union or too closely allied to the United States. We have to live with that, and if neutrality is the result of a concentration on internal problems, raising the standard of living of the people and so on, particularly in the underdeveloped countries, I would accept that. It's part of our own history for over a hundred years. I should look with friendship upon those people who want to beat the problems that almost overwhelm them, and wish to concentrate their energies on doing that, and do not want to become associated as the tail of our kite.

control. There was already a long-standing tendency of certain groups in the U.S. to join with European counterparts in replacing colonialism with neo-colonialism. It was this tendency that Kennedy opposed.

In supporting economic development and the right of Third World countries to maintain their independence and neutralism, Kennedy was staking out a policy which was clear in principle. He knew what he wanted: to assist economic development and independence. He favored economic planning and felt that other nations had a right to work out their own economic programs. He also knew what he was against: both Western domination of or suppression of the economies of Third World nations, either openly and formally (colonialism) or indirectly and subtly (neo-colonialism or imperialism), and Soviet or Chinese imperialism, a variant form of imperialism involving political or military domination. He also was opposed to entrenched élites in Third World nations who refused to support political reform and economic development within their own nations.*[19]

As demonstrated during the Cuban missile crisis, Kennedy's opposition to colonialism and his reluctance to use military force in the Third World did not translate into passivity toward the Soviet Union. The Soviet government's decision in 1962 to put long-range nuclear missiles, along with complementary forces, into Cuba while it practiced diplomatic deception and double-talk led to the famous confrontation in October.[20] While Kennedy would be criticized for going too far (risking nuclear war) or not far enough (failing to invade Cuba), the events did demonstrate his willingness to "stand up" to the Soviet Union. Similarly, he demonstrated a clear resolve in resisting attempts by the Soviet Union to intimidate the U.S. and force Kennedy to abandon his commitment to preserve the status of West Berlin.[21] There is also little doubt about his determination to maintain U.S. military capabilities and to succeed in the economic and scientific competition with the Soviet Union, including, of course, the area of space exploration.

Kennedy's determination to deal with the Soviet Union from a position of strength and his willingness to confront it when necessary do not, however, add up to reckless militarism or obsessive anti-communism as some have suggested.[22] Kennedy repeatedly challenged the Soviet Union to a different kind of competition. In his inaugural address he challenged the Soviets to use the "wonders of science" for economic progress and space exploration instead of militarism.[23] In a speech at the United Nations 32 months later, Kennedy

---

* Sorensen (p. 602), summing up Kennedy's attitudes about this, wrote that Kennedy was extremely disturbed by "the attitude of that 2 percent of the citizenry of Latin America who owned more than 50 percent of the wealth and controlled most of the political-economic apparatus.... They had friendly ties with U.S. press and business interests who reflected their views in Washington. They saw no reason to alter the ancient feudal patterns of land tenure and tax structure, the top-heavy military budgets, the substandard wages and the concentration of capital. They classified many of their opponents as 'Communists,' considered the social and political reforms of the Alianza [Alliance for Progress] a threat to stability and clung tenaciously to the status quo. Kennedy at all times kept the pressure on—stirring the people in his trips to Mexico, Colombia, Venezuela, and Costa Rica, using what influence he had through OAS and AID to give preference to those governments willing to curb the holdings and privileges of the élite. It was a revolution, he said over and over, and 'those who make peaceful revolution impossible will make violent revolution inevitable.'"

proposed "a new approach to the Cold War" in which the military competition and hostilities would be replaced by a competition to improve life through science, technology, and education.[24] In this speech, in which he also proposed that the U.N. commit itself to "helping bring to all men the fruits of modern science and industry," Kennedy was once again displaying that central commitment, so evident in his national program, to scientific and technological progress. Here, it was offered as a way out of the arms race and of endless confrontation. Hardly the suggestion of an obsessive militarist! In his policies toward underdeveloped nations there was always a more complex agenda than merely countering the spread of communism. That agenda, as indicated before, included his refusal to embrace the tradition of Western domination over Third World nations with its anti-development economic policies.

Kennedy's views in this regard have been testified to by numerous analysts of his policies,[25] some of whom served in the Kennedy administration and had first-hand knowledge of those policies.* Sorensen, who knew Kennedy well for ten years and who served as Special Counsel to Kennedy while he was president, insisted that Kennedy's policies represented a change of U.S. direction and that those leaders in the Third World who sought national independence and economic progress recognized this and appreciated it. Sorensen observed:[26]

> In time most of the neutralist leaders came to respect Kennedy's concepts of independence and diversity and to respect the man who put them forward. They recognized that a subtle shift in attitude had aligned the United States with the aspirations for social justice and economic growth within their countries—that land distribution, literacy drives and central planning were no longer regarded in the U.S. as communist slogans but as reforms to be encouraged and even specified by our government—that this nation's hand was now more often extended to leaders with greater popular backing and social purpose than the "safe" rightwing regimes usually supported by Western diplomats—and that the United States had a president who both understood and welcomed the nationalist revolution and believed that the most relevant contributions from his own country's experience were not its concepts of private property or political parties but its traditions of human dignity and liberty.

Kennedy's support for economic development and Third World nationalism and his tolerance for government economic planning, even when it involved expropriation of property owned by interests in the U.S., all led to conflicts between Kennedy and élites within both the U.S. and foreign nations.[27]

In the next chapter we will deal in considerable detail with the most important of those conflicts. For now the focus will be on some of the specific foreign policy decisions made by Kennedy which, along with his economic development

---

* Chester Bowles, who held three different positions during Kennedy's presidency, expressed some frustration with Kennedy but felt that his own support for Third World nations' aspirations was opposed primarily by Secretary of State Rusk and what Bowles called "Acheson-oriented Cold War elements in the State Department and in the White House" (pp. 358-59, 366, 433).

initiatives, demonstrate that his discussions of economic and political change were more than just words.* We will focus on actions taken by Kennedy, usually against the desires of most of his advisers, which illustrate his intention to shift the U.S. away from a path it had taken during much of the twentieth century, that of becoming the successor to England and other colonial powers in the domination of weaker nations.

When Kennedy went against his advisers on foreign policy, it was usually because he rejected the idea that the U.S. had a right to control economic and political events in other nations. In quite sharp contrast to his strong military stand against the powerful Soviet Union, Kennedy was reluctant to employ military force against smaller and weaker nations. This reluctance was completely consistent with his comments in 1959, quoted earlier, where he rejected "the pageantry of imperialism."

Chester Bowles** cited the following decisions made by Kennedy against a majority of his advisers:[28] refusing to invade Cuba during the Bay of Pigs disaster; refusing to intervene in the Dominican Republic following the assassination of Trujillo; refusing to introduce ground forces into Laos; refusing to escalate our involvement in Vietnam; backing U.N. policy in the Congo; and backing India in its disputes with China and Pakistan. In making these decisions, Kennedy was repeatedly affirming his idea of U.S. foreign policy against those who either shared the neo-colonialist attitudes of various economic interests in Europe and the U.S. or viewed all interests of Third World nations as unimportant compared to the ongoing conflict with communism.

Considering the multitude of factors involved in any significant foreign policy decision, it is reasonable to conclude that consistency across a series of such decisions indicates underlying principles. In all the decisions listed by Bowles, President Kennedy would have had to consider the level of support or opposition to his views among members of his administration, other government agencies, Congress, his party, and the nation at large. He would have needed to consider the short- and long-term consequences of his decisions in terms of his broader goals, the interests of the peoples or nations involved, and the issues of peace and war, particularly as they relate to the U.S.-Soviet relationship. There is consistency in Kennedy's decisions and there seems little doubt that it was based on the principles he stated with respect to the goals of economic development and independence for Third World nations.

Laos

Immediately upon becoming president, Kennedy was faced with a situation in Laos in which the Laotian communists, the Pathet Lao, were temporarily aligned with neutralist forces in a battle against rightwing forces led by General Phoumi

* Paper (pp. 343-44) suggested that there was more image and rhetoric than substance in Kennedy's policy toward Third World nations. The bulk of the evidence indicates Paper was wrong.

** Bowles's three positions in the Kennedy government had been: Under Secretary of State, Special Representative and Adviser on Asian, African, and Latin American Affairs, and Ambassador to India.

Nosavan, actively supported by the CIA in the months preceding Kennedy's inauguration.[29] Events were thought to be leading to a possible communist domination of Laos and increasing dangers to South Vietnam and Cambodia. North Vietnam had a small but important force fighting with the Pathet Lao, and there was a possibility of Chinese involvement. The Soviets, although apparently reluctant to become directly engaged, were giving assistance to the Pathet Lao. Although most U.S. press commentary and sentiment in Congress was opposed to the commitment of U.S. forces, the press and Republican leaders were openly against any coalition or compromise government that would give the communists significant power. The Joint Chiefs of Staff and elements of the CIA and State Department supported military intervention, with the Joint Chiefs taking the position during much of this time that the U.S. had to be willing to use nuclear weapons if necessary. At least two members of Kennedy's administration, Secretary of Defense Robert McNamara and the head of the State Department's Policy Planning Council, Walt Rostow, favored a more aggressive military policy.[30] Also, on the day before Kennedy took office, President Eisenhower emphasized to him the problems in Laos and advised that U.S. forces might be needed.[31]

Although Kennedy went through the preparations for deployment of U.S. forces, he consistently displayed an intention to avoid military intervention. He had stated in his first press conference in January of 1961 that Laos should be an independent country free of domination by either side.[32] He rejected the recommendations to commit forces to Laos to preserve the existing rightwing government and instead opted to support the formation of a neutralist, coalition government.[33] For many reasons, including the internal political situation and the emerging war in Vietnam, this solution would not be ultimately successful. Kennedy's decision not to commit troops may well have been influenced by practicalities such as the problems presented by Laos's geography, or it may have been determined by too much talk by military officials of the possible need to use nuclear weapons to win. The primary reason, however, may simply be the obvious one. That is, the use of military force against a country in a region so recently liberated from French domination could not but seem a continuation of those colonial policies in a new form. As we have seen, Kennedy had no interest in pursuing economic domination of Third World countries. He seems quite logically to have had a similar dislike for the use of the United States' political and military power against backward and weaker nations. This seems to be true in the other crisis he faced in the early months of his presidency, the Bay of Pigs adventure, even though his administration was responsible for continuing U.S. involvement in the covert attempts to overthrow the Castro government.

The Bay of Pigs

The Bay of Pigs invasion involved the landing, at Playa Girón, Cuba, of a Cuban exile force, organized, armed, and trained under Central Intelligence Agency auspices, to overthrow the increasingly pro-communist government. Although this project had been in the works for some time, Kennedy's advisers were not told anything about it in the foreign policy briefings they received during the campaign.[34] The plan was developed during the end of the Eisenhower administration and implemented in April of 1961, three months after Kennedy took office. The project was the creation of Eisenhower's Secretary of Defense Thomas Gates, Director of CIA Allen Dulles, and Dulles's Deputy Director of Plans Richard Bissell.[35] President Eisenhower was apparently kept in the dark concerning important aspects of the invasion plan,[36] and President Kennedy would end up feeling he had been victimized by misinformation and even outright deception.[37]

It is clear that Kennedy only reluctantly permitted this operation to go forward and that he consistently viewed it as essentially a Cuban affair. There are many reasons for his decision to go along with the CIA and Pentagon leaders, who also may have agreed to this based on bad intelligence.[38] Immediately after the invasion, Kennedy cited the following list of arguments given to him by his briefers to convince him to approve the venture: that there was widespread discontent in Cuba; that the anti-Castro Cubans were well trained and ready to go; that both seasonal concerns and increasing Soviet military aid to Cuba made it a now-or-never proposition; that the anti-Castro force would be hard to handle if not allowed to go ahead; that the invasion force could easily escape to fight a guerrilla war if the invasion did not initially go well.[39]

Kennedy felt he had been misled in all these areas, i.e., given "the treatment."[40] Dulles had not only conveyed optimism about the operation, he had in effect told Kennedy he was absolutely certain of its success.*[41] According to Wyden,[42] Kennedy went along primarily for two reasons. First, there would be a national revolt against Castro's government, and, second, the invaders could easily escape the landing site to fight a guerrilla war. Wyden noted that, in fact, neither was remotely possible. The location of the invasion site and the nature of the surrounding terrain made easy escape impossible. There was also no chance of a popular uprising against the government; however, the CIA had done everything to convince Kennedy it was not only possible, but virtually certain. In the process, the Agency appealed to Kennedy's dislike of communism and dictatorship and, perhaps, to one of the few motives that would cause him to intervene in a Third World country, i.e., to give support to a popular movement. As Sorensen put it,[43] Kennedy could see no reason to prevent Cubans who were upset by the direction their revolution had taken from attempting to take it back.

This idea of lending support to a popular revolt seems to have been critical in overriding Kennedy's continuous reluctance and doubt.[44] Kennedy was told a month before the invasion by Dulles and Bissell that there was already an organized resistance in Cuba involving thousands of people and that the invasion

---

* In the midst of the deterioration of the invasion, Allen Dulles displayed a very strange level of detachment and disinterest, choosing to discuss an upcoming Washington dinner instead of being briefed on the developments in Cuba (Wyden, pp. 265-66).

would get active support from as much as one-fourth of the population. The CIA falsely reported to Kennedy in April, just before he gave the go-ahead, widespread active opposition to Castro.[45] Shortly before approving the invasion, Kennedy received an extremely positive evaluation of the exile force from a respected Marine colonel and received a further spurious CIA evaluation that not only portrayed the whole country as in a state of quiet revolt, but also claimed that the Cuban army was so penetrated by anti-Castro forces that it probably would not fight.[46]

These evaluations turned out to be wildly inaccurate. There is a serious question whether these massive failures in intelligence were honest mistakes or part of a strategy to manipulate Kennedy into a situation in which he would have only the following choices: He could fail to give direct military assistance to this doomed operation and later feel greater pressure to use military force somewhere else; or he could use U.S. military forces and, in effect, destroy his credibility in the Third World as a leader who opposed Western military intervention. From beginning to end, Kennedy was on record, publicly and privately, that under no circumstances would the U.S. commit its military forces against Cuba, and he essentially lived up to this promise.[47] In spite of these statements and decisions, and in spite of the apparent understanding of them by the CIA, the Pentagon, and the Cuban exile force, the operation was coordinated and carried out by all of them as if it were assumed Kennedy would deploy U.S. forces if requested.[48] This strange behavior, the terribly misleading reports of the CIA, and the great enthusiasm of Dulles and others in promoting the operation all suggest the possibility of intentional manipulation of the new president. That Kennedy suspected such is certainly not a result of paranoia.

The men who dreamed up the Bay of Pigs invasion had already misled and deceived Eisenhower. Secretary of Defense Gates, a veteran of Naval Intelligence who went on to become president and then chairman of the Morgan Guaranty Bank, allegedly ordered the 1960 Gary Powers U-2 flight that undermined Eisenhower's summit with Khrushchev. He did this against Eisenhower's specific orders to suspend those flights. Without authorization, he also put U.S. forces on alert during the summit.[49] Another architect of the Bay of Pigs fiasco, Richard Bissell, was the man who developed and ran the U-2 flights and almost certainly played a role in the Gates-Gary Powers mess.[50] As was later discovered by Kennedy, Bissell had also disobeyed his direct orders and used American pilots (four of whom were killed) at the Bay of Pigs.[51] Ultimately, Kennedy refused to commit U.S. forces to the operation, despite the pleas of the CIA, the Pentagon, and most of his top advisers, such as McGeorge Bundy* and Dean Rusk.[52] And, in the end, the mission failed, and Kennedy decided to sack Dulles and Bissell.[53]

---

* Bundy was a long-time friend and former student at Yale of CIA Deputy Director Bissell (Wyden, pp. 10-18).

Kennedy would not change his determination to oppose communism, but this fiasco only strengthened his reluctance to use U.S. military power against Third World nations and was, along with the decision on Laos, the beginning of an ongoing policy split with not just the CIA and the more aggressive leaders in the military, but also those within or outside of his administration who wanted to pursue an imperial policy. Two and a half years later, November 18, 1963, Kennedy returned to the issue of Cuba in a speech in Florida.[54] There he observed that the problems of poverty and underdevelopment "will not be solved simply by complaints about Castro, by blaming all problems on Communism or generals or nationalism." Even though Kennedy was to be tempted to engage in another military venture, Vietnam, it would be pro-development and anti-imperialist goals that guided most of his decisions.

The Congo

One of those decisions involved yet another crisis with which Kennedy was confronted in the first weeks and months of his presidency. In the Congo crisis he would be confronted in a very clear way by the two evils he spoke so much about. The Congo had received, rather abruptly, its independence from Belgium in 1960. In the turmoil that followed, a multitude of groups contended for power, but two were of particular concern to Kennedy. One was the Soviet-backed supporters of Patrice Lumumba, the first premier of the independent Congo, who had been deposed by President Joseph Kasavubu in September 1960 and assassinated in a CIA-backed operation several days before Kennedy took office. These forces were allied around Antoine Gizenga, Lumumba's successor. The second group was led by Moise Tshombe, the president of the secessionist state of Katanga, with backing from financial and mining interests in Great Britain, Belgium, and France.

Sorensen emphasizes Kennedy's concern with the communist threat in his account of the events:[55]

> The Kennedy Congo policy was largely an extension of the Eisenhower policy. Its aim was the restoration of stability and order to a reunited, independent and viable Congo, free from Communist domination and free from both civil war and cold war conflicts.

Chester Bowles[56] and Roger Hilsman,[57] both members of the Kennedy administration, place greater emphasis on Kennedy's opposition to the imperialist policies of Great Britain and Belgium. Bowles described the situation:[58]

> Since 1960, when the Congo became independent, it had been beset with dissension and violence. The basic issue was whether the copper-rich province of Katanga, which was controlled politically by Moise Tshombe, would be permitted to become a separate state or whether the Congo would exist as a united country. Belgium had

substantial financial interests in Katanga, which it was assumed Tshombe could be trusted to protect.

Bowles said that this became an issue of "nationalism versus colonialism," pitting British, French, and Belgian financiers who owned the copper mines in Katanga against nationalist forces.[59] Whatever Eisenhower's personal views may have been, it appears that the government that Kennedy took over was heavily biased in favor of old European interests. Bowles said that the Joint Chiefs, the Defense Department, and the European Bureau of the State Department all sympathized with Belgian interests and felt that ex-colonial areas in Africa should "end up as spheres of influence of their former colonial rulers."[60]

The conflict between Kennedy and the forces seeking to perpetuate European control of resources in the Congo was clear and quite open. Kennedy would publicly identify the Union Minière copper company as a source of the problems, and Great Britain would warn the Kennedy administration and the United Nations against any attempt to impose a solution.[61] It also appears that the Central Intelligence Agency was actively involved on the British-Belgian side at the time Kennedy took office.[62]

Kennedy would, over a period of almost two years, pursue a policy of supporting United Nations efforts, including the use of military forces, to prevent the breakup of the Congo. The Kennedy-U.N. policy ultimately succeeded in January of 1963. In the short term at least, this was one situation in which Kennedy successfully opposed imperialist or neo-colonialist interests in the U.S. and Europe and also prevented an expansion of communism in Africa. An independent and unified Congo (Zaire since 1971) was preserved, even if, as Kennedy noted in September of 1963, the difficult task of economic development remained.[63] There was to be further political and military conflict in the Congo in 1964 and 1965.

Kennedy faced a similar array of political forces in his attempt to work out a constructive relationship with Indonesia. The country was led by President Ahmed Sukarno, who possessed excellent credentials as a nationalist leader. Sukarno had helped organize the Indonesian Nationalist Party in the 1920s and became president of the newly independent nation in 1949. While 1949 ended several centuries of Dutch rule over Indonesia, the Netherlands in 1960 still controlled West New Guinea, and in that year Sukarno began a campaign to force the Netherlands to transfer control of this territory to Indonesia.[64] When Kennedy took office, the U.S. relationship with Sukarno's government was not good, due to a considerable degree to an attempt in 1958 by the CIA to overthrow Sukarno.[65] This interference in Indonesia was largely the effort of Secretary of State John Foster Dulles and his brother, CIA Director Allen Dulles.[66]

Within the country, Sukarno was straddling rightwing forces in the military and a strong indigenous communist movement. There was also an active Soviet and Chinese interest in the Indonesian-Dutch conflict. Within the U.S. State Department and the CIA there was strong support for the Netherlands.[67] As was the case with the Congo, Kennedy went against the neo-colonialists in his own government and essentially supported Sukarno's views over those of the Dutch. Indonesian preparations in 1962 for military action against the Netherlands and Kennedy's pressure on the Dutch led to Dutch capitulation and an agreement to transfer the territory to Indonesia in 1963.[68]

While Kennedy's actions were apparently not quite fast enough nor emphatic enough to completely satisfy Sukarno,[69] his policies did represent something qualitatively different from both the previous attempts to undermine Sukarno and the subsequent policies of President Johnson. They were, in the political and diplomatic arena, another indication that Kennedy meant to steer a course away from neo-colonialism while still attempting to counter Soviet or Chinese expansion.*

Vietnam

Probably the most widely debated foreign policy issue of the Kennedy administration is Vietnam. Literally hundreds of journalists, historians, government officials, and others have written articles or books dealing to some extent with Kennedy's Vietnam policy and his intentions.** The discussion here will be as brief as possible. It is true that we can never know for certain what Kennedy would have done. However, given Kennedy's record of both statements and actions, the burden of proof should rest with those who claim that he would have followed the same general policy as his successor, Lyndon Johnson.

Kennedy's position on what was a multi-faceted political and economic problem was quite consistent. He was against a continuation of Western colonialist domination of Vietnam. He did not want to see a communist takeover of the region. He favored support of an anti-communist government in Vietnam, or South Vietnam, as long as such a government would offer social, political, and economic progress and could thereby acquire the support of the population. He opposed a massive commitment of U.S. forces to fight a war that he felt the Vietnamese had to fight primarily on their own. Writing just prior to becoming president, Kennedy observed:[70]

> Indochina presents a clear case study in the power of the anticolonial revolution sweeping Asia and Africa. What has happened also demonstrates that national independence can lead to genuine resistance to Communism. It is a long, sad story with a hopeful chapter, but the end not in sight.
>
> On a trip to Asia in 1951 I saw firsthand that in Indochina we had allied ourselves with a colonial regime that had no real support from the people.

---

* In one case Kennedy had to override the advice of his normally anti-communist advisors (Rusk, Bundy, and McNamara) in making a decision to increase military aid to India in the midst of India's confrontation with Communist China (Bowles, p. 439).

** The release of Oliver Stone's film *JFK* in 1991 alone triggered hundreds of newspaper and magazine articles.

In a 1954 speech in the Senate,[71] Kennedy first said that he could support "some commitment of our manpower" to prevent communist domination of Indochina but he then qualified this with the following:

> But to pour money, material, and men, into the jungles of Indochina without at least a remote prospect of victory would be dangerously futile and self-destructive.... Moreover, without political independence for the associated states, the other Asian nations have made it clear that they regard this as a war of colonialism; and the "united action" [quoting John Foster Dulles] which is said to be so desperately needed for victory in that area is likely to end up as unilateral action by our own country. Such intervention, without participation by the armed forces of the other nations of Asia, without the support of the great masses of the peoples of the associated states, with increasing reluctance and discouragement on the part of the French—and, I might add, with hordes of Chinese Communist troops poised just across the border in anticipation of our unilateral entry into their kind of battleground—such intervention would be virtually impossible in the type of military situation which prevails in Indochina.

Kennedy then quoted his own remarks from 1951, when he had criticized our alliance with the French effort to retain its empire and had emphasized that successful resistance to communism depended on indigenous popular sentiment.

Kennedy was, for a time in the 1950s, impressed with the efforts of South Vietnam's President Diem to rally the population to the anti-communist cause.[72] Kennedy came into office hoping to support that effort. Consistent with his remarks over the course of a decade, however, President Kennedy would remain emphatically opposed to making Vietnam an American war, and he remained convinced that the war could not be won without the broadbased popular support of the Vietnamese people.[73]

During his presidency he consistently rejected recommendations to introduce U.S. ground forces, and, according to numerous sources, he became increasingly inclined to extricate the U.S. military altogether.[74] In rejecting an expanded military involvement, Kennedy went against the Joint Chiefs and a host of high-level people in his government, including Dean Rusk, Robert McNamara, and McGeorge and William Bundy.[75]

Any interpretation of Kennedy's policies in Vietnam must also take into account the substantial evidence indicating that he was victimized by slanted and sometimes grossly inaccurate intelligence reports.[76] Misrepresentations of important aspects of the situation in Vietnam (*e.g.*, level of popular support for the communists versus the Saigon government; estimates of enemy troop strength and casualties) seemed to be intended to convince Kennedy that things were going well, that our allies were increasing their support among the people of South Vietnam, and that increased U.S. efforts would be effective. For a time this misleading intelligence elicited from Kennedy a partial commitment, but even that was waning by 1963.

In the end, four points are clear. First, Kennedy did not want to see Vietnam or neighboring countries come under communist rule. Second, he was consistent in his opposition to the U.S. acting like or in fact being a neo-colonialist successor to France, and he continuously looked to the South Vietnamese government to implement social and economic reforms and to build popular support for its opposition to communism. Third, while he allowed the U.S. commitment to grow, he consistently resisted pressures to commit the U.S. to a general war in Vietnam. Fourth, it was not Kennedy but Johnson who drastically expanded U.S. involvement.

In every situation involving a Third World nation, Kennedy's decisions were based on a number of considerations. These included the determination to avoid neo-colonialist actions, a willingness to support opposition to communism if it had popular support and included progressive political and economic policies, and a reluctance to use U.S. military power against smaller nations. These considerations, plus a concern with domestic political realities, produced at times what appeared to be ambiguous policies.

This was not, however, a reflection of lack of principle or determination. Both of those traits were demonstrated in a multitude of choices and actions related to domestic and foreign policy. The apparent ambiguities resulted instead from the clash between Kennedy's purposes and the complex situations and purposes of diverse opponents.

President Kennedy tried to put the United States on the side of development. He also attempted to put the United States on a course which transcended the conflict between communist revolution and entrenched and reactionary interests determined to continue long-standing policies of suppressing progressive economic development. He proposed increased cooperation among nations to achieve economic development, and he attempted to reorganize both foreign aid and lending programs to facilitate development. He was not only tolerant of, but actively supportive of, government economic planning within and among nations, stopping short of the total state control that was associated in many communist nations with totalitarianism. Kennedy was against any attempt to replace the direct colonial domination of Third World nations with an informal system of economic control backed up by the national economic and military resources of the United States.

Logically enough, Kennedy was willing to confront the Soviet Union when he thought it was necessary (Cuba and Berlin) and tempted to intervene in Third World nations if he thought there was indigenous popular resistance to communist forces (Bay of Pigs and Vietnam). But in Cuba he consistently tried to minimize direct U.S. involvement, and in Vietnam he did less than most of his advisers proposed and ultimately refused to commit the U.S. to war. His political and military decisions elsewhere (Laos, Indonesia, Congo) were very consistent with his stated objections to colonialism, or anything like it, as were his economic initiatives and his personal attitudes and actions toward independent Third World leaders.

Kennedy's domestic program was coherently and consistently oriented toward the goal of making life better for as many people as possible. His purposes in international policy were much the same, even though the methods for achieving this could not be as direct. Technological and scientific progress, the expansion of productive capacity, and rising real levels of material consumption were the ingredients of his overall commitment to economic progress. Space exploration, service in the Peace Corps, and the goals of reducing poverty and eliminating racial injustice provided adventure, challenge, and moral purpose. All of these goals were in harmony with one other, providing a concern for both the spiritual and the physical well-being of people, thereby expressing what many would consider the best elements of Western civilization.[77]

To some it may not be readily apparent that there could be opposition to Kennedy's efforts to use government to stimulate economic progress, but such opposition did exist. This opposition arose as a reaction to both his domestic and his international policy, and opposition to both often came from the same groups of people. What is perhaps surprising about this opposition is that it was not restricted to the *means* employed by Kennedy, *i.e.*, government actions to shape economic decisions. It extended even to the *goal* itself, *i.e.*, economic progress—global and national. Much of this opposition was very specific, and it was publicly stated. Even when the opposition was not so open, it was nevertheless clear and is part of the public record. It all adds up to a rather amazing confrontation between a president bent on driving the country and the world forward and a combination of old forces determined to go in the opposite direction.

FOUR

Kennedy's Opponents

President Kennedy was well aware of the significant opposition to his policies. This was reflected in public comments and in remarks in private conversations. This chapter examines Kennedy's own, generally accurate, identification of those opponents, in banking and big business, and in the media organizations aligned with those interests.

His understanding of this opposition was indicated by his response to a reporter's question during a 1962 news conference.[1]

> Q: Mr. President, there is a feeling in some quarters, sir, that big business is using the stock market slump as a means of forcing you to come to terms.... [T]heir attitude is "Now we have you where we want you." Have you seen any reflection of this attitude?
> Kennedy: I can't believe I am where business, big business, wants me!

The president's riposte indicated not only how conscious he was of opposition, but also how acutely aware he was that his opposition was not "business" in general, but a numerically much smaller though more powerful group.

After an appearance before the Business Council, made up of leaders of top banks and corporations, Kennedy later privately observed that this was the only audience that did not "rise to its feet upon the entrance of the President of the United States."[2] This organization, known as the Business Advisory Council until 1962, was created in 1933 and had a semi-official relationship with the government until a dispute arose with the Kennedy administration over this special relationship. Kennedy felt that it was improper for this élite group to have special access to government officials and information that other businesses and the public did not have. Meetings between government officials and Council representatives continued after this disagreement, but on a less formal and less frequent basis.[3]

Whether Kennedy disliked bankers in general, as suggested by Irving Bernstein,[4] he was concerned about their attitudes toward him and their ability to affect his policies. Kennedy indicated to Sorensen, apparently in 1962, that he had reason to think that in 1960 American bankers had triggered a run on gold that was timed to undermine him politically, by suggesting a possible panic upon his election. He was determined not to be vulnerable to such tactics in 1964.[5]

It interested President Kennedy that there was hostility toward him even though the economy as a whole and most businesses did extremely well during his presidency.* In one of his last speeches, delivered to the Florida Chamber of Commerce on November 18, 1963,[6] Kennedy discussed the fact that "many" businessmen believed that his administration was antibusiness. In part, he said the following:

> The hard facts contradict these beliefs. This administration is interested in the healthy expansion of our economy. We are interested in the steady progress of our society, and it is in this kind of program, in my opinion, that American business has the largest stake. Why is it that profits are at an all-time high in the nation today? It is because the nation as a whole is prospering. It is because our Gross National Product is rising from $500 billion to $600 billion, a record rise of $100 billion in three years—thirty-six months. It is because industrial production in the last three years has increased 22 percent and personal income 15 percent. It is because, as the *Wall Street Journal* pointed out last week, the United States now leads most of Western Europe in the rate of business expansion. For the first time in many years, in the last eighteen months our growth rate exceeds that of France and Germany. It is because, as *Fortune* magazine recently pointed out, corporate profits in America are now rising much faster than corporate profits overseas. It is because these profits have not been eaten up by an inflationary spiral. And finally, it is because we have reversed the dismal trend toward ever more frequent recessions, which are the greatest enemy of profits. By next April, with the indispensable help of the pending tax cut bill, the United States will be sailing with the winds of the longest and strongest peacetime economic expansion in our nation's entire history.**
> I do not say that all this is due to the administration alone, but neither is it all accidental. The fiscal and monetary policies which we have followed are the key factors in whether the economy moves toward a path of expansion or restriction. In

---

* Paper (pp. 151, 153) says that the evidence shows that most businessmen did not view the administration as antibusiness, but there was considerable hostility among business leaders "on Wall Street and elsewhere." This is generally accurate, but vague.

** Many of us have probably been made cynical about the use of this sort of rhetoric and about political leaders' claims that the country is doing well. But as the evidence shows, Kennedy's claim that the country was enjoying an unusually high level of economic progress was accurate.

the last three years, American business and industry have directly benefitted from a host of our legislative and administrative actions, which increased corporate flow, increased markets at home and abroad, increased consumer purchasing power and increased plant modernization and productivity. And still other steps have been taken to curb the wage-price spiral. In the first six months of 1963 there was less time lost in strikes than in any other period since the Second World War.

I do not say that these actions were taken for the benefit of business alone. They were taken to benefit the country. Some of them were labeled pro-business, some of them labeled anti-business, depending upon the viewpoint of the opposing groups. But that kind of label is meaningless. This Administration is "pro" the public interest. Nor do I say that all of these policies could please all American businessmen all of the time. So long as the interests and views of businessmen frequently clash with each other, no president could possibly please them all.

Most businessmen, though perhaps not most business spokesmen, are associated with small business. They ask the government for assistance to protect them against monopoly, to assure them of reasonable credit, to enable them to participate in defense contracts. And both large and small business work with the various arms of the administration every day on trade, transportation, procurement, balance of payments, and international business affairs. They do not show the hostility, which is so often described, or find that our policies and personnel are so incompatible with their own.

The hostility came, in the president's view, not from the majority of businessmen, but from certain segments of big business and from "business spokesmen." Whether he was referring to organizations such as the Business Council or to the media, or to both, is not clear. As for the media, there is some irony in his use of *Fortune* magazine and the *Wall Street Journal* in his own defense. Not only had Kennedy reportedly expressed displeasure and anger with both of these publications,[7] but they were, in fact, two of the most hostile critics of Kennedy and his economic policies. Both spoke for leading financial and business interests. Both were related in numerous ways to the two most influential financial groups in the United States—Morgan and Rockefeller. Those connections will be discussed after we examine the assault on Kennedy that appeared in *Time-Life-Fortune* and the *Wall Street Journal*.

The "Free Enterprise" Repudiation of Kenendy: The Lucepress

At the time of Kennedy's election, Henry Luce's media empire, then made up primarily of *Time*, *Life*, and *Fortune* magazines, was one of the nation's most influential opinion shapers.* Henry Luce had started *Time* magazine in the early

---

* This media empire has since grown tremendously to include, among other components, *People* and *Money* magazines; Warner Studios; Little, Brown and Scott Foresman book publishers; HBO Video; and the Channel One Cable Service.

1920s with help from the families of two partners in J.P. Morgan & Co., a relative of a Rockefeller partner, and a number of individuals who had been, with Luce, members of Yale University's élitist Skull and Bones society.[8] Some of these relationships were probably rooted in Luce's family history. His father also graduated from Yale (1892) and was a close personal friend of Mrs. Cyrus Hall McCormick, heir to the International Harvester fortune.[9] The McCormicks became related through marriage to the Rockefeller family and had business associations with the Morgans.[10] There were connections between *Time-Life-Fortune* and particularly the Morgan interests during Kennedy's presidency.

Henry Luce entered Yale in 1916, was admitted to Skull and Bones in 1919, and went on to study at Oxford. Luce once described himself as "a Protestant, a Republican, and a free-enterpriser."[11] This image is, to say the least, incomplete. That self-description suggests what Richard Nixon might have called "cloth-coat Republicanism," an image of competitive business, small-town values, mainstream Christianity, middle-class politics. In reality, Luce was quite different. Consistent with his personal and family background, Luce's conservatism was more aristocratic. He admired royalty, at times showed open disdain for the Constitution and democracy, and expressed in the 1920s and 1930s an approval of Mussolini's fascism and at least an ambiguous attitude toward Hitler.[12] Luce traveled in the highest social circles in both the United States and Europe. His friends and acquaintances included Prince Bernhard of the Netherlands, the Duke and Duchess of Windsor, Lady Astor, Winston Churchill, John D. Rockefeller III, John Foster Dulles, and Robert M. Hutchins.[13]

These are not the social contacts of even most fur-coat Republicans. Luce's lifestyle also often varied greatly from that self-description. Long before drug experimentation became common on university campuses, Luce and his wife were ingesting LSD, at times in the company of such avant-garde drug users as Aldous Huxley and Christopher Isherwood.[14] Luce advocated such experimentation to the top people at *Time, Life,* and *Fortune,* and in 1957 *Life* magazine printed a 17-page article by a J.P. Morgan vice-president, R. Gordon Wasson, praising psychedelic drugs.*[15]

Luce was obviously far from a conventional, middle-class Republican of the 1950s. He was by education, wealth, and social connections a full member of the upper class. Within that class he was a leading defender of the U.S. position in the world, at times clashing with those who favored greater integration of the U.S. Establishment with those of England and Europe.** Luce's notion of the U.S. role globally and his conception of "free enterprise" are, along with his

---

* *Life* apparently reversed its position nine years later, after LSD use had spread to the counterculture. In March of 1966 the magazine printed a severe criticism of LSD (Lee and Shlain, p. 150).

** Luce's brand of American patriotism led him in the early 1950s to attack Arnold Toynbee's assertion that the U.S. was merely a peripheral part of European civilization. Similarly, he questioned the loyalty of prominent figures such as Arthur Schlesinger, Jr., and Eleanor Roosevelt (Swanberg, pp. 465-66, 470) because they accepted a view similar to Toynbee's.

aristocratic leanings, reflected in Time, Inc.'s often vitriolic attacks on President Kennedy's policies.

In February 1963, *Fortune* observed[16] that the unfriendly attitudes of many businessmen toward "Kennedy & Co." could be explained. Even though Kennedy was pursuing a policy of giving tax relief to business, *Fortune* suggested there was "some general characteristic of this Administration" that business suspected and opposed, but the reasons for this opposition had not been "clearly formulated." *Fortune* went on to suggest that the "trouble can be found in the Administration's tendency to employ the vast discretionary powers of the federal government toward whatever ends the men in power consider desirable." In this context, the article cited Kennedy's confrontation with the steel companies, his support of labor in its dispute with companies in the aerospace industry, and the manner in which he pressured private interests to provide the resources to "ransom" the Cubans captured by Castro during the Bay of Pigs fiasco. The Lucepress, both before and after this critique of Kennedy, rejected much more than these specific actions taken by Kennedy.

In June of 1961, *Fortune*[17] simultaneously criticized Kennedy for being insufficiently activist in foreign policy (*i.e.*, not fully backing the Bay of Pigs invasion of Cuba) and all too activist in domestic policy. Luce's magazine then accused the president of having "little understanding of the American political economic system," of pursuing policies that threatened to "undermine a strong and free economy," and of attempting to implement controls which would "erode away basic American liberties" and lead to "resentment and anger" at his policies.*[18] *Fortune* said that Kennedy was seeking to implement "a master government plan" in an economy that operates "by means of millions of individual decisions in response to the free play of prices, wages and profits." Specifically, they called his investment tax credit an "elaborate gimmick" and an example of Kennedy's attempts to "manipulate the economy." They criticized the Kennedy tax proposals that continued tax breaks for profits made through productive investment in underdeveloped countries while taking those benefits away from investments in developed countries.[19]

In the following year, John Davenport, one of *Fortune*'s three managing editors, intensified the ideological campaign. Kennedy was now portrayed not only as a misguided, overzealous president, but as a reactionary and a cultist. Davenport's article[20] began with the following:

> The trouble with the New Frontiersman is not that he is too radical but that he has missed the bus. In a literal sense he is reactionary; he belongs to a cult that is as old as Diocletian.**

* Nowhere in this "free enterprise" assault on Kennedy is there an acknowledgment that all modern economies feature some level of concentrated economic power (*e.g.*, in the creation of money and the establishment of interest rates) or that there was in some U.S. industries a long history of organized economic power (*e.g.*, banking, oil, steel).

** The reference is to the Roman Emperor's efforts at price controls.

Continuing in this vein, Davenport[21] accused Kennedy and unnamed advisers of being out of touch with modern history because they didn't recognize that government in "our day" must be restricted essentially to national defense, the maintenance of law and order, and the provision of a sound and dependable currency system. Davenport then referred to Walter Lippman's assertion that anyone attempting to direct the economy was a "reactionary." As it happens, the idea of government being propounded by *Fortune* is rooted in the seventeenth-century, pre-industrial ideas of John Locke, and Kennedy's originate more in the eighteenth, nineteenth, and twentieth centuries. Ignoring for the moment the absurd argument that Kennedy was a Diocletian reactionary, we will continue to focus on *Fortune*'s objections to his policies.

Davenport argued[22] that people like Kennedy base their political philosophy on economics, and that the economics requires interventionist government. This attitude, he said, permeated Kennedy's messages to Congress and was implicit in his "constant talk" of moving America forward. This is, of course, substantially correct. Davenport singled out for specific criticism[23] Kennedy's intimidation of the steel companies, his failure to heed David Rockefeller's admonition concerning a balanced budget, and Kennedy's determination to keep interest rates down.

In a 1963 article, *Fortune*[24] accepted Kennedy's tax reductions even though they would produce a deficit. *Fortune* did so, however, based on the conditions that the deficit would be temporary and that there would be no increases in government spending. If this was a concession, it was an extremely limited one, for the article continued the Lucepress barrage against Kennedy by advising that the real wise men in economic policy were such enemies of government action as Adam Smith, Friedrich Hayek,* and Milton Friedman.[25] The article continued by describing as "especially unfortunate" Kennedy's attempt in 1962 to have Congress give the president discretionary powers "to manipulate the tax level against the business cycle."**[26] Later in 1963, *Fortune*[27] encouraged Congress to prevent Kennedy from using tax and budget policy as "instruments for managing the economy" and criticized Kennedy and his advisers, Kermit Gordon and Heller, for using budget deficits to promote growth rather than for the much more limited purpose of countering recession.

It is hard to imagine a more emphatic repudiation of a president, at least within limits normally observed by major media entities. (Indeed, some specific attacks did go beyond even the *Fortune* characterization of Kennedy as a reactionary.)

---

* Hayek (pp. 70-73) viewed any and all attempts to use government to mold the economy as threats to freedom. He was opposed to what is known in the U.S. as implied powers, which allow government some flexibility in promoting the interests of the nation and instead suggested limited government operating under fixed rules. Like most supporters of these views, Hayek and Friedman talk as if there were no concentrated private power and, instead, create a fictitious image of a decentralized, market-driven economy.

** These proposals are described in Chapter Two, in the section on "The Federal Budget, Deficit Spending and Money," *supra*, page 27.

Fortune was among the leaders in rejecting virtually every major aspect of Kennedy's domestic economic program. These "free enterprise" assaults on Kennedy were presented in an extraordinarily biased way. The attacks on the president's efforts to steer the economy toward real growth in production were made in the context of two unstated and unproven assertions. One was an implicit notion that there were no parts of the U.S. economy operating on the basis of concentrated economic power and featuring a type of coordination and planning. This was false, ignoring known realities in areas such as commercial banking and the petroleum industry, and, to some degree, the steel and auto industries. The second assumption posited the existence of a clear body of evidence showing that all government measures to shape the economy had historically been failures, and that maximum freedom for private enterprise, even if it is highly organized, had always led to positive results. In the next chapter we demonstrate that both of these assumptions are, to say the least, dubious. The Lucepress was not very interested in a careful review of facts, but was primarily concerned with portraying Kennedy as a threat to the free-enterprise system and to liberty itself. This line of criticism extended to the president's foreign policy. This should not be surprising; as demonstrated earlier, there was a consistency between JFK's domestic and foreign programs. Both were organized around the goal of economic progress.

Early in 1962 the editors of *Fortune* expressed their concern that the Alliance for Progress and other Kennedy administration programs were being heavily influenced by the doctrine of the Economic Commission for Latin America, a group established in 1947 under United Nations auspices. *Fortune* charged that this doctrine favored government *dirigisme*, that is, a type of economic nationalism which included economic planning to achieve rapid growth. *Fortune* advised that it would be "insane" for the Kennedy administration to embrace this *dirigisme** and turn its back on those in Latin America who favor "sound money, higher productivity in exportable goods, and internal free enterprise."[28] What this quite literally meant was that *Fortune* wanted Latin nations to pursue a conservative economic policy focused not on internal development and improving the standard of living, but on fulfilling the traditional role within colonial and neo-colonial relations of exporting wealth and allowing foreign domination of their economies. This was precisely the policy that Kennedy had repeatedly rejected.

In January and March of 1963 *Fortune* published a series of articles critical of Kennedy's foreign policy. Some of this criticism focused on the president's support of anti-colonialist efforts even where this policy offended powerful interests in Europe. Kennedy was charged with "vulnerable and/or discreditable

---

* The *Round Table*, a publication representing the views of part of the British upper class, observed in 1965 that private enterprise in the U.S. was "terrified" of *dirigisme* but could live with and benefit from other kinds of government involvement in the economy, such as President Johnson's programs (*Round Table*, 1964-65: 256).

acts in foreign policy—such as forcing the Dutch to surrender West New Guinea to Indonesian blackmail" and with "promoting U.N. charter violation in the Congo."[29] In both of these cases President Kennedy was pursuing his policy of opposing continued domination of Third World nations by Western economic interests. The president was also accused of waging the greatest effort in U.S. peacetime history to control and manage the news. This alleged manipulation, it was claimed, was going on in the area of foreign policy and in domestic matters (*e.g.*, Kennedy was accused of trying in 1962 to suppress information about the budget deficit).[30] The primary focus remained, however, JFK's economic policy. In January, Julio E. Nuñez, a Harvard-educated, Cuban-American investment banker, accused Kennedy[31] of turning his back on those élites in Latin America who were attempting "to promote sound limited government and free economies." Shortly after this, *Fortune* published an extensive and emphatic repudiation of the president written by *Fortune* editor Charles J. V. Murphy. Murphy had been one of Kennedy's severest critics after the Bay of Pigs failure and would be one of the media's most emphatic supporters of the war in Vietnam.[32] In March of 1963 it was the president's commitment to economic development that was at issue.

Murphy's broadside at the Kennedy program was quite comprehensive, not in detailed analysis but in its overall condemnation of both Kennedy's methods and his goals. Murphy asserted[33] that whatever success was being achieved through foreign aid was neutralized by excessive population growth, but then went on to focus on the basic means and ends of Kennedy's policies. He claimed that the aid program, which was in the form of "technical assistance (mostly grants) and soft loans for long-range economic development" had no "unifying economic policy other than a wearied assumption that the U.S. must somehow satisfy the universal lust for industrialization and growth. And the process has clearly got out of hand."[34]

What he described as "lust" was, and still is, a desire for a decent life. What he described as a "wearied assumption" was in fact something that had not been the basis of Western policy toward underdeveloped nations. While Kennedy's attitudes about this were probably not unique, they were at odds with a far more "wearied" set of assumptions, *i.e.*, that the peoples of Africa, Latin America, and Asia were to be perpetually poor exporters of raw materials, agricultural products, and payment on debt.

Murphy made his position clear[35] by suggesting that any economic assistance that might be provided should be accompanied by "a combined effort to organize the capacity of the underdeveloped countries to produce more and more primary commodities for export, the only path for those countries toward true 'self-sustaining' growth and social stability."

In hindsight, it seems obvious that this was double-talk which attached a couple of nice-sounding words to what was a clear proposal that the economic position of most people in the world should never change. The difference between these views and those of President Kennedy could hardly be more stark.

Along with this rejection of Kennedy's attempt to use aid and soft loans to assist economic development, Murphy admonished the president for engaging in negotiations on a nation-to-nation basis, which bypassed the international financial community and co-opted U.S. producers by linking aid to purchases of goods made in the United States.

There was also criticism of Kennedy's failure to attach tough conditions or requirements to these loans. This referred to the demand noted earlier that recipients of loans and aid adhere to a conservative government spending policy and open up their countries to more foreign investment.* Murphy[36] made some of these points as follows:

No "self-sustained" growth is going to come from the Alianza [Alliance for Progress] billions unless the client nations brace themselves for the most elementary fiscal disciplines. Some technicians suggest that without these the most salutary course for the U.S. might be to give no money at all. But because Kennedy has staked so much of his personal prestige on making the Alianza work, it is doubtful that Bell could nerve himself for so drastic an action, even with governments as profligate as Brazil.** Nevertheless, long second-thinking has prompted a basic question: Would it not have been wiser to seek a cure for Latin America's economic woes through an international apparatus that included the major European nations, long bankers to that region and its first market?

This suggestion that nation-to-nation loans and aid should be dropped in favor of arrangements that would achieve more "fiscal discipline" and greater involvement by European lenders accompanied other criticisms of the role that national considerations were playing in Kennedy's policy.

The Kennedy administration was assisting projects in poorer nations based on an agreement that capital goods and technical services be purchased from U.S. producers. Murphy argued[37] that this practice amounted to a "subsidy for U.S. business" and, because it enlisted business self-interest, often supported projects that were inappropriate. Murphy buttressed his assertions by referring to the sources of these criticisms of Kennedy:[38]

a new and formidable criticism is gathering strength in the American business community. That businessmen are critical is not so surprising as the nature of the

---

* These demands are much the same as those known as "conditionalities" in relation to loans to debtor nations made under the auspices of the International Monetary Fund (IMF). The standard package of IMF conditionalities is as follows: abolition or liberalization of foreign exchange and import controls; devaluations of the exchange rate; domestic anti-inflation measures (including control of bank credit, higher interest rates, limits on government spending, higher taxes, elimination of special government subsidies, elimination of price controls); and greater hospitality to foreign investment (Payer, p. 33).
** One year after this article was published, Brazil's "profligate" government was overthrown by a clique of military officers. The new military leaders were immediately recognized by the Johnson administration, and the coup leaders were rewarded with financial aid (Payer, p. 155).

new criticism; it puts industry itself in a culpable role in foreign aid. This line of attack comes principally from Eugene Black, who retired two months ago as president of the International Bank for Reconstruction and Finance, George Champion, chairman of the board of the Chase Manhattan Bank, and Herbert V. Prochnow,* president of the First National Bank of Chicago, himself a former deputy Under Secretary of State for Economic Affairs in Eisenhower's Administration.

The critical businessmen were leading bankers; the culpable businessmen were manufacturers who benefited from Kennedy's credit and aid policies. The point of view represented in Murphy's critique of Kennedy, and in other *Fortune* articles, was, in essence, that of the international financial community.

The criticism of Kennedy's international economic policy was aimed at the purposes of aid and loans, the manner in which the policy was carried out, and the roles to be played by nations and private interests, particularly banks. The Luce press stated clear preferences. Poorer nations should remain primarily exporters of raw materials and agricultural products. They should not "lust" after industrialization. Those nations should pursue very conservative governmental policy and keep their economies open to foreign penetration. Aid and trade should be left, as much as possible, to private enterprise under the guidance of international finance.

Kennedy's initiatives were significantly at odds with all of those preferences. His foreign aid program was supposed to further economic development and free Third World nations from the backwardness and inferiority which were central to colonial and neo-colonial arrangements. He favored nation-to-nation agreements and was willing to bypass the private banks and the "free market." He showed no interest in aggressively demanding that recipients adhere to the other conditions for aid favored by the international banking community.

Those criticisms of international policy were, for the most part, identical with the attacks on Kennedy's national economic program. He was criticized for his attempts to intervene in the private economy for the purpose of stimulating growth. In domestic matters he was labeled a "reactionary" and a Diocletian cultist. In global policy he was accused of feeding the lust for industrialization and for showing a disregard for private interests, free enterprise, and the world's financial leaders.

This series of *Fortune* articles provides a very clear statement of the disagreements with Kennedy's policies that were being voiced by the financial community. *Fortune* magazine was directed at people working in the banking and corporate worlds and was preaching to those most easily, or already, converted. The same kind of criticism was displayed in the more widely read *Life* magazine. The readership of *Life* was much larger than *Fortune*'s and was more than twice

---

* Both Prochnow and Black had strong connections to Rockefeller interests. Black served as a director of Chase Manhattan, and the First National Bank of Chicago was interconnected with Rockefeller financial interests (Lundberg, 1975, p. 40; Collier and Horowitz, 1976, p. 416).

that of *Time* magazine.[39] Because it was geared to a more general audience, its criticisms were less technical.

The early evaluations of the Kennedy administration in *Life* were mixed or positive. On his domestic economic agenda, *Life* had some vaguely stated concerns about future policy decisions,[40] but tentatively concluded that, "Some of his proposals are good, some bad; but at least there is not a wild idea among them, and no radically new policy commitments." Early in 1962[41] *Life* graded JFK's foreign policy and gave him an "A." *Life* approved his tough stand on Berlin, the development of the Peace Corps, his efforts toward arms control, and his dealings with U.S. allies. The Lucepress also supported the increased commitment to South Vietnam, noting that it was part of "Kennedy's determination to make sure that Vietnam will save itself." Finally, *Life* gave its approval of Kennedy's trade policy and his support of U.N. involvement in the Congo; both of these were lauded for their potentially adverse effects on the global influence of communism.

In mid-1962 the tone of *Life*'s examination of Kennedy's domestic policy changed, and he was criticized for treating economic problems as "technical" problems, thereby giving too little attention to the overall importance of economic "freedom."[42] *Life* also advised the president to take an anti-union position and to avoid big-spending in his economic program. Criticism of Kennedy was more intense in 1963, and although *Life* did not again assign a grade to Kennedy, it appears that it would not have given him even a "gentleman's C." In March of 1963,[43] *Life* described Kennedy's use of deficit spending as reckless and careless. It quoted Wisconsin's Senator William Proxmire, who called some of Kennedy's proposals for 1964 "downright shocking," and referred to the concerns being expressed by Governor Nelson Rockefeller of New York.

Much of the criticism in *Life* focused on the federal budget and deficits, but other Kennedy actions were also given less than passing grades. Although the Lucepress generally championed "free enterprise," which would seemingly put it on the side of decentralized and competitive markets, it attacked President Kennedy and the Department of Justice, headed by Robert Kennedy, for blocking or opposing mergers in the railroad and airline industries.[44]

In keeping with its normal rhetoric, *Life*[45] accused Kennedy of interfering with the free flow of international investments with his proposal to increase taxes on purchases by Americans of foreign securities. In this piece, *Life* restated its objection to Kennedy's deficit proposals and quoted David Rockefeller's advice to Kennedy, which was contained in the Rockefeller-Kennedy letters published earlier in *Life*. Finally, the November 22 issue of *Life* indicated its concern that President Kennedy was disengaging from Vietnam, asserting that, "It is *not* a time to relax or schedule U.S. manpower withdrawals in time for our 1964 elections."[46] (This comment by *Life* certainly supports the view that, shortly before his death, Kennedy had indeed decided to reduce or eliminate our military involvement in Vietnam, certainly that the Establishment feared such a move.)

The *Wall Street Journal* and Others

In light of the severe treatment of Kennedy in *Fortune* and *Life*, it makes sense that his reviews would be negative in the *Wall Street Journal*, a paper strongly associated with leading financial and corporate circles. As with the Lucepress, it is perhaps surprising to see the depth and breadth of the hostility. Also of interest is the extent to which the *Journal*'s condemnation of Kennedy conformed to that in the Lucepress. They were not identical; the Lucepress was, for example, a more enthusiastic proponent of the use of American military power. There was on most issues, however, a similarity in outlook, even to the point of using the same terms and historical referents. Whether this was merely a case of one following the other or of likes thinking alike, or an example of organized propaganda is not completely clear. What is clear is that most, if not all, of Kennedy's critics were associated in some way with the others and were part of a generally coherent group.

The *Wall Street Journal* was started in 1889 as part of Dow, Jones & Company. Dow, Jones was created in 1882 as a financial news company by Charles Dow, Eddie Jones, and Charles Bergstresser. Control of Dow, Jones passed in 1902 to Clarence Walker Barron and his wife Jessie. Marriage brought Hugh Bancroft into the Barron family in 1907, and from 1912 to 1933 the enterprise was run by Clarence Walker Barron or Hugh Bancroft.* In 1930 the various publications of the Barron family and Dow, Jones were organized into a single trust named the Financial Press Companies of America (FPCA).[47]

At the time Kennedy became president, the editorial policy of the *Journal* reflected the views of the directors of Dow, Jones; the Bancrofts; *Wall Street Journal* President Bernard Kilgore; and Editor Vermont Royster.[48] The *Journal*'s view of Kennedy was harsh from the beginning. It had already flunked Kennedy for his economic policy before he took office, and an unfriendly exchange occurred in January of 1961 between Kennedy and Royster.[49] Weeks before the inauguration, the *Journal* editorialized that Kennedy should resist the inclination to create a "planned economy." It noted his comments about pursuing the spirit of the Employment Act of 1946, and advised him that the purposes of that act (*i.e.*, maximizing employment, production, and purchasing power through government action) were purely a response to the depression and were not relevant to the 1960s. Finally, it warned against big spending in either domestic or foreign areas.[50]

The *Wall Street Journal*'s criticisms of Kennedy, beginning before he took office, continued after he was dead. Near the end, the *Journal* was even more harsh in its condemnation of the president's policies than it had been at the

---

* Mary Bancroft, Hugh's daughter, was a long-time close friend of Henry Luce. She was also very close to such notables as psychoanalyst Carl Jung and CIA Director Allen Dulles. Mary reportedly clashed with Luce on some issues, with her views representing élites in the U.S. who wanted more cooperation with British or European interests, while Luce favored a leading role for the American Establishment (Mosley, pp. 189-202, 272; Swanberg).

outset.* On October 15, 1963, it accused the Kennedy administration of giving mere "lip-service to economic freedom" while pursuing a foreign aid program that favored socialism and a domestic program that led to bureaucratic control of the economy. The paper charged that Kennedy's policies reflected a hostility to the "philosophy of freedom."[51] A couple of weeks later, it continued this assault, repeating what by that time had been almost continuous criticism of excessive spending, budget deficits, and easy money.** It characterized the Kennedy administration as following perhaps the "most restrictive and reactionary economic policy" in U.S. history. The *Journal* claimed that government activity was crowding out private enterprise, that government was overregulating the economy and interfering in private investment abroad. It concluded by claiming that Adam Smith's free-market economy was being replaced by the "corporate state," wherein the State directed everything without necessarily nationalizing the major organs of production and distribution. This, the *Journal* concluded, "smacks heartily" of eighteenth-century mercantilism.[52]

During the final week of Kennedy's life, the *Journal* acknowledged that there was general prosperity, but claimed there was an uneasiness about Kennedy attributable to his attempts to control the economy, as well as to excessive spending and the growth of government. In a separate article it said that Kennedy's foreign aid often fostered "statist and socialistic institutions."[53] Even after Kennedy's death, the repudiation of his policies continued. The *Journal* noted its differences with Kennedy concerning the proper role of government and referred to the Kennedy spending policy as "economic nonsense." The paper praised Johnson for his apparent recognition that these policies were mistaken.[54]

Concerning foreign aid, the *Journal* had repeatedly[55] accused Kennedy of encouraging state planning, statism, and/or socialism. It criticized Kennedy for having increased the Eisenhower administration's practice of providing soft loans (long-term with little or no interest) and recommended that Kennedy follow more closely the policies of the World Bank.[56] The *Journal's* point of view in foreign policy was less nationalist and less militaristic than most of what appeared in the Lucepress. Like the Lucepress, however, it did take Kennedy to task for betraying European allies (*e.g.*, Belgium and the Netherlands) in the interest of a rigid policy of opposing colonialism.[57]

There were numerous attacks on the Kennedy administration's tax, budget, and monetary policies. There was specific criticism of Kennedy's decision to

---

* In his 1969 book, *John F. Kennedy and the Business Community*, Heath (p. 125) claims that criticism of Kennedy was less harsh in 1963 than in 1961 and early 1962. This may well have been true of most businessmen and some business spokesmen. It is not accurate for the media analyzed here, nor is it accurate for leaders in the financial community and the foreign policy Establishment. The same objections have to be made to Bernard Nossiter's (1964, pp. 2, 41-42) claims that business attitudes toward Kennedy became less critical after Kennedy's confrontation with U.S. Steel.
** It was noted in Chapter Two that Kennedy got the cooperation of the Federal Reserve in keeping interest rates down. There were reports that this cooperation was secured only because Kennedy was putting intense pressure on the Fed's chairman (Nossiter, 1961, p. A4).

engage in deficit spending in order to sustain growth, suggesting that Kennedy's policies would "make even Lord Keynes turn in his grave." The *Journal's* rhetoric suggested that the man in the White House was a dangerous radical, an incompetent, a madman, or all three. Kennedy was referred to as a "potential threat" to the national interest, as "living in a dream-world" and indulging in "deep and damaging delusion," and as a failure on the "economic test."[58]

All of this criticism was part of one overriding accusation leveled against Kennedy: the charge that he was attempting to use the powers of his office and of the federal government to influence and direct economic processes. As we have seen, it was indeed true that Kennedy sought to influence and shape economic decisions in order to increase the nation's capacity to provide a higher standard of living and to solve economic and social problems. Under Kennedy, the *Journal* complained,[59] the government had become the "self-appointed enforcer of progress." It was this tendency in Kennedy, more than any particular policy, that infuriated the Lucepress and the *Wall Street Journal.*

The *Journal* criticized specific policies (Kennedy's actions toward U.S. Steel, his proposal to put a tax on the purchase of foreign securities from foreigners and on long-term loans to foreign borrowers, and his proposal to tax the earnings of foreign subsidiaries of U.S. companies), but saved its most in-depth critique for Kennedy's overall attempt to enforce progress.

In October of 1962 it suggested that Kennedy and his advisers were moving toward a "managed economy." This, they said, was "a flop in the days of Diocletian* and of the mercantilists" as well as in various communist and socialist programs. Elsewhere the *Journal* expressed misgivings about the "effect of the totality of all the Administration's economic and social programs" and claimed that many "can see in the unchecked expansion of Government and its controls the very specter of compulsion that our political institutions were designed to prevent." In the *Journal's* view, Kennedy's actions were leading toward "all-encompassing Government," a violation of eighteenth-century principles which limited the government's role to national defense, maintenance of order, and preservation of personal liberty. The attempt by Kennedy to shift decision-making power to government was an encroachment on the "grand design of liberty itself."[60]

Other than highly qualified approval of certain tax breaks for business, there was very little about Kennedy's economic policies that the *Journal* did favor. Even Kennedy's commitment to supporting research and development came under fire. The *Journal* criticized its size and cost ($14 billion, accounting as of 1963 for two-thirds of all R & D), the rate of increase (a "speed that is staggering"), and its impact on university programs (making them "top-heavy on science at the expense of other disciplines").[61] There was no praise of

---

* As noted earlier, John Davenport, managing editor at *Fortune*, in October of 1962 also associated Kennedy with the Roman Emperor Diocletian and implied that Kennedy was a reactionary and a cultist. This reflects either great coincidence in outlook or a coordinated ideological campaign.

Kennedy's commitment to the principles of competition and the free market when his Justice Department aggressively opposed mergers in its 1963 actions against Continental Can Co., ALCOA, and the Colonial Pipeline Company.*[62] This lack of appreciation for these efforts does make sense. It was not interference with the decentralized, competitive sectors of the economy that was ever at issue; it was Kennedy's effort to shift decision-making away from large-scale, concentrated private powers to the federal government that aroused the ire of opinion shapers at places like *Fortune* and the *Wall Street Journal*.

It was on behalf of organized powers that these media forces waged their war of ideas. One of those powers comprised the leading banks in the country, a group whose influence with Kennedy was on the decline in 1963.

As described in the *Wall Street Journal* in October of 1963,[63] there was an ongoing shift within the Kennedy administration on global monetary policy. According to the *Journal* analysis, the shift began late in 1962, as the "activists" in the administration supplanted the "conservatives." The conservatives were identified as Secretary of the Treasury Dillon,** Under-Secretary Robert V. Roosa, and the Federal Reserve Board. The activists, also described as "Kennedy lieutenants" and "the professors," were led by CEA Chairman Walter Heller, former Kennedy assistant Carl Kaysen, Under-Secretary of Commerce Franklin D. Roosevelt, Jr., and Under-Secretary of State George Ball.

The *Journal* suggested that the conservatives wanted to deal with U.S. balance-of-payments problems by reducing the amount of money available in the economy and cutting government spending. The activists rejected this, arguing that it was counterproductive for "the U.S. or any other nation" to adopt such policies to deal with transitory balance-of-payments problems. Around these kinds of issues the battle to see who would determine policy was being waged. According to the *Journal*, the activists didn't "entirely trust bankers," and Kennedy had come to the same view. Rightly or wrongly, the article concluded, "Mr. Kennedy has come increasingly to believe that large and global banking problems are too important to be left entirely to bankers."

Around this time, the Bank for International Settlements, one of the most influential of international financial institutions, recommended that the Kennedy administration allow all interest rates to rise.[64] While Kennedy seemed to be in no mood to have policy dictated by bankers, he must have been sensitive to the

---

* The Colonial Pipeline Company was part of the cooperative effort among the major oil companies to control the distribution of oil. The top companies were and are involved in many such joint ventures. According to testimony in the early 1970s before the Senate Subcommittee on Antitrust and Monopoly, the Colonial Pipeline Company was jointly controlled by Mobil, Texaco, Gulf, Standard of Indiana, and Atlantic Richfield (Blair, 1976, pp. 137-39).

** Whatever the level of support given by Dillon to Kennedy at the beginning, it appears that they definitely parted ways in 1962. During that year Dillon joined David Rockefeller in pressing Kennedy to reduce government spending, excepting defense. Rockefeller and Dillon were then and later willing to accept increases in spending for the war in Vietnam. Rockefeller and Dillon joined in 1965 with fellow Chase Manhattan directors, such as John J. McCloy, to create a formal group to promote the war (Collier and Horowitz, 1976, pp. 410, 416).

significance of this institution. It represented the wishes of the central banks of the leading economies of the world, including the U.S. Federal Reserve Bank. While Kennedy thought that banking was too important to be left to bankers, the members of this international bank thought that financial policy could not be left to nations and their politicians.[65] The *Wall Street Journal* was in agreement with that view.

The Lucepress and the *Wall Street Journal* were, based on both the extent of the coverage and the importance of the publications, the leading critics and media opponents of Kennedy's policies. Such criticism did, however, appear in other media. One of these, *Newsweek* magazine, was owned by what some thought of as the "liberal" or even "leftwing" *Washington Post*.[66] Whatever its image might have been in various sectors of American society, its views of Kennedy were almost identical to those of the Lucepress and the *Journal*.

The opposition to Kennedy was expressed primarily in the regular column, "Business Tides," written by contributing editor Henry Hazlitt. Hazlitt took the president to task for a multitude of sins. Among these were Kennedy's attempts to increase his own discretionary powers, his tax policies (including the proposed tax on earnings of U.S. business abroad and the withholding tax on dividends and interest), "reckless" welfare spending, allegedly discriminatory application of anti-trust laws, and excessive support of unions. Like *Fortune* and the *Wall Street Journal*, Hazlitt's articles contained frequent and emphatic criticisms of budget policy, deficits, easy money, and excessively low interest rates. Foreign aid was criticized for directly promoting national planning, socialism, and welfare-statism.[67]

The Lucepress, the *Wall Street Journal*, and *Newsweek* hammered away at President Kennedy's policies, condemning specific actions as well as Kennedy's use of presidential powers to shape the economy. In doing so, they spoke not for the country nor for business in general, but for highly concentrated economic power organized around America's leading financial institutions. They were not defending competition and the free play of entrepreneurship, but were rather engaging in a conflict with Kennedy over whether it would be private or public power that molded the future. The interests of old money, of status and privilege, came into confrontation with the most direct expression of a democratic republic—an elected and popular president acting on behalf of the nation's interests. Actually, these publications were more than just mouthpieces for financial groups and oligopolistic oil companies, they were part of the network of families and institutions that are at the very top of what is generally called the Establishment.

The Lucepress, the *Wall Street Journal*, and Morgan-Rockefeller

As was noted at the beginning of this chapter, Time, Inc., was more than just "Lucepress." While the available evidence indicates that Henry Luce was indeed a force within this media empire, it is just as clear that other powerful forces were part of this operation, perhaps the dominant part. These others are part of a network of individuals and families who tie together a wide assortment of institutions and organizations, stretching from top banks and oil companies to foundations, think tanks, the media, and the intelligence community.

At the center of this network, and highly visible in the Time complex, were people associated with the two most significant financial groups in the United States—Morgan and Rockefeller.*

Writing about the early years of Time, Inc., Ferdinand Lundberg pointed out[68] that in the 1920s Luce got financial help to start the company from Harry Davison, a Morgan banking partner and classmate of Luce's at Yale, and from other wealthy people including E. Roland Harriman. Lundberg went on to say that Time, Inc. in the 1930s was "owned by the inner circle of contemporary American finance, and the policies of its publications down to the smallest detail consistently reflect its ownership."

In the early 1960s various financial services were provided to Time by Morgan Guaranty Trust, Drexel & Co. (long affiliated with Morgan), and Chemical Bank (Rockefeller).[69] Time's historical relationship with Morgan interests and the Harrimans and the more recent connection to Rockefeller were also reflected in the makeup of Time's board of directors and management. For example, Maurice T. Moore, one of Time's directors who was married to Henry Luce's sister, was a member of the law firm of Cravath, Swaine & Moore (previously known as Cravath, Henderson, Leffingwell and de Gersdorff). This law firm worked closely with J.P. Morgan, Harriman's Union Pacific Railroad, and Brown Brothers & Co. before it merged with the Harriman bank. Handling most of this work for Cravath was John J. McCloy of whom we will see more below. A partner in that law firm, Russell Leffingwell, became chairman of J.P. Morgan in 1948. Leffingwell also served as chairman of the Morgan-Rockefeller-led Council on Foreign Relations from 1946 to 1953 (he was succeeded by McCloy). In addition to these connections to Morgan, Moore was a director of the Rockefeller-controlled Chemical Bank.[70]

---

* In the discussion that follows these two groups will be identified simply by the family names. There is a great deal of information available on both groups, but it is also incomplete. The Morgan group, which is not family dominated, has its origins in the mid-nineteenth century banking and trading business of Junius Spencer Morgan. In the 1850s and 1860s Junius and his son, John Pierpont, also became involved in London banking, establishing a U.S.-British connection of immense importance. In the early 1960s the Morgan group included Morgan Guaranty Trust, Morgan Stanley, and the London-based Morgan Grenfell. These institutions and the families involved in them were in control of or interconnected with dozens of other companies, including some of the largest insurance companies and industrial corporations in the world. The Rockefeller group emerged in the post-Civil War period as leaders of the Standard Oil Trust. In Kennedy's time the center of this group comprised the Chase, Chemical, and National City Banks. Like Morgan, however, these interests controlled or were tied to a multitude of other financial and corporate interests, and the Morgan and Rockefeller groups themselves were intertwined. Readers not familiar with this history might look at the following works listed in the Bibliography: Chernow; Collier and Horowitz (1976); Kotz; Lundberg (1937); Medvin; Myers; Quigley (1966, 1981).

Another Time director, Thomas J. Watson, Sr., was the chairman of International Business Machines Corporation (IBM), which had been financed originally by Morgan and had a continuing relationship with the Morgan Bank. Watson was also a director of Bankers Trust, which had been affiliated with Morgan.[71] At least four other directors of Time had some kind of connection to Morgan.*

Six of Time's fourteen directors were members of the Council on Foreign Relations (CFR), as was Time's senior vice-president, C.D. Jackson. There were at least two directors connected to each of the following: the Committee for Economic Development, the Ford Foundation, the Aspen Institute, and the Encyclopedia Britannica, which was partly owned by the University of Chicago. There are a multitude of other connections among these individuals and organizations, and they were all part of the opposition to Kennedy. The nature of these relationships can be illustrated by looking at C.D. Jackson's friend and adviser John J. McCloy.

Jackson, besides being Time's vice-president and Henry Luce's righthand man, had a career in intelligence activities. In the 1940s and early 1950s, Jackson frequently worked for or with John J. McCloy on psychological warfare operations and covert operations. In 1953 Jackson was appointed the chief of the Psychological Strategy Board, a White House agency which he used to promote covert operations. Jackson's friendship with McCloy by itself would have linked Time to many private and public centers of power. During his career, which began long before and lasted long after Kennedy's presidency, McCloy was chairman of the Chase Manhattan Bank, of the CFR, and of the Ford Foundation; president of the World Bank; High Commissioner in Germany after World War II; and a representative of the major oil companies. McCloy played a significant role in the creation of the Office of Strategic Services, forerunner of the CIA, and later helped to work out a relationship between the Ford Foundation and the CIA that allowed the foundation to fund CIA activities. Also, in the 1950s McCloy helped to initiate a practice whereby private banks cooperated directly with the International Monetary Fund in establishing conditions for loans to other nations, an arrangement circumvented by Kennedy policies. McCloy's close friends ranged from the Rockefeller family to Texas oilman Clint Mur-

---

* The other four directors were Artemus Gates, Paul Hoffman, Roy Larsen, and Frank Pace, Jr. Gates was president of New York Trust, which had been connected historically to Morgan. The New York Trust was taken over by Chemical Bank in the 1950s, representing either the replacement of Morgan by Rockefeller interests or an interweaving of the two groups. Paul Hoffman, once chairman of the Studebaker-Packard Corporation and a founder of the Committee for Economic Development, was a director of United Air Lines, in which Morgan stock control was large and perhaps dominant. Roy Larsen was said to be a close friend of both Thomas Lamont, vice-chairman of Morgan Guaranty, and Paul Cabot, a director of Morgan Guaranty. Frank Pace was a director of Continental Oil Company which had been created in a merger arranged by Morgan and which was interconnected with Morgan Guaranty's board of directors as of the early-1970s. (Chernow, pp. 496, 530, 561; Hyman, p. 101; Kotz, p. 161; Lundberg, 1937, p. 36-37; Marquis *Who's Who*, 1962-63; Moody's Investors Service, 1964; Swanberg, p. 514; Welles, p. 414).

chison, and included the top men at institutions as varied as the *Washington Post* and the CIA.*[72] It is this network for which *Time-Life-Fortune* spoke, as did the *Wall Street Journal*.

Lundberg[73] once described the *Wall Street Journal* as the "central organ of finance capital." In the early 1960s the *Journal*'s parent company, Dow, Jones, utilized the services of Morgan Guaranty and First National City Bank. The chairman of First National was James Stillman Rockefeller,** a descendant of the William Rockefeller wing of the family, who was also related to numerous wealthy families, including the Stillmans, Dodges, and Carnegies.[74]

Morgan interests were also represented on the small board of directors of Dow, Jones. Of the seven directors, two were executives of the company and two were members of the Bancroft family. The other three directors had some connection to Morgan interests, direct for one, indirect for the other two. The direct connection between Dow, Jones and Morgan was Carl J. Gilbert, who was a director of Morgan Guaranty Trust and, more significantly, the brother of a Morgan partner and related to a future (1980s) chairman of the Morgan Stanley investment bank.[75] Gilbert was a member of the Council on Foreign Relations. Also a member of the CFR and of the Committee for Economic Development was Dow, Jones director Harold Boeschenstein. He was a director of the International Paper Co., in which Morgan Guaranty was the leading stockholder,[76] and the Ford Motor Co., as well as president of Owens-Corning Fiberglass Corporation. Boeschenstein was, with Henry Luce, a trustee of the American Heritage Foundation. The third director, James White, served with Gilbert as a director of the Fiduciary Trust Co. of Boston.[77]

Even at *Newsweek*, where contributing editor Henry Hazlitt was repeating many of *Time*'s and the *Journal*'s criticisms of Kennedy, there were similar connections. In 1963 the chairman of *Newsweek* and the *Washington Post* was Frederick S. Beebe. Besides being a member of the CFR and a close friend of Allen Dulles, Beebe had previously been with the Morgan-related law firm of Cravath, Swaine & Moore.[78] Benjamin Bradlee, the Washington bureau chief of *Newsweek*, who had been married twice to members of upper-class families (Saltonstall and Pinchot), was related through his mother to a partner of the same law firm and was close to Richard Helms,*** who was Allen Dulles's deputy

---

* According to McCloy's biographer (Bird, pp. 496, 542), McCloy never thought much of Kennedy and was sensitive to the fact that Kennedy had never sought ties to Establishment institutions or with people at the CFR.

** An early rivalry between Morgan and the Stillman-Rockefeller interests came to a head in a contest over control of the Northern Pacific Railway. The National City Bank was backing E.H. Harriman in his attempt to wrest control from Morgan-backed James Hill. The resolution of this conflict also ended the general rivalry, with Morgan becoming a stockholder of City Bank in 1909 and J.P. Morgan, Jr., serving for a time as a director of the City Bank (Kotz, pp. 38-39).

*** The world of inherited wealth and connections is small. Helms's grandfather, Gates W. McGarrah, was on the board of the Astor Foundation, which, along with the Harrimans, had owned *Newsweek* until it was passed on to the Washington Post Company. McGarrah had also been the first president of the

and soon-to-be director of the CIA.[79] *Newsweek*'s editor-in-chief, Osborn Elliot, was also a member of the CFR.

By the early 1960s the Council on Foreign Relations, Morgan and Rockefeller interests, and the intelligence community were so extensively inbred as to be virtually a single entity. The Morgan and Rockefeller groups had always been dominant forces within the CFR, Morgan people being more prominent until the early 1950s, when the Rockefeller interests filled the positions of leadership. The CFR was also from the beginning tightly interconnected with leaders of the British establishment.[80] The connection to England and the overall internationalist nature of the CFR reflected, in part, the English-American origins of Morgan Banking and the worldwide banking and oil activities in which both Morgan and Rockefeller were (and are) deeply involved. Not only has the Rockefeller family continued to have significant holdings in the oil companies that once were part of its Standard Oil Company, but also the major oil companies and major banks, especially Chase, National City Bank, Morgan Guaranty, and Morgan Stanley, had become extensively intertwined by Kennedy's time.[81] These banking and oil interests by themselves make the Rockefeller and Morgan groups leaders of the internationalist sector of U.S. banking and business. Both groups are also tied to other upper-class groups around the world, from London and Paris to Saudi Arabia and Kuwait. Like their colleagues and friends at the Bank for International Settlements, they would have little tolerance for a president who interfered with their decisions or made their interests secondary to the needs of nations or of people in general.

The global interests of the Morgan and Rockefeller groups led to a natural involvement in the formation and development of the Central Intelligence Agency. A full account of these relationships would require a separate book. The relationships were extensive and covered the entire history of the CIA and of its forerunner, the Office of Strategic Services (OSS). For example, William Donovan, who is usually credited with organizing the OSS during World War II, began his intelligence career working as a private operator for J.P. Morgan, Jr.[82] Allen Dulles, who was in 1963 the most senior member (since 1927) of the board of directors of the Council on Foreign Relations, was director of the CIA from 1953 until his dismissal by Kennedy. Dulles was associated with both the Rockefeller and Morgan groups.*[83]

Swiss-based Bank for International Settlements, which later clashed with the Kennedy administration over economic policy. This international bank was created in 1929 with input from Morgan interests through their representative, Benjamin Strong. At the end of World War II the Roosevelt administration, due in part to allegations that the bank had cooperated with the Nazis, made an unsuccessful attempt to eliminate this bank. The bank had been connected with the pro-Nazi I.G. Farben Company. I.G. Farben interests were saved after the war by the efforts of people such as John J. McCloy. (Bird, p. 368; Davis, pp. 132-34; Epstein; Hersh, p. 160; Quigley, 1966, pp. 324-26, 512-13.)

* As has been noted before, the establishment world is quite small. Allen's brother, John Foster, was a close friend of John D. Rockefeller III and served as chairman of the Rockefeller Foundation. He was succeeded by Dean Rusk, who later served as Kennedy's Secretary of State. Also on the board of the Rockefeller Foundation at that time were John J. McCloy and Robert A. Lovett of Brown Brothers,

Kennedy faced external opposition in the media attacks on his policies, and he was saddled with an intelligence community that had more enduring connections to his opponents than to him. This problem of opposition from both outside and inside the administration can be illustrated by looking at David Rockefeller's criticism of Kennedy and the split that existed within the Kennedy administration.

David Rockefeller and the Internal Opposition to Kennedy

During Kennedy's presidency, David Rockefeller was emerging as one of the leaders of the financial community and of the upper class in general. He was president of Chase Manhattan Bank—in line to become its chief executive—and he was vice-president of the Council on Foreign Relations.

In July of 1962, *Life* magazine featured an exchange of letters between David Rockefeller and President Kennedy.[84] In this public and somewhat polite airing of differences, Rockefeller offered praise for some of Kennedy's actions, but he ultimately located the source of the country's economic problems in the president's policies. Claiming to reflect the concerns of bankers in the U.S. and abroad, Rockefeller advised the president to make a "vigorous effort" to control government spending and to balance the budget. He also suggested to Kennedy that interest rates were being kept too low and too much money was being injected into the economy. In his reply, Kennedy either rejected or ignored these arguments.

Rockefeller's concern for what he called "fiscal responsibility" was also expressed in a report issued around this time by another influential group with which Rockefeller was involved. This was the Committee for Economic Development, which was created in the early 1940s and largely made up of leaders from the major non-financial corporations in the U.S., including two of the directors of Time. In 1958 this organization created a Commission on Money and Credit, which included David Rockefeller as a member, to do a study on national economic policy with a focus on money and credit. Although the report, issued in 1961, contained a multitude of diverse recommendations, probably reflecting input from a large staff, there was some continuity in theme. The report claimed that the government's spending, taxation, and monetary policies should be geared to stabilization of the economy. In this view, actions such as tax reductions and increases in money supply were only appropriate during downturns in the economy.[85] In these basic areas, the recommendations were in direct conflict with the course Kennedy would eventually take. There was also a

Harriman (Bowles, pp. 299-300; Collier and Horowitz, 1976, p. 281). Like Henry Luce, the Dulles brothers and Morgan people such as J.P. Morgan, Jr., and Thomas W. Lamont had an affinity for far-right politics, including that of a fascist or Nazi nature (Chernow, pp. 214-15, 283; Hersh, pp. 46, 52, 69, 120, 135). The Morgan Bank and its top people, *e.g.*, Lamont, were also close to those at very top of the British Establishment, including the royal family, the Barings, the Astors, Lord Lothian, and Montagu Norman. Among these people (Lothian and Astor) there was in the 1930s at the least a tolerant attitude toward Hitler (Chernow, pp. 79, 171, 202, 207, 261, 435, 637).

difference in emphasis on the topic of international economic relations. The commission wanted the government to make free trade and private initiative central in U.S. foreign policy.[86] This and related issues brought Rockefeller into conflict with Kennedy over the Alliance for Progress.

Rockefeller was opposed to Kennedy's foreign policy from the beginning, critical of what he viewed as too much government involvement in and too little emphasis on the creation of the right kind of investment climate. These views were expressed in personal statements and in a report issued in 1963 by Chase Manhattan.[87]

In 1966 Rockefeller reacted to criticism of U.S. activity in Latin America in an article he wrote for *Foreign Affairs*, the official publication of the Council on Foreign Relations. In defending the contribution to Latin economies by U.S. business, Rockefeller noted the investment figures for 1964 and said that the main reason for alleged recent success was a change of the "policy which prevailed in the early years of the Alliance of placing too much emphasis on rapid and revolutionary social change and on strictly government-to-government assistance."[88] He later[89] referred to the "overly ambitious concepts of revolutionary social change which typified the thinking of many who played an important part in the Alliance in its early years."

When David Rockefeller ventured to publicly condemn Kennedy's policies, he was adding his personal prestige to the campaign run by Morgan-Rockefeller-related media. These interests were also represented within the Kennedy administration, and they attempted to steer Kennedy in certain directions, with little success.

As noted above, there was a clear split within the Kennedy administration over economic policy. The Kennedy group, which included Walter Heller and FDR, Jr., opposed the Dillon-Federal Reserve group, which spoke for the major banks. Dillon was a close associate of David Rockefeller's and a director of the Chase Manhattan Bank. The Federal Reserve, particularly the New York regional bank, has always been tightly interconnected with Morgan and Rockefeller banking. William McChesney Martin, the Fed's chairman, would become a supervisor of the Rockefeller family's trust fund.[90]

People with similar connections were also represented in the administration's foreign policy decisions. For example, Collier and Horowitz point out[91] that when the decision was made to go ahead with the Bay of Pigs invasion, many of the people involved were close friends or associates of David Rockefeller, including Secretary of State Dean Rusk, Secretary of the Treasury Douglas Dillon, CIA Director Allen Dulles, McGeorge Bundy, and A.A. Berle, Jr. Essentially the same group, according to Sorensen,[92] had pushed Kennedy toward intervention in Laos, and, in Kennedy's view, it was Allen Dulles's CIA that had maneuvered him into going along with the Bay of Pigs action.[93]

Kennedy's problems with some of these people were almost certainly not a complete surprise to him, although the deceptions and manipulations may have been. He had been at odds with this foreign policy establishment—including

Dillon, who was now part of his administration—even before his election. In 1957 Kennedy said in a Senate speech that the U.S. had to respond to the desires of people in Asia and Africa to be free of both Soviet and Western imperialism. In that speech he criticized Dillon and Henry Cabot Lodge for their support of French imperialist policy toward Algeria.[94] In the same period he was also in conflict with Secretary of State John Foster Dulles, Allen Dulles's brother, and Dean Acheson* over the same issue.[95] He had disagreed with John Foster Dulles and others when they wished to intervene in Indochina in 1954 on the side of France.[96]

In these conflicts, as well as those discussed earlier, Kennedy was coming up against those people variously referred to as the East Coast Establishment, Wall Street, finance capital, the higher circles, etc.** The label is not important. In the end they all refer to Morgan interests, the Rockefellers, and the many other wealthy and influential families allied with them (including Harriman, Cabot, Lodge, Dillon, Bundy).

Kennedy's ideas about the responsibilities of the presidency, his attitude about economic progress and the role of the federal government in achieving that progress, his view of foreign aid and foreign policy, and his recommendations and actions in a variety of specific areas disrupted or threatened to disrupt an established order. In that established order, in place for most of the century, major government decisions were to serve or at least not disrupt the privately organized hierarchy. Many in the upper levels of this hierarchy, most emphatically those in and around Morgan interests, were—and still are—involved in a special relationship with the British establishment.*** Their ideas about the world are similar to, if not direct imitations of, those of that older British élite rooted in inherited wealth and titles and organized in the modern world around control of finance and raw materials.

---

* John Foster Dulles and Dean Acheson represented the two tendencies in the U.S. foreign policy establishment that were mentioned earlier. These two groups probably agreed much more than they disagreed, as is suggested by Kennedy's difficulties with both. John Foster Dulles and Henry Luce, for example, favored a somewhat more dominant and independent role for the U.S. establishment, while people such as Acheson, Harriman, Allen Dulles, and Charles J.V. Murphy of Time, Inc. favored closer cooperation with upper-class interests in England and Europe. The latter group, the internationalists, seem to have been the dominant group in Kennedy's time and to have become more so since then. At any rate, this seems to be an in-house split that only occasionally erupted into serious conflicts. The Rockefellers appear to have felt sympathy for both tendencies and straddled these two factions in the early 1960s; those around Morgan would have been in the internationalist group.
** Why did Kennedy bring these people into his administration? Perhaps only Kennedy could answer this question. Possible answers would include the following: He didn't want to antagonize such interests from the beginning by excluding them. He thought he could co-opt some of them. He underestimated the extent to which they would oppose him. He expected to have a clearer reading of political realities by having them nearby. He wasn't going to allow them to dictate policy whether in or out of his administration. He did not have alternatives who could get past Congress.
*** A clear description of this special relationship was provided by Carroll Quigley in *Tragedy and Hope* and in *The Anglo-American Establishment*. Quigley's work may now attract increased attention because he was one of President Clinton's professors at Georgetown.

In this worldview, the Anglo-American upper class should maintain its global position by suppressing progress elsewhere and by preventing or containing disruptive changes within England and the United States. Important decision-making power should be kept in private hands, or, if necessary, in government agencies under their influence. From this perspective, Kennedy must have looked like a wild man. Economic growth, scientific and technological progress, expanding opportunity, development in the Third World, and social justice were the goals for Kennedy, not preservation of the class structure. Not only were the government policies he undertook intended to further this disruptive agenda; in many specific instances those policies meant that decision-making power was being taken over by the author of that agenda. Even where Kennedy's efforts meant only changes in the rules, these changes were intended to alter investment patterns and tax burdens in a way not in tune with upper-class interests.

Seen in this context, the rhetoric of the *Wall Street Journal*, *Fortune*, *Life*, and *Newsweek* makes sense. Also understandable is the unusual spectacle of a private establishment figure such as David Rockefeller going public to person-ally challenge the president. Rockefeller's *Life* magazine admonishment was polite; the polemics elsewhere were not. To label a popular president a cultist, a reactionary, a threat to freedom, was to engage in serious conflict with the democratically elected leader of the Republic. It suggested great anger, and it indicated a frustration produced by Kennedy's failure to heed the criticism.

President Kennedy's refusal to surrender to the pressures from such powerful forces* was a demonstration of courage. In discussing the meaning of courage,[97] Kennedy said:

> A man does what he must—in spite of personal consequences, in spite of obstacles and dangers and pressures—and that is the basis of all human morality.

His repeated efforts on behalf of economic progress and justice demonstrated the highest form of morality.

President Kennedy, not satisfied with the drift of the 1950s, had promised to get the country moving again, and in many ways he had done that. The end of his presidency also marked a shift in the direction of the country. We will turn first to changes that were almost immediate, and then we will look at later events from the perspective represented in President Kennedy's goals and policies.

---

* In one of the supposedly definitive books on President Kennedy, Arthur Schlesinger, Jr., managed to write over a thousand pages which never touched on most of Kennedy's economic initiatives, never mentioned Morgan or David Rockefeller, and barely touched on the attacks on Kennedy. In this way he could wind up portraying the John Birch Society as a prime opponent of President Kennedy.

FIVE

Short-Term Changes

President Kennedy's assassination was a disastrous event. Not only did the country lose an energetic and attractive leader, but also an extremely intelligent and courageous president who was willing and able to assert the country's interests and the interests of people in general against some of the most powerful forces in the world. For that reason, his presence in the White House made a big difference in the world, and his loss would have been mitigated only had he been replaced by someone with similar goals, abilities, and determination. His replacement did not fit that description.

It is true that Lyndon Johnson would speak of economic growth and progress, although in some important ways without consistency. It is also true that Johnson would preside over the enactment of the Medicare program, although it seems that the success of that legislation was virtually assured at the time of President Kennedy's death.[1] In some way Johnson also carried forward efforts in civil rights and proposed a variety of other social programs. These are not insignificant matters, but it is nevertheless a fact that across a range of the most important issues, Johnson presided over a series of changes that reversed or undermined Kennedy's policies. For the most part, these changes were in line with what Kennedy's opponents wanted.

In foreign policy the changes came quickly, and they were dramatic. Whereas Kennedy had been sympathetic to leaders and political groups in underdeveloped countries who were committed to independence and development, Johnson proved to be quite willing to use power against those same people. Under Johnson the Alliance for Progress became merely a tool for policies which once more were serving neo-colonialist interests. In domestic policy there would no longer be a steady stream of proposals aimed at reshaping the flow of money and investments; LBJ would not be called a cultist, a reactionary, or an enforcer of progress.

We begin with the redirection of foreign policy, which was expressed in actions taken against a popular, pro-development group in the Dominican Republic.

The Foreign Policy Shift

At the end of April 1965, the Johnson administration ordered an invasion of the Dominican Republic to prevent an alleged communist takeover. Among the people involved in this decision, which led to the deployment of about 23,000 U.S. soldiers, were LBJ, Secretary of State Rusk, Secretary of Defense McNamara, McGeorge Bundy, and Thomas C. Mann from the State Department. Mann was one of the people directly involved in carrying out David Rockefeller's request that Kennedy's Alliance for Progress be dumped.[2]

This intervention was on behalf of rightwing forces opposed to the return to power of groups loyal to exiled President Juan Bosch. Bosch had been elected in 1962, and his government was supported by President Kennedy, who had viewed the Bosch government as a potential success story for both democracy and development supported by the Alliance for Progress. When Bosch was overthrown in September of 1963 by reactionary forces led by General Elias Wessin y Wessin, Kennedy suspended diplomatic relations and economic aid. LBJ reversed this policy.[3]

Bosch's administration, which was backed by over 60 percent of the voters in the 1962 election, was the first legally elected government in the Dominican Republic in 38 years. On September 25, 1963, the Bosch government was overthrown and replaced by a junta led by military officers and civilians, including a Yale-educated millionaire who was one of the key people charging Bosch with communist sympathies. Within hours of the coup, President Kennedy ordered the suspension of diplomatic relations and an end to economic aid. On October 4 President Kennedy announced that all military and economic assistance personnel were being withdrawn from the Dominican Republic. According to news accounts, these decisions were "made personally by President Kennedy" and "served emphatic notice that the programs would not be readily resumed." Kennedy's immediate condemnation of this coup was repeated in other capitals as Venezuela, Mexico, Bolivia, Costa Rica, and Puerto Rico quickly gave support to deposed President Bosch and, at least indirectly, to Kennedy. By mid-October the leaders of the coup were accusing the Kennedy administration of interfering in the Dominican Republic and complaining about the U.S. government's attitude toward the junta.[4]

President Kennedy would be assassinated in five weeks, while Bosch would go into exile in Puerto Rico. That situation continued until early 1965, when Bosch supporters and other opponents of the military government organized a revolt against the junta with the purpose of restoring constitutional government.

Johnson, Rusk, Assistant Secretary of State for Inter-American Affairs Thomas Mann, and others were opposed to the restoration of the popular Bosch or of political figures representing Bosch's policies, and they justified intervention with claims that communists were leading the revolt and would end up controlling it. Relying in part on information supplied by the British vice-consul in the Dominican Republic, the Johnson administration decided to portray the Bosch supporters, led by Colonel Francisco Caamaño, as dupes of a nebulous gang of extremists with communist connections. From Puerto Rico, Bosch vehemently denied this, pointing out that there were few communists in the Dominican Republic and that they were fragmented and without capable leadership. "These Communists," said Bosch, "could not even manage a hotel, let alone take over a country." He said that there was "absolutely no justification" for U.S. military intervention. Bosch's views were supported by other leaders in the Dominican Republic and by at least a substantial part of the Dominican people.[5]

None of this influenced Johnson or his advisers, and—with the often-used, and untrue, claim that American lives were in jeopardy—the United States invaded the Dominican Republic. Johnson thus ended up using U.S. military power against much the same forces described by Kennedy 18 months earlier as democratic and progressive. The junta protected by this intervention was substantially the same one that Kennedy had opposed.

A similar change, just as drastic, occurred in U.S. policy toward Brazil. As previously noted, Kennedy was criticized in 1963 for continuing foreign aid to Latin American countries that had failed to adopt policies favored by the banking community and the International Monetary Fund (IMF). In that context, Brazil was singled out by Charles J.V. Murphy, writing for *Fortune*,[6] as an example of a Latin nation that refused to adopt the domestic austerity program and the free-market policies demanded by the IMF.* João Goulart's government not only resisted these demands, but Goulart also had moved in 1962 to limit the profits that could be taken out of Brazil, and he had initiated legal action against the mining concession held by the M.A. Hanna Mining Company.[7]

In 1964 John J. McCloy** worked with the CIA, the Johnson administration, and both U.S. and Brazilian military officials to organize a coup against Goulart. That Goulart was an elected president with widespread support and was not a communist mattered little. The coup, code-named Operation Brother Sam in

---

* It was in that article that Murphy referred to various bankers' criticisms of Kennedy's foreign aid policy and went on to cite Brazil as an example of one of those countries where the Kennedy administration was wrongly trying to "satisfy the universal lust for industrialization and growth" (Murphy, p. 210). When Murphy wrote this article, he may have been aware of opposition to Brazil's government within the CIA. Murphy was close to Frank Wisner, a protégé of Allen Dulles's. Wisner had been involved in the 1957-58 attempt to overthrow Indonesia's Sukarno government (Hersh, pp. 307, 414-20).

** This was a busy time for McCloy. Besides organizing this coup, he was serving on the Warren Commission, and he was going to London to attack publicly the policies of President Charles de Gaulle of France (Bird, pp. 550-53).

Washington, was supported by the deployment of a U.S. naval carrier task force to the Brazilian coast to provide arms and oil to the Brazilian military. These actions, called a turning point for U.S. policy in Latin America by McCloy's biographer, were on behalf of the Hanna Mining Company* and other U.S. interests with investments in oil refining and land.[8]

On April 1, 1964, Goulart was overthrown. The next day President Johnson officially recognized and congratulated the new government. Two weeks before this coup, Mann had announced a policy stressing the protection of U.S. private interests in Latin America.** Mann would also be one of the key figures involved in the U.S. invasion of the Dominican Republic in the following year. In their history of the Rockefeller family, Collier and Horowitz[9] point to the coup in Brazil and Mann's policy statements as events signifying a reversal of Kennedy's Alliance for Progress policies.

The new military government in Brazil, headed by General Humberto Castello Branco, quickly came to an agreement with the IMF. According to Cheryl Payer,[10] during the next three years this led to a severe business depression, a rash of takeovers by foreign investors, and growing inequality among the populace.

The relationship between President Kennedy and Brazil's President Goulart had been at times a tense one. There is, however, no evidence available that President Kennedy had decided to back a rightwing coup. Specifically, Kennedy did not take up the defense of the Hanna interests as did LBJ. Moreover, Johnson and Mann carried out an almost total change in policy, openly de-emphasizing land reform, democracy, income redistribution, and nation-to-nation coordination of aid. After the new government led by General Branco had taken measures to protect Hanna's mining interests and had used direct military intimidation to force the Brazilian Congress to accept the IMF's austerity program, Johnson referred to these actions as "courageous economic policy decisions."[11]

It is more than difficult to imagine Kennedy giving such wholehearted support to a military revolt of this type. It is, in fact, impossible to conjure up such an image, given that the purposes of this revolt were thoroughly at odds

---

* There was a historical relationship between Hanna and the Rockefeller interests with which McCloy was so long involved. This went back to an almost life-long connection between John D. Rockefeller, Sr., and Mark Hanna. Hanna had also been well-acquainted with and responsive as a Senator to J.P. Morgan, Sr. (Chernow, p. 77; Collier and Horowitz, 1976, p. 12; Lundberg, 1937, pp. 57-60).

** In 1958 Senator Kennedy (1961, pp. 174-75) observed in a speech given in Puerto Rico that "Latin Americans do want to use American capital within their own political and economic framework. They resent our insisting upon a larger role for their private enterprise, which cannot cope with many of their problems, or a larger role for our private investors, who have limited their interests almost entirely to extractive industries and to only five countries (Brazil, Cuba, Mexico, Venezuela, and Chile)." The Johnson administration and CIA support of this coup was intended to protect those private investors involved in extractive operations. This emphasis on extractive investments had long been part of the exploitative orientation of colonialist and neo-colonialist economic interests. It was that orientation that President Kennedy rejected, viewing it as both wrong and not in the real long-term interest of the United States.

with his foreign aid policy, his general support for reforms, and his opposition to neo-colonialist interests. There were indications that policy had changed even before these April 1964 events.

As noted earlier, President Kennedy had tried to repair the U.S. relationship with Indonesia, a relationship severely damaged by the CIA-backed 1958 coup attempt against the Sukarno government and by U.S. State Department backing of the Netherlands in its dispute with Indonesia. Within weeks of taking office, LBJ changed the policy toward Indonesia by refusing to sign a directive to continue economic aid. Abandoning Kennedy's sympathetic policy, Johnson proceeded to back a British policy of isolating and punishing Indonesia.[12] This immediate change indicated a more general shift in U.S. policy.

Sukarno would not accept what he viewed as continuing British dominance of the newly formed Malaysian Federation and opposed official recognition of Malaysia by the United Nations. By early January 1965, the British were already building up their military forces in Malaysia and would have 11,000 troops there before the month ended. Several months later the Sukarno government withdrew from the IMF and the World Bank and seized properties owned by major U.S., British, and Dutch companies (including Standard Oil of New Jersey, Mobil, Standard Oil of California, Texaco, Royal Dutch Shell, and Goodyear Tire and Rubber).[13]

With significant prodding and support from Johnson's CIA, the situation deteriorated into a bloody civil war ending in the ouster of Sukarno's government. The Johnson administration held off complete normalization of relations until the new government had time to re-establish protection of and freedom for foreign investors and had agreed to adopt the policy recommendations of the International Monetary Fund.[14]

No one can say with certainty that events in these countries would have been different had President Kennedy lived. But it is clear that U.S. policy would have been different, and, given the overwhelming power of the United States, that might easily have been a critical factor in one or all of these situations.

The Johnson administration's changes in policy toward the Dominican Republic, Brazil, and Indonesia indicate a pattern. Vietnam policy was probably part of that pattern. A number of those who knew Kennedy and others who were involved with or have studied the Kennedy government believe that, shortly before his assassination, he had decided to pull out of Vietnam. *Life* magazine[15] had noted and criticized Kennedy's decision to begin withdrawing U.S. troops from Vietnam. He had resisted pressures to escalate U.S. involvement, and at the time of his death about 16,000 U.S. troops were in Vietnam;* under Johnson

---

* Kennedy is usually charged with putting all but six or seven hundred of these soldiers into Vietnam. The truth is probably not that simple. Fletcher Prouty points out that some of the 16,000 were in the region prior to Kennedy's presidency and were transferred into Vietnam. He points specifically to a 1,000-man Marine helicopter unit which was based in Thailand, but flew missions over Laos and Vietnam. When it was transferred to Vietnam in 1961, it was counted as part of the JFK buildup (Prouty, 1989).

it would become 543,000. There were about 50 U.S. combat fatalities during Kennedy's presidency; before the war ended, over 47,000 Americans—and hundreds of thousands of Vietnamese—would die in combat.

There is some evidence that U.S. policy in Vietnam changed within 24 hours of President Kennedy's death.[16] It certainly changed within months, as talk of bringing troops home and of Vietnamese responsibility was replaced with new affirmations of U.S. commitment, and, in 1965, a much bigger troop buildup began. The simplest explanation, and one that fits with all of the known facts, is that Kennedy was suppressing a tendency that was released under Johnson. In other words, there was constant pressure for escalation of U.S. involvement through both the Kennedy and Johnson administrations. What changed is that an independent president concerned with economic and social progress and opposed to a U.S. neo-colonialist role was replaced by a president who was both more compliant and more willing to go to war against communists, even if it meant embracing neo-colonialist policies. Perhaps nobody, including Johnson himself, could say whether it was Johnson's anticommunism, his fear of appearing weak, his worries about the political consequences of a communist victory, or his submission to Establishment figures that produced that compliance.[17] What is certain is that before, during, and after the Kennedy presidency, most of the top foreign policy people were in favor of U.S. intervention in Vietnam. They were the constant force behind a policy that would not only wreak massive death and destruction on Southeast Asia, but also tear the United States apart and spawn a drug epidemic in the United States.

The commitment to a neo-colonialist policy in Southeast Asia goes back to the early 1940s, when the Morgan-led Council on Foreign Relations concluded that the U.S. ruling class should seek to control this region. The attraction was threefold. There were a variety of raw materials, the control of which would mean both money and economic power. The area was a major producer and exporter of rice and therefore a potential source of influence over consuming nations. Finally, the region was viewed as a strategic location in relation to important sea and air routes. From the early 1940s through 1963, leaders within the CFR stated and restated their view that this area had to be held.[18]

In 1951, the CFR and Britain's Royal Institute for International Affairs created a study group, with money from the Rockefeller Foundation, to work on Anglo-American relations, including U.S.-British policy toward Southeast Asia. Among the leaders from the U.S. were Morgan stalwarts such as John W. Davis and Henry M. Wriston. The Royal Institute had been created in 1919 to perpetuate British power in the world, and it helped to create the Council on Foreign Relations as part of an effort to link England's upper class and its foreign policy interests to those of the United States. Both Morgan and Rockefeller people were closely associated with the Royal Institute and with the aristocrats and financiers who created it. The CFR-Royal Institute study group was one of a number of CFR groups to recommend domination of Southeast Asia, and the CFR's views were well-represented in the Eisenhower administration by the Dulles brothers.[19]

Supporters of expanded involvement who served under both Kennedy and Johnson included National Security Adviser McGeorge Bundy, Secretary of State Dean Rusk, Secretary of Defense Robert McNamara, and Ambassador to South Vietnam Henry Cabot Lodge.* In 1964 William Bundy, McGeorge's brother, became a director of the CFR and was also appointed by LBJ to the position of Assistant Secretary of State for Far Eastern Affairs. In that position he was an important advocate of escalation.[20] With the exception of McNamara, all these men were CFR members. In fact, many of the most important advocates of U.S. involvement in Vietnam, both within and outside of the government, were members of the Board of Directors of the CFR.**

In one of the most detailed accounts of the events leading to fullscale war in Vietnam, John Newman[21] presents evidence indicating that Johnson was not only continuously supportive of escalation, but as vice president was also involved in deceiving President Kennedy about the real political and military situation in Vietnam. Newman also thinks the evidence shows conclusively that policy changed when Johnson succeeded Kennedy.*** Newman concludes[22] that Kennedy had intended to withdraw, but he also criticizes Kennedy for not making this policy public and waging an honest fight for his decision. He then asks if this duplicity was merely to achieve reelection or on behalf of a higher, nobler cause, or both. Since Kennedy did publicly discuss bringing soldiers home and was publicly criticized for this, it is not altogether fair to portray Kennedy as deceptive. It is true that there were ambiguities in his public comments, and it does appear that this was related to concerns about the 1964 election.[23]

From Kennedy's own perspective, the reelection and the higher, nobler cause were in fact inseparable. If Kennedy was not reelected, who would be there to fight for the tax policies and the other measures intended to raise the standard of living? Who was going to push for the new direction represented in the Alliance for Progress? Who would be willing to contest the power of private bankers to set the economic agenda at home and abroad? Who would resist the kinds of policies that were ultimately adopted for Brazil, the Dominican Republic, and Indonesia? Who would provide active presidential leadership on behalf of progress? The answers to these questions are the same—nobody. Kennedy almost certainly believed that. His reelection and potential impact on policy in the future were more than sufficient justification for his attempts to manage politically the situation in Vietnam.

---

* These individuals are frequently described as Kennedy men (*e.g.*, Goodwin, p. 196; Wofford, p. 339). Other than the fact that Kennedy had appointed them, there is no basis for such a characterization.
** The list would include Allen Dulles, David Rockefeller, John J. McCloy, and Henry M. Wriston (Council on Foreign Relations, 1963; Shoup and Minter, pp. 246-47).
*** Fletcher Prouty's 1992 account of Kennedy's actions reaches the same general conclusion about the policy shift that occurred when Johnson took over. The two books do differ on some of the important events surrounding this change, and they differ on the relative importance in these events of the military versus the intelligence community. Prouty's focus on the intelligence community seems more accurate.

The changes in policy involving Vietnam and the other cases described here were consistent with a basic shift in international economic policy. When David Rockefeller[24] observed in 1966 with great satisfaction that the Alliance for Progress was no longer what it had been under Kennedy, he was indicating that the challenge to neo-colonialist economic policy was gone. *Fortune* magazine had criticized Kennedy for being too interventionist in economic affairs but not interventionist enough when it came to using military power. What these interests wanted was a president who would support private domination of resources, markets, and credit with the authority of the U.S. government and, if necessary, with military and covert action. Kennedy's intention to pursue government-to-government coordination for development purposes and his determination to avoid using military force to subdue nationalist forces in the Third World caused the Establishment to view him as the major problem in world affairs.

Lyndon Johnson had no intention of being an enforcer of progress, and the *Wall Street Journal*, Lucepress, and those they spoke for had no reason to charge him with this—and they didn't. Johnson would continue talking about development and the problems of poverty, here and abroad, but he would be far more passive than President Kennedy, allowing influence and power to return to the organized sectors of big banking and business. His passivity in economic affairs was matched by his compliance in foreign policy. Ironically, what might seem on the surface to be the height of boldness and activism—the use of military power—actually reflected Johnson's willingness to go along with an Establishment that he at times resented but also feared. John Kennedy interrupted an ongoing process which involved the consolidation of economic and political power in increasingly well-organized upper-class groups. Lyndon Johnson's time in office allowed a resumption of that process in domestic affairs no less than in foreign policy.

Change in Domestic Policy

President Kennedy's promise to get the country moving again was a reaction to real problems developing in the 1953 to 1960 period. Actions taken to prepare for and fight World War II had brought the economy out of the Great Depression, and the war was followed by an eight-year period in which the overall investment and growth performance was very good. The next eight years, leading up to Kennedy's presidency, however, had featured stagnation and three recessions.[25] During the years affected immediately by Kennedy's policies, 1962 to 1964 or 1965, the U.S. economy returned to and even exceeded the rapid growth displayed in the pre-stagnation period of 1948 to 1953.[26]

What Kennedy attempted to effect, with some success, in the three years he was in office, was a moderate peacetime version of federal policy during World War II. That war was paid for primarily through borrowing and deficit spending on an unheard of scale. Government borrowing, lending, and spending generated a virtual industrial revolution, force-feeding the development of new productive capacity in many industries. This growth provided the basis for the postwar prosperity that Kennedy thought was threatened by the recessions and stagnation after 1953. The huge expansion of debt and the growth in the money supply during World War II did not lead to significant problems after the war, because these were accompanied by rapid growth in real production.*

President Kennedy did not seek anything close to the level of deficits incurred during World War II, and by almost any standard they were modest.[27] The deficits were combined with stable interest rates, an adequate expansion of money and credit, the investment tax credit, rapid expansion of some government programs,** and, in terms of the general economic climate, Kennedy's focus on the things that would generate future economic progress (*e.g.*, various tax reforms, support for education, science, and research). Although many of the reforms he sought in order to reduce speculation and to channel investment into productive purposes did not get through Congress, he could rightly claim some credit for the prosperity and progress evident in the 1961 to 1966 period.

In an economy far more rooted in real production than today's, there was a 5 percent growth rate by 1964. Wages and profits were rising, unemployment fell in 1964 to 4 percent, and there was a high level of optimism.[28] It is also clear that when President Kennedy was killed in 1963, he viewed the progress already underway as something to be deepened and continued. That was not to be, and although it would be some years before the economy really began to unravel, there were some negative developments that appeared soon after Kennedy's death.

During the 1953 to 1960 period the Federal Reserve System had contributed to two recessions by reducing the availability of money, and this "tight money" policy played a role in the third recession of that period.[29] Kennedy was determined either to prevent these downturns altogether or at least to reduce their severity. Also, during the 1950s interest rates had risen during most years and had more than doubled during the decade. The prime rate, charged by large banks to corporate clients, had been at 1.5 percent from 1939 until 1947, even though the government was incurring some of the largest deficits in history. It rose during the 1950s and was 4.82 percent in 1960. Under Kennedy it declined slightly to 4.5 percent, where it remained until 1965. It then began rising, and

---

* In the years 1942 to 1946 the federal government spent each year more than twice what it took in, or, to put it another way, over half of the budget was deficit-financed. The deficits were in real terms far bigger than anything that occurred in the 1980s or early 1990s. These deficits financed government spending and loans to business which produced what Greider (p. 324) has called an industrial revolution. Greider cites electronics, petrochemical synthetics, aircraft, and shipbuilding as industries built up during the war. Other examples of growth and development would include expansion of U.S. capacity to produce aluminum ingots from 200,000 tons in 1941 to 6,200,000 tons in 1944. Between 1939 and 1944 the production of rails almost doubled, and steel output rose by more than 50 percent. In 1939, 355 locomotives were produced; in 1945 it was 3,213 (Department of Commerce, 1965; Greider; Taus; Tax Foundation, 1979). According to his biographer (Bird, p. 131), John J. McCloy wrote a government memo during World War II that warned against the continuation of planning after the war.
** Included here would be international economic aid linked to purchases of U.S. goods, the space program, and health, education, and welfare.

by 1969 was at 7.96 percent, then thought of as an extremely high level.*[30] In his detailed analysis of economic trends from 1948 to 1969, John Kendrick[31] concluded that the strong economic improvement which began in 1961 ended in 1966 and was followed by a three-year period of marked slowdown.**

The 1960s began with Kennedy's aggressive program "to get America moving again." That program was accompanied by his emphasis on progress in science and technology, in production and the standard of living, and in the areas of social justice and international peace. With Johnson in office the policy toward underdeveloped nations returned to the neo-colonialist direction that had existed throughout much of the century. The purposes of the Alliance for Progress were abandoned in favor of those private interests that sought both dominance over and suppression of the economies of the underdeveloped world. Kennedy's sympathy with independent Third World leaders was replaced by renewed aggression. His efforts to shift some of the decision-making power away from organized private groups to the federal government came to an end. Johnson's willingness to go to war was accompanied by timidity when it came to government's role in promoting progress both within the United States and internationally.

Economic progress was a central goal in Kennedy's policies, something he viewed as good in itself and as a basis for social justice. During the 1960s, after Kennedy was killed, the atmosphere began changing. Writing in the early 1970s, John W. Kendrick[32] observed that in the 1960s

> the intellectual climate changed appreciably. No longer is economic growth accepted uncritically as a national goal. Increasing emphasis is being placed on the costs of growth, in the forms of pollution and other environmental deterioration and the social disorganization attributed by some in part to technological advance and other dynamic economic changes.

---

* There have been various arguments made about the relationship between government deficits and interest rates, with some arguing it is deficit spending that drives up interest rates either by fueling bankers' fears of inflation or by raising the demand for available money. Interest rates began rising in 1965 even though the Johnson administration deficits for 1965 and 1966 were lower than the three Kennedy years. While these numbers and trends would not be proof of anything for many involved in these debates, it is hard to see deficit spending as the reason for the increases that began in 1965 (Council of Economic Advisers, 1983, pp. 240, 248).

** The growth of the 1960s is often portrayed as continuing into 1969 (Greider, p. 331). This image is based on the broadest possible measures of growth (including government spending), while Kendrick's assessment is based on trends in capital formation, investment, and productivity. In terms of real growth and long-term effect, Kendrick's approach makes the most sense. His conclusions indicate the success of the Kennedy administration, and they contradict all arguments that attribute 1960s prosperity to Vietnam War spending. The slowdown in the economy in 1966 could have had many causes. Among those, however, may have been the rise in the prime rate from 4.5 percent in 1964 to 5.6 percent in 1966. Also, according to Rowen (p. 278), Johnson decided within 48 hours of Kennedy's assassination to cut back the budget for 1965. This not only produced a budget smaller than that planned by Kennedy, but one that was smaller than 1964's.

The growing criticism of growth and technological progress that Kendrick refers to was in many ways more extreme than these comments suggest and went beyond a reasonable concern for air and water quality and specific problems such as chemical dumping. The criticism often amounted to a rejection of the modern world and its peoples and cultures. It contrasted sharply with Kennedy's outlook and goals. Much of this change in intellectual climate did not well up from the general population, but came from the same circles of power that appeared so often in the conflicts over Kennedy's policies.

Kennedy, Johnson, and the "New Conservationism"

President Kennedy's use of the powers of his office and of the federal government to promote economic progress was met with fierce criticism from Morgan-Rockefeller-related interests. Underlying this criticism was the perception that Kennedy was challenging the private centers of power and making himself the "enforcer of progress." The conflict, as we have described it so far, revolved primarily around the issue of who would shape the economy—the elected president or hereditary wealth centered in banking, oil, and other big businesses. Contained in the hostile reaction to Kennedy's efforts to change the flow of investments, alter tax rules and burdens, challenge monopolistic power, and promote development were hints that some in the Establishment did not share the president's goal of rapid economic progress.

This is suggested in the charge that Kennedy was promoting in his foreign aid policy "the universal lust for industrialization and growth" and that he was wrong to make economic development the primary goal of foreign policy. This suggestion that industrialization, development, and growth are not legitimate goals makes sense in the context of the conflict between Kennedy and Morgan-Rockefeller interests over foreign policy. The economic development Kennedy was supporting threatened Establishment control of Third World economies. Given Kennedy's commitment to national and global economic progress, it is not surprising to find that Kennedy was not receptive to a growing effort to condemn scientific and technological progress and economic growth. Johnson, however, was receptive to this condemnation, just as he was willing to take U.S. foreign policy back to a neo-colonialist direction and to abandon Kennedy's domestic efforts to use tax, budget, and monetary policy to promote economic progress.

In the late 1950s and early 1960s, a longstanding inclination among some members of the upper class was about to become a national issue. This inclination was to redefine achievements in science and technology as either evil actions threatening to nature or as futile attempts to reduce human suffering that was said to be the result of overpopulation. This tendency, partly articulated as a worldview in the writings of Thomas Malthus, takes what might be reasonable concerns over issues such as air and water quality and embeds them in an ideology deeply hostile to economic progress and to the majority of human beings.

Malthus's work appeared around 1800 and appealed to classes of people in England preoccupied with preserving their wealth and social position. Malthus offered to British aristocrats, financiers, landowners, and even some involved in the growing areas of manufacturing and commerce a justification for continuing large-scale poverty and a rationale for opposition to government intervention in the economy.

Malthus argued in two versions of his *An Essay on the Principle of Population*[33] that population tended to grow faster than agricultural output. In the later, much expanded version, he focused on ways in which this population growth could be kept in balance with food production. Malthus divided these ways into what he called preventive and positive checks. Preventive checks are those that reduce the numbers of people born. Primary is moral or self-restraint, including non-marriage, late marriage, and efforts to avoid reproducing. Also mentioned are forms of promiscuity and vice which do not increase reproduction. Positive checks are those that eliminate existing human beings. Malthus's list includes war, severe labor, unwholesome occupations, extreme poverty, exposure, poor care of children, and what he calls natural checks—epidemic, plague, and famine. All of the preventive and positive checks are "resolvable into moral restraint, vice and misery."[34]

Malthus was enthusiastic about the effects of plague and famine on human population. He wrote:[35]

> Famine seems to be the last, the most dreadful resource of nature. The power of population is so superior to the power in the earth to produce subsistence for man, that premature death must in some shape or other visit the human race. The vices of mankind are active and able ministers of depopulation; and often finish the dreadful work themselves. But should they fail in this war of extermination, sickly seasons, epidemics, pestilence, and plague, advance in terrific array, and sweep off their thousands and ten thousands. Should success be still incomplete, gigantic inevitable famine stalks in the rear, and with one mighty blow, levels the population with the food of the world.

Suffering and death are not viewed here as the enemies of mankind, but rather as the just punishment for a profligate humanity. Going even further, Malthus advocated explicitly that government and society should adopt a policy of allowing the destitute to die. This view is expressed in his assault on parish relief and the poor laws.* Malthus argued that

---

* The parish relief system, which developed in the 1500s, was a result of national statutes, or poor laws, which established responsibility at the local level for the church and local officials to provide relief to the poor within a particular area, or parish. In Malthus's time, beginning three years before the publication of his first essay, the Speenhamland System, a variation of parish relief, provided some food and money assistance to the very poor. In 1834, partly as a result of Malthus's criticisms and the recommendations of Benthamite political economists, this system was transformed into one in which relief was given only to those who would work in regulated workhouses.

there is one right which man has generally been thought to possess, which I am confident he neither does nor can possess—a right to subsistence when his labour will not fairly purchase it.

He recommended that public notice be given that no one born after a certain date, some time in the very near future, be eligible for any form of relief. Generations to come then would have "no claim of right on society for the smallest portion of food." Acknowledging that charity would become the only possible hope for survival, he went on to say that the uncertainty this creates for the poor is desirable as it will force the poor to save more or face the threat that their families will starve to death; this will discipline the poor not to have children they cannot care for. To assist in this last goal he suggested that a shortage of housing would be beneficial as it would discourage early marriage and large families.[36] Malthus's ideas about food production and population became thoroughly intertwined with his Social Darwinism (long before Darwin's name was associated with this doctrine) and his defense of the status quo. His arguments about poverty led him to an early version of the resource-scarcity argument from which he also derived a kind of free-enterprise polemic against government efforts on behalf of economic progress. Denying the possibility of expanding resources through human effort, Malthus repeatedly asserted[37] that redistribution was the only way to alleviate poverty in the short run, and that this was only delaying inevitable poverty and misery. Speaking again about the poor laws, Malthus asserted:[38]

Poor-laws, indeed, will always tend to aggravate the evil by diminishing the general resources of the country; and in such a state of things can exist only for a very short time; but with or without them, no stretch of human ingenuity and exertion can rescue the people from the most extreme poverty and wretchedness.

This convergence of arguments about resources and social policy was ultimately expanded by Malthus into a general defense of upper-class interests and government passivity. His pessimism, his claim about resources, and his defense of privileged interests come together in this passage:[39]

In the actual circumstances of every country, the prolific power of nature seems to be always ready to exert nearly its full force; but within the limit of possibility, there is nothing perhaps more improbable, or more out of reach of any government to effect, than the direction of the industry of its subjects in such a manner as to produce the greatest quantity of human sustenance that the earth could bear. It evidently could not be done without the most complete violation of the law of property, from which everything that is valuable to man has hitherto arisen.

Here the system of property replaces the system of nature as the reason that limits exist. Having merged the political and the natural,[40] Malthus relieves government and the wealthy from all responsibilities for economic conditions, inequality, and poverty.[41]

> That the principal and most permanent cause of poverty has little or no direct relation to the forms of government, or the unequal division of property; and that, as the rich do not in reality possess the power of finding employment and maintenance for the poor, the poor cannot in the nature of things, possess the right to demand them....

Malthus[42] also thought that people would be less likely to challenge established authority if they saw overpopulation as the cause of social problems.

At the time that Kennedy was in office, an updated version of Malthus's argument was about to appear. By the 1970s this modern version would provide a more comprehensive critique of the industrial world than did Malthus, but one that offered a similar rationale for abandoning economic progress. In the new version, raw materials scarcity would become a primary focus, and population growth would be viewed as a multifaceted problem which threatened not only to exhaust allegedly scarce resources but also to threaten the environment. Industrialization would come under attack for accelerating resource depletion and damaging the environment. Overpopulation, resource scarcity, and the evils of increased production and consumption would become a rationale in the 1970s and beyond for economic problems actually caused by human actions.

The pessimism promoted by these views would not only justify a lack of economic progress but also discourage the search for solutions in government action and economic reform. Arguments about scarce resources, limits to growth, and too many people wanting too much would be logically attractive to economic interests seeking profit through restricted output, price fixing, and financial manipulation. Such ideas are also inherently appealing to established upper classes who worry that economic progress will disrupt existing political and social relationships.

Although most of this was to unfold in the years after Kennedy's death, there were some early indicators of these later developments. Some of that can be seen in a divergence of outlook between Kennedy and elements of the new conservation movement and in Kennedy's stated disagreements with those proclaiming overpopulation to be a major problem. Views that were at odds with Kennedy's stated commitment to technological progress and rising standards of living emanated from three interrelated groups: a Rockefeller-led government commission, the more extreme part of the old conservation movement, and the Aspen Institute.

The Outdoor Recreation Resources Review Commission (ORRRC) was created by Congress in 1958, and President Eisenhower named Laurance Rockefeller as its chairman. The ORRRC's report was issued in 1962, and there was much in the report that was narrowly focused on recreation. However, it also recommended government policy that would restrict economic growth and repeatedly used rhetoric that was anti-industry, anti-technology, and anti-growth. Except for a few specific suggestions related to recreation, President Kennedy ignored the ORRRC's recommendations and polemics.

The tone of the report was decidedly anti-modernist. Describing factories as "dark satanic mills," citing Jefferson's image of the city as a place of "rootlessness," and describing the radically anti-modern John Muir as a "mainstream" thinker, the report suggested that contact with nature is a spiritual experience and at the core of the nation's character. The report also mentioned issues that were not yet major, but would become so later in the 1960s and early 1970s. These invoked the image of "scarce resources" and linked recreation to the broader issue of pollution.[43]

The Commission's report criticized earlier federal policies for putting flood control, irrigation, and the generation of hydroelectric power ahead of the preservation of rivers for recreation. It not only recommended the expansion of territory designated for recreation or as primitive areas, but also urged legislation flatly prohibiting the use of any parkland for schools, hospitals, freeways or other purposes without replacement lands.[44] The legislative proposals had a huge anti-growth potential, entirely preventing public officials from weighing the comparative benefits of different land uses.

Collier and Horowitz[45] say that Laurance Rockefeller's leadership of this commission was part of his change from "a gentleman conservationist into a statesman in the emerging environmental movement." At the same time that he sent this report to President Kennedy, his American Conservation Association began spending almost a million dollars promoting the report and also organized 150 notables to disseminate its views.

Although President Kennedy made Rockefeller head of an Advisory Council on Recreation, the president's policies concerning technology, growth, and resources, and his constant emphasis on progress clearly showed that he had a different agenda.

In his February 23, 1961, message to Congress on "Natural Resources" President Kennedy[46] made some passing references to conservationism but quickly identified resource development and "long-range planning for national economic growth" as his goals. In this eight-page message there were at least six separate references to growth and development, plus numerous specific proposals for water resource and energy development. While there are some recommendations on parks and recreational areas, there is no indication that Kennedy shared the anti-industrial sentiments expressed in the Rockefeller report. There was also no acceptance of ORRRC calls to limit severely the use of parklands or to reduce flood control efforts.

In his 1962 message on conservation, President Kennedy[47] referred to the ORRRC report and supported the general goal of expanding recreational opportunities and parklands. Consistent with his overall commitment to technology, industrial progress, and growth, he continued to emphasize development. He specifically asserted that mineral resources were "for practical purposes" not fixed or limited, but were instead created through advances in technology.* For example, he placed great emphasis on efforts to expand energy production and to keep energy prices down. Finally, he never embraced the imagery of the Rockefeller report which implied a conflict between modern production and nature. Consistent with his concern for human life, his overall commitment to progress, and his cultural optimism, President Kennedy believed that people could use science and technology to create a better world (the very opposite of the Malthusian worldview). He was not indifferent to nature, but his values and outlook were Western, Judeo-Christian, democratic, and progressive. The Rockefeller report was drawing on a different tradition.

Reflected in the rhetoric of the Rockefeller report were values that had long been present in the American conservation movement and soon would be given new influence as an upper-class imprint on the new conservationism and environmentalism. Laurance Rockefeller was a major figure among conservationists, and he was active in taking what had been a small and decidedly élitist movement and transforming it into a force with much broader political impact. The popularization of this previously exclusive preoccupation, however, did not lead to any moderation of its views; if anything the opposite occurred.

The American conservation movement, begun in the 1890s, had always included some people who had a general disdain for the modern, industrial world. This part of the movement had been anti-materialist, anti-urban, and technophobic, and some of its leaders embraced pagan or pantheistic views at odds with Judeo-Christian views of the relationship between human beings and nature. The movement in general had been decidedly élitist and was permeated with racist sentiments.**

The more extreme views were associated with the part of the movement that developed out of the radically anti-modernist ideas of John Muir, the founder in the early 1890s of the Sierra Club. In the 1960s, much of the conservation movement was shifting to a more pointed opposition to industrial technology and economic growth.[48] Oddly, this development did not make the movement more exclusive or politically marginal. In fact, this change was accompanied by an aggressive effort to attract popular support. In the growth of the conservation movement and its transformation into the environmental movement, the Rockefeller family played an important role.

In 1947 Laurance Rockefeller and Fairfield Osborn started the Conservation Foundation. In 1953 the Rockefellers worked with the Ford Foundation on a conference which led to the establishment of Resources for the Future, and in 1957 Laurance Rockefeller formed the American Conservation Association. In

---

* In a November 18, 1963, speech defending his economic policies Kennedy (1964, p. 231) referred to the abundance of raw materials.

** An ostensibly non-partisan account of these notions can be found in Stephen Fox's *The American Conservation Movement* (pp. 289-92; 322-24; 347-73). More critical discussions of many of the same issues are provided in books by Richard Neuhaus and William Tucker. These two focus on the way aristocratic and élitist views came to the fore in the growth of environmentalism in the 1970s. Neither author, however, examines the events of the 1960s.

the 1950s, Laurance had also been a leader in other conservation groups, including the Hudson River Conservation Society.[49] These activities extended a family involvement that went back to the early 1900s.

Closely related to conservation was another cause with which the Rockefellers had long been involved—the Malthus-like effort to portray overpopulation as the cause of poverty and underdevelopment.

The population control movement, long interconnected with conservationism, was also growing when President Kennedy took office. Among the many upper-class figures involved in this, few were more important than John D. Rockefeller III.* In the early 1950s he established and headed the Population Council, which came to play a major role in spreading population control policies to underdeveloped countries. The Council led the expansion of the population control effort that began around 1962. A committee created in 1958 by President Eisenhower to review military security matters concluded that population growth was a primary cause of instability and backwardness.** The 10-man committee included Rockefeller associate John J. McCloy and other notables, such as investment bankers Joseph M. Dodge and William H. Draper, Jr. (the committee was informally called the Draper Committee). Draper, a partner at Dillon, Read, and Co., would organize the Population Crisis Committee in 1965 to act as a lobbying force in Washington, D.C. St. Louis millionaire Hugh Moore assisted Draper in creating the Crisis Committee, and in the 1950s he paid for newspaper ads and pamphlets warning about the danger of a "population bomb."[50]

McCloy, Draper, the Ford Foundation, and Rockefeller interests were connected to another group which was also very critical of the economic goals that President Kennedy saw as central parts of his program. This group was associated with the Aspen Institute based in Aspen, Colorado, and was becoming in the 1950s and early 1960s very critical of scientific-technological progress, industrial society, and economic growth. Aspen was one of the first organizations, if not the first, to begin talking about the possibility of moving the United States away from science-technology-oriented growth.

The Aspen Institute developed out of a 1949 conference organized to celebrate the bicentennial of the birth of Goethe. The primary organizers of the

---

* In a not very critical book, Demerath (pp. 34-35) describes the population control movement, or "family planning establishment," as "a visible and respectable spinoff of the more general Eastern Establishment, that influential and polished combination of 'old boys,' talented professionals, and great wealth that operates in so many circuits of top U.S. power. The family planning establishment represents the Eastern Establishment's interests in population, particularly in foreign population growth. These interests run mainly to the control of natural resources, raw materials, investments, and markets, all of which tend to get translated by the Eastern Establishment as the need for law-and-order and national security."

** In 1959, when this committee issued its report, the Stanford Research Institute published a study with a similar view. Both reports made population control a national security issue. The July 1961 issue of *Foreign Affairs* included a brief discussion of these reports in an article asserting that there was a population problem and that the "core of the problem" was a declining death rate (Zlotnick, 1961).

conference were Guiseppe Borgese, Robert M. Hutchins from the University of Chicago, and Paul Paepcke, head of the Container Corporation of America and also a trustee of the University of Chicago and a director of Encyclopedia Britannica.* When Aspen's formation was announced, an official statement was issued; it included the following:[51]

> At the midpoint of the twentieth century, when men's lives are dominated more than ever by science, men need the elevation and liberation of a sound humanism. In a world which almost worships science and technology, we must rediscover the moral and spiritual truths which will enable men to control science and all its machinery.

Obviously Aspen's version of humanism was very different from John Kennedy's. For Kennedy, science, technology, and industry were a part of human creativity and human progress. They were a means to eliminate suffering and a basis for social justice. Around 1950, when this Aspen statement was written, most of the world's nations were in dire need of that science and technology, and a third of the people in the U.S. were living in poverty. This Aspen outlook is the same that underlay the charge that Kennedy was promoting a lust for industrialization.

According to Aspen's chronicler, Sidney Hyman,[52] Paepcke thought that in the immediate aftermath of World War II, too many people were preoccupied with material security. Paepcke's attitude, coming at the end of four years of war and ten years of extremely hard times, can only be attributed to an aristocratic indifference. Certainly, the leading figures in Aspen's development during the 1950s and 1960s were part of the untitled American aristocracy.

The president of Aspen from 1957 to 1963, and then its chairman, was Robert O. Anderson. Anderson was chairman of Atlantic Richfield, a corporate offspring of the Rockefellers' Standard Oil complex. Anderson, who was also the primary source of funding for Aspen in the early 1960s, was at various times director of the Chase Bank and of CBS, president of the Dallas Federal Reserve Bank, and a trustee of the University of Chicago. On the eve of President Kennedy's inauguration, Anderson began a series of seminars on the role of science in society, and in 1962 a number of different programs were begun on environmental issues. It is clear that the drift of these seminars and programs was an extension of Aspen's stated purpose of devaluing technology and industrial production.[53]

---

* In the early 1960s, Time, Inc. director Gaylord Freeman was also a director of Aspen and of the Container Corporation. Henry Luce was a director of the University of Chicago-affiliated Encyclopedia Britannica. Luce and his wife were participants in Aspen seminars, and Luce helped to start Aspen seminars for businessmen. Alvin Eurich, president of Aspen in the 1960s, once worked for Time, Inc.; he was also chairman of the Stanford Research Institute and was the director of the Ford Foundation's Fund for the Advancement of Education. The chairman of the fund was Time director Roy Larsen, friend of Paul Cabot (director) and Thomas Lamont (director, vice-chairman) of Morgan. (Hyman, pp. 26, 100-2, 172-73; Marquis *Who's Who*, 1962-63; Swanberg, p. 514.)

This work would later be carried on by Joseph E. Slater, who became Aspen's resident in 1969. Slater had worked for General William Draper in Europe following World War II, and he viewed Draper, John J. McCloy and Paul Hoffman as his mentors. Hoffman was, among other things, a director of Time, Inc. and the Encyclopedia Britannica and a trustee of the Ford Foundation. From 1953 to 1957, Slater was chief economist for the Creole Petroleum Company, a subsidiary of Standard Oil of New Jersey. In 1957 he went to work with McCloy at the Ford Foundation and in 1960 became the director of its International Affairs Program. Slater was involved in the founding of the Institute for Strategic Studies in London, which had an ongoing relationship with Aspen and was the model for the International Institute for Environmental Affairs, organized in the early 1970s by Slater and Robert O. Anderson.[54]

Slater was heavily involved in activities leading to and following the appearance of the new conservationism-environmentalism. Following a brief stint as a deputy to an assistant secretary in Kennedy's State Department, a job from which he resigned because of frustration with Kennedy (reasons unknown), Slater worked on environmental issues at the Ford Foundation and went on in the late 1960s to help Anderson plan the first Earth Day. Around this time he was describing Aspen's purpose as one of dealing with problems of materialism and of "overwhelming scientific and technological developments."[55] That people around Aspen were still not fond of Kennedy years later is suggested by Lyman's[56] 1975 reference to a Kennedy proposal on recreation as the "so-called Wilderness Act."

Expressing what had been the goals of Anderson, Slater, and the institute, Robert M. Hutchins said in a 1969 Aspen speech that the United States had to make a painful transition to a less production-oriented, post-industrial society.[57] That had not been President Kennedy's idea of the future, nor was it part of the values and goals that motivated President Kennedy to override the "free-enterprise" objections of Establishment interests. Kennedy showed no signs of embracing these extreme views, and he certainly was not inclined to see science, technology, and production as evils.*

President Kennedy did clearly state his objections to any attempt at making alleged population problems part of U.S. foreign policy, and he clearly rejected overpopulation as a primary explanation for poverty and underdevelopment. It true that the Kennedy administration agreed to have information on fertility research disseminated to other countries, but this did not mean that Kennedy would attempt to impose population control on anyone. It would be Johnson who committed the U.S. to limiting population growth, both at home and abroad.[58]

On December 9, 1959, then Senator Kennedy discussed various issues with John Fischer, editor-in-chief of *Harper's* magazine. Besides criticizing John

---

President Kennedy's entire economic program was an indirect repudiation of these reactions against the modern world. Secretary of the Interior Stewart L. Udall and Senator Gaylord Nelson both reported Kennedy's general lack of interest in conservationist causes (Paper, pp. 154, 240, 367).

Foster Dulles's foreign policy and affirming his commitment to economic development, Kennedy stated his views on population growth and economic problems in underdeveloped countries:[59]

Q: In these underdeveloped countries, do you think they can ever solve their economic problems as long as their population keeps rising at the rate of about 3 percent a year, doubling every forty years?

Kennedy: Well, I would think it was a population increase closer to 2 percent. But then you have to have an annual rate of increase of at least 6 per cent in your gross national product, so that you have a 2 per cent increase to take care of the population increase, another 2 per cent to provide increased standard of living of the population, and another 2 per cent to provide increased momentum in the years ahead. In terms of food, at least, if you provided for the kind of agricultural production increases necessary, if you provided for the calorie output per acre in India that you have in Japan or even in Western Europe—which is not impossible with new fertilizer, the control of water and education of the farmers—you could increase that production faster than the population. We've had a population increase in the United States which was as great as any place in the world, but our food production increases faster. Those with whom I've talked at the experimental stations of the Department of Agriculture point out what the Dutch and the Japanese produce per acre; and would indicate that increased productivity in the United States, which is really a technological explosion in the United States in food production (which is the heart of our agricultural problem), is going to continue; and that, with a concentrated technological effort, it can be done in other areas of the world also.

I think it's possible to sustain a growth where the resources of the world, if properly managed, could increase faster than the population. I'm not saying it's going to be done, but it can be done, and that must be our goal.

Q: Am I right, however, in thinking that no nation, except possibly Communist Russia and Communist China, has ever achieved annual growth rates of 6 per cent a year for a considerable period? It's much greater than we ever achieved.

Kennedy: I would think that since the war the countries of Western Europe and Japan, which started at a rather low level—I'd have to recall their exact growth rate, but I would think that their growth rate was in several instances bigger than that. Economists such as Professor Rostow and others believe that the Indians could do it, in their third five-year plan, if they receive sufficient foreign assistance. What is the alternative? I think we must do it. Otherwise you just say you're going to ration poverty among an increased number of people.

Q: Do you see any hope at all of slowing up the rate of population increase?

Kennedy: You mean through birth control?

Q: By any method whatever.

Kennedy: Of course, the population increase is a matter of more children surviving and adults living to an older age, which gives us an immediate problem now. I'm not sure that the mathematical predictions of doubling the population every forty years will be fulfilled. Once the average person around the world can hope to reach three

score and ten, once nine out of ten children live through the first year rather than two
or three out of ten, I don't think you're going to get that arithmetical, geometrical,
doubling every forty or fifty years.

Now, on the question of limiting population: as you know the Japanese have been
doing it very vigorously, through abortion, which I think would be repugnant to all
Americans. Some other countries have instituted programs of birth control, including
the Indians. Their success has been rather limited. Most people consider their families
to be their families, and that it is other people's families that provide the population
explosion. The techniques are rather imperfect, and it should be remembered that in
the experience of the countries which have used them, these techniques have not had
a significant effect on the population increase expected. As you know, the Chinese
were pushing it for a while, but are not now.

Q: They have appeared to abandon it.

Kennedy: So have the Russians, who believe this policy would indicate the inability
of the Communist system to solve its problems. I believe it is a judgment which the
countries and the people involved must make as to whether they wish to limit their
population. Since it involves so personal a decision I think it would be unwise for
the United States to intervene.

In this exchange President Kennedy thoroughly rejects the Malthusian views
ɔmoted by the population control movement. He questions the factual basis
their arguments, rejects abortion as a population control method, emphasizes
 possibility and desirability of achieving high levels of economic growth, and
ncludes by saying that it would be "unwise" for U.S. to impose population
ntrol policies on other nations. Kennedy went on to say that both those who
pose population control and those hoping to limit population growth should
port development assistance.*

President Kennedy's views on population growth were described as an im-
diment to population control in the July 1961 issue of *Foreign Affairs*.[60] His
position to the population control movement's views parallelled his attitudes
out and differences with the anti-modernist views of many conservationists
 the anti-growth ideas of the Aspen Institute's leaders. President Kennedy's
mitment to science, technology, and economic progress had led him to adopt
icies that were vehemently attacked by people in and around the Morgan-
ckefeller complex. They had criticized Kennedy for becoming the "enforcer"

---

ennedy felt that those who opposed population control should support policies that help create the
nomic growth for growing populations. In regard to those wanting less population growth, he is
ost certainly referring to demographic transition theory, which maintains that changes set in motion
:conomic development and rising standards of living lead to lower population growth rates. In that
ry, economic progress reduces infant mortality rates, eliminating a reason to have many children,
produces movement to cities and less need for labor-intensive agricultural production (Simon, pp.
-87). In fact, the population densities of both Africa and South America were well below that of the
ted States, which was itself a small fraction of the population density of countries that are today
ng the most prosperous nations in the world (*e.g.*, Germany, Belgium, Netherlands, Japan).

of progress. Upper-class interests in the conservation-population control mo
ment, often connected to the Rockefellers, were challenging progress itself.
doing so, they were attacking the ends of Kennedy's programs while rela
upper-class interests assaulted the means to that end, *i.e.*, active gove
ment.*

President Johnson, on the other hand, embraced the conservationist-popu
tion control movement and either tolerated or initiated other changes wh
indicated a shift away from the attempt to promote national and internatio
economic progress. In the short term, Johnson's adoption of the "new conser
tionism" was probably most important as a symbolic commitment, rather tha
shift that meant immediate major changes in the economy.

The importance of this symbolic action should not, however, be undere
mated. President Johnson was the first national leader to make these issues
important part of the nation's goals. Also, the new emphasis on the evils
economic growth and human reproduction coincided with and was consist
with Johnson's retreat from Kennedy's domestic and foreign policy.

President Johnson

Exactly six months after assuming office, President Johnson defined aspect
his Great Society program in a speech to a university audience in Ann Art
Michigan.[61] The themes in this speech did not present a complete departure fr
Kennedy policies. There were the stated goals of ending poverty and ra
injustice, and of expanding educational opportunity. Johnson also said that
Great Society "rests on abundance and liberty for all." Mixed in with th
comments, however, were themes which contradicted Kennedy's stated ap
ciation for science, technology, and industrial production, and in many w
made the speech self-contradictory.

> Your imagination, your initiative, and your indignation will determine whether w
> build a society where progress is the servant of our needs, or a society where ol
> values and new visions are buried under unbridled growth. For in your time we hav
> the opportunity to move not only toward the rich society and the powerful society
> but upward to the Great Society.

He went on to describe the Great Society as

> a place where the city of man serves not only the needs of body and the demands o
> commerce but the desire for beauty and the hunger for community.
> It is a place where man can renew contact with nature. It is a place which honor
> creation for its own sake and for what it adds to the understanding of the race. It i

---

* Implicit in this is a possible political strategy for this part of the upper class. It could tolerate a presi
who talked about economic progress but did little or nothing to secure it, and could tolerate
government activism as long as it was not for the purpose of enforcing progress.

a place where men are more concerned with the quality of their goals than the quantity of their goods.

President Johnson then emphasized the needs of a growing population, implying that quantity of goods and growth, bridled or unbridled, would still be important. In a way bordering on the incoherent, he immediately shifted to his fear that "open land is vanishing" and that the expansion of cities is eroding the time-honored value of "communion with nature."

The incoherence continued as Johnson emphasized the goal of making our cities great, but followed that with more fears that the opportunity to commune with nature was being lost.

> The water we drink, the food we eat, the very air that we breathe, are threatened with pollution. Our parks are overcrowded, our seashores overburdened. Green fields and dense forests are disappearing.
> A few years ago we were greatly concerned about the "Ugly American." Today we must act to prevent an ugly America.
> For once the battle is lost, once our natural splendor is destroyed, it can never be recaptured. And once man can no longer walk with beauty or wonder at nature his spirit will wither and his sustenance be wasted.

While there was nothing necessarily contradictory in valuing both cities and nature, there was a real tension in Johnson's emphasis on building a better urban environment while he also voiced dire warnings about growth, and he located man's real home in nature.

Summing up, he warned that the people were in danger of being "condemned to a soulless wealth." He also made the following mysterious remark: "Within your lifetime powerful forces, already loosed, will take us toward a way of life beyond the realm of our experience, almost beyond the bounds of our imagination."

The powerful forces and the new way of life were undefined. Was this the same post-industrial society being discussed at the Aspen Institute? Was it a society guided by the anti-modernist goals of the mobilized conservation movement? President Johnson's assertion that the human spirit developed from experience of nature is a view found in the ORRRC report.

On February 8, 1965, two messages were sent to Congress that demonstrated Johnson's commitment to what he was now calling the "new conservation." At the beginning of his message concerning wilderness preservation, Johnson[62] quoted Ralph Waldo Emerson: "In the woods we return to reason and faith." This sentiment is not only anti-modern, it suggests an attraction to some sort of nature religion. Whatever Lyndon Johnson's personal feelings might have been, it is almost impossible to imagine President Kennedy saying anything like this. In the other message, "Natural Beauty of our Country," Johnson[63] invoked images long associated with anti-modernist politics. He warned that urbanization and growth were crowding people into cities and cutting them off from nature and that the "darker side" of modern technology threatened our air, water, soil and wildlife.

Johnson also announced that Laurance Rockefeller would be chairman of an upcoming White House Conference on Natural Beauty, this to focus on a public education campaign "needed to alert Americans to the danger to their natural heritage and to the need for action."

In his February 1966 State of the Union Address,[64] President Johnson continued with the new conservationist themes but also pointed proudly to improving economic conditions and high levels of growth. He hoped for a budget that no longer was in deficit, but warned that greater spending might be required for the war in Vietnam. Twice he emphasized that the U.S. was embarking on a new foreign aid policy that made the control of population growth a primary goal. In their analysis of the development of today's population control movement, Peter Bachrach and Elihu Bergman[65] called President Johnson's initiative a "watershed" development.* In the years immediately following, a Population Office was created within the Agency for International Development (AID) in 1966, the position of Special Assistant to the Secretary of State for Population Matters was created in 1967, and, under Johnson and Nixon, the AID funds allocated for population control activities increased from $10 million in 1966 to $125 million in 1971.[66]

Johnson's adoption of the population control cause and the new conservationism represented a qualitative shift away from traditional politics and from President Kennedy's emphasis on economic progress.[67] In the short term, the practical impact of this was probably small, but it was a significant development in what would become a war of ideas between supporters of economic progress and those who believe that the overriding problems of the late-twentieth century are too many people, too much industrial production, and too much consumption. There is nothing to indicate that Lyndon Johnson had ever had a significant involvement with these issues until he began speaking about them as president. Here, too, he was going along with Establishment pressures, just as he was willing to redirect foreign policy and to play a more passive role in the national economy.

The combination of Johnson's personal inclinations and his compliance allowed upper-class interests to gain or regain influence over the direction of the country. President Kennedy had challenged that influence in many important areas. Kennedy's success in making that challenge was aided by his personal traits, his attractiveness as a political figure, and his ability to touch people through his speeches. He showed a large capacity for hard work and a great

---

* The actual development of population control policy indicates that Schlesinger (p. 604) was really stretching things when he claimed that it was President Kennedy who laid the groundwork for population control efforts. President Kennedy's views were essentially at odds with this movement, and his concessions to it were tiny when compared to the aggressive commitment of Johnson.

determination to make that work pay off. None of these traits would have mattered that much, however, had they not been attached to a leadership strategy and a set of substantive goals. Without the strategy and goals, his presidency would not have been that significant, and his death would be an individual tragedy, made larger only by his symbolic importance as leader of the nation.

President Kennedy was the kind of national leader who actually promotes the general welfare and the kind that a country needs most when that welfare is threatened by powerful groups. For three years, Kennedy fought against certain tendencies within those groups, and immediately after his death some of those tendencies were reasserted. Within ten years of Kennedy's death the progress he had fought for was disappearing as those tendencies became expressed in a most flagrant and destructive way.

SIX

Long-Term Changes

In his introduction to Kennedy's *The Strategy of Peace*,[1] Allan Nevins noted that "since Franklin D. Roosevelt the Democrats have cherished Jeffersonian ideals but acted on Hamiltonian ideas." Nevins made this remark before Kennedy took office, and he offered little explanation of its meaning. As it turned out, Kennedy's policies were in spirit and even in detail thoroughly Hamiltonian. This is what generated the intense conflict with the Morgan-Rockefeller sector of the ruling class over national economic policy. Kennedy's international economic policy extended Hamilton's principles to the global arena, and this produced a similar confrontation with essentially the same opponents.

Hamilton came from a humble background. His abilities, hard work, an advantageous marriage, and the opportunities presented by revolutionary times allowed him to rise to the position of aide to General George Washington. He played a prominent role in the debates surrounding the writing of the Constitution and in the development of the federal government after the revolution. He was selected by Washington to be the first secretary of the treasury, and he remained a significant figure in American politics until 1804, when, at age 47, he was killed by Aaron Burr.*

As adviser to President Washington and as Secretary of the Treasury, Hamilton attempted to instigate a social revolution "in the face of powerful vested interests in the status quo."[2] Hamilton moved against the rule of oligarchy, the

---

* According to William Hoffman (p. 108), the pistols used in the duel in which Burr killed Hamilton, who, consistent with his opposition to dueling, never fired at Burr, are among David Rockefeller's prized possessions.

103

networks of people whose wealth was based on inherited property. He wished to see a nation develop that was not dominated by hereditary power, privilege, or status, and he had a particular dislike for the world of the agrarian oligarchy. During the revolution, he believed the country was being ruined by "money making men" engaged in price-gouging, speculation, and market manipulation. He became convinced that greed and the market could undermine the welfare of the nation and that when this was happening, the government had to intervene.[3]

While Hamilton accepted the idea that the economy should be based on private property, markets, and the profit motive, he rejected the central premise of laissez-faire that economic forces should be allowed to operate without government intervention. Hamilton believed strongly that government should shape the rules to channel private profit motives into actions that benefit the entire nation. Taxes and other government policies should promote industry and productivity while discouraging actions that impede development.[4] Hamilton was the primary architect of the Washington administration's economic policies, and those policies repudiated the same free-market ideas that the *Wall Street Journal* and *Fortune* used to attack Kennedy. Two of Hamilton's most important legacies were his proposal for a national bank and his recommendations for stimulating the development of manufacturing.

The bank proposal was submitted in 1790 as part of Hamilton's overall goal of utilizing spending, money creation, tax policy, and trade policy to channel money into useful investments.[5] With a mistrust of bankers at least equal to Kennedy's, Hamilton sought to organize the bank so that private bankers could be involved, but not dominant. He used the Bank of England as an organizational model, but viewed that bank as an instrument of British ruling-class power and attempted to structure the American version to serve U.S. national economic needs.[6]

Hamilton's most direct opponent in this endeavor was Thomas Jefferson, who attempted to convince Washington that the bank was unnecessary and that it would be unconstitutional. Jefferson, James Madison, and the Southern plantation class opposed the bank, and after Hamilton succeeded in having it established, they worked with Aaron Burr in an attempt to undermine Hamilton's program.[7]

In proposing the bank, Hamilton had specific concerns. He worried about the tendency of private interests to protect their position by promoting restrictive policies in the creation of money and credit. He also mentioned specifically that the bank, by providing adequate capital and credit, would allow the country to cope with trade deficits by stimulating investments in production rather than by reducing consumption.[8] In his specific arguments as well as in his general defense of the bank, Hamilton had one overriding goal—to develop the United States as a productive, manufacturing nation. To that end he submitted to Congress in the next year a report on manufacturing.

In his 1791 proposals on the promotion of productive investments, Hamilton again rejected free-enterprise ideas and attacked those claiming that only agricultural production created wealth. Hamilton offered an active government program, which he defended in general by underscoring government's obligation to promote the general welfare.[9] It was this view of the Constitution and the role of government that Kennedy echoed when he gave his view of the powers of the presidency, and this outlook permeates his explanations for and justifications of many of his actions.

Hamilton energetically defended the government's right to use spending, taxation, and trade policy to promote economic growth and diversity. He suggested that government powers be used to reward invention and creativity, assist new industries, and, in general, stimulate production.[10] He argued that taxes should generally be higher for the rich, and he specifically rejected most taxes that fall equally on rich and poor.* Hamilton's views on debt and deficit spending were, like Kennedy's, derived from his overall conception of economic progress. In short, Hamilton argued[11] that debt and deficit spending could be very useful as long as the increases in money and credit led to investments in technology and industry. Hamilton pointed out that an expansion of government debt without accompanying growth in the economy would lead to a growing tax burden simply to pay interest, and that the commitment of an increasing part of government revenue to servicing debt would reduce the government's flexibility in dealing with new problems.

Kennedy as Hamiltonian

Kennedy, like Hamilton, was committed to using the powers of the presidency and of the federal government to promote economic progress. As we have noted, Kennedy attempted to shape the federal budget so that spending stimulated technological progress and industrial modernization. He was determined to prevent interest rates from rising, and he wanted to see enough growth in money and credit to allow the economy to grow with little or no interruption. This was a continuing concern to him, and the issue gained importance in 1963. His support of bigger deficits was linked to his determination to sustain high levels of investment and growth.

Kennedy proposed a variety of tax changes aimed at discouraging short-term, speculative, and nonproductive investments and at encouraging production-ori-

---

* As with Kennedy, there are many different accounts of Hamilton's policies and of Hamilton as a person. An exploration of the various images of Hamilton would take up more space than seems appropriate or necessary in this book. Hamilton has often been portrayed as some sort of élitist or conservative. However, his concerns for the well-being of people in general, his actions, and the conflicts in which he became involved all show that his values, outlook, and goals were completely consistent in principle with what was best in the Roosevelt-Kennedy tradition. Beside his very progressive and activist philosophy of government, Hamilton was one of the few emphatic and active opponents of slavery in his time and was among the few leaders to argue then that there was equality of ability between blacks and whites (McDonald, pp. 21, 34). Anyone interested in Hamilton or the issues of his time might begin by reading Forrest McDonald's definitive biography, then Hamilton's proposals on the bank, manufacturing, and credit, and his contributions to what became the *Federalist Papers*.

ented investment. He sent tax reforms to Congress in an attempt to redirect foreign investments away from Europe and Canada to the U.S. and to Third World nations. He proposed measures that would have taken tax advantages away from individuals and institutions involved in taking money out of the U.S. He also suggested measures to curtail the special privileges enjoyed by U.S. multinationals involved in oil and other raw materials. Kennedy was determined to see a rapid expansion of the country's energy production, and he viewed cheap energy as an essential condition for economic growth and prosperity. His program was very supportive of scientific research and technological progress, which he viewed as the key to overcoming potential resource problems.

In these efforts, Kennedy offered a twentieth-century version of Hamilton's policy; in principle it was identical. President Kennedy's efforts to carry out this program were criticized and condemned in the most severe fashion. No other president in the 20th century, with the exception of Roosevelt during World War II, had so actively sought to shape the direction of the nation's economy. In this regard, Kennedy can be compared to only a handful of presidents, which might also include Washington, following Hamilton's advice, and perhaps Lincoln. Kennedy deserves to be recognized in history as one of our nation's most important advocates for progress. His general goal was to make the 1960s a decade of growth and prosperity at home and of economic development in the poor nations of the Third World. The 1970s brought the progress of the 1960s, and of the better part of the 1940-1966 period, to a halt. The 1960s had featured rising real income, shrinking poverty, and a growing potential for future progress. In the 1970s those trends changed, replaced by falling real income and rising poverty and by deterioration in the overall investment process. This decline would continue in the 1980s, accelerating in some areas, and become part of the way business is done.

In the early 1970s, banking and oil interests, interwoven as the core of the U.S. establishment's economic power, rocked the U.S. economy with stunning increases in the cost of money and energy, probably the two most important items in a modern economy. The boards of directors of the major banks in the Morgan-Rockefeller orbit (Chase, Chemical, City Bank, Morgan) had in 1972 at least 17 connections, in the form of common directors, to oil companies.[12] This plus a variety of other relationships between bankers and oilmen suggested a virtual identity of interests.[13]

The prime interest rate, the trend-setting rate offered by major banks to corporations, had begun rising again in 1965 and stood at 8 percent at the end of the 1960s. It continued upward in the early 1970s, reaching 10.8 percent for 1974. This extraordinarily high rate coincided with rapid increases in energy prices, and the two together jolted the U.S. economy and did even worse damage to the development prospects of the Third World. In 1970, President Nixon had replaced Martin at the Federal Reserve with Arthur Burns, publicly instructing Burns to keep interest rates down and keep the money supply expanding.[14] Interest rates did go back down into the 4.5-5.0 percent range in 1971 and 1972, but surged upward again in 1973. Whatever Nixon's real views were about the rising interest rates, he was probably no more capable of reacting to this problem than he was of dealing with the oil crisis, for during 1973, his administration was engulfed by the Watergate scandal.[15]

The Energy Crisis

President Kennedy had repeatedly stressed the importance of creating an abundant and growing supply of cheap energy.[16] By 1969, oilmen were heading in a different direction, looking for ways to drive the price of energy upward. A 1969 Standard Oil of California (SoCal/Chevron) study indicated that the primary impediment to higher prices was an abundance of oil.[17] As events were to show in the 1970s, there was a way to solve this "problem"—create shortages and illusions of shortages and use the fictional scarcity to justify higher prices.

Such ideas were certainly not new within the oil industry. Back in the 1870s, John D. Rockefeller, Sr., had noted the advantages of producing "less oil than the world required."[18] In 1914, Standard Oil of New Jersey claimed that the U.S. had only ten years' oil supply left, and price increases followed.[19] In the midst of an attempt by U.S. oil companies to gain access to Middle East oil, then dominated by British and French interests, the U.S. Geological Survey issued a report in 1920, based on information from the oil companies, saying that supplies were precarious and that the U.S. would have to either reduce its consumption or depend on foreign sources.[20]

In July of 1928, after six years of negotiations, Standard Oil of New Jersey (later Exxon) and Standard Oil of New York (later Mobil) were admitted as partners in the Iraq Petroleum Company, joining British Petroleum, Royal Dutch Shell, and Compagne Française Pétrole.*[21] Later in the year, the representatives of Standard of New Jersey, British Petroleum, and Royal Dutch Shell met at the Achnacarry Castle in the Highlands of Scotland to discuss the world oil situation. The meeting, joined at some point by other oilmen, such as William Mellon of Gulf, led to an agreement, known as the "As Is Agreement of 1928" or the "Achnacarry Agreement." The agreement represented an attempt to stabilize the existing division of the world market, establish a process of fixing prices, and produce agreements to limit production. This arrangement was soon to be publicly justified in terms of the need for conservation.[22] While the effectiveness of this plan has been questioned, there is no doubt about the

---

* Oil companies have used different names over the years. The following are the top international companies with earlier or alternate names in parenthesis: Exxon (Standard Oil of New Jersey, Esso, Humble Oil Co.), Royal Dutch Shell, British Petroleum (BP, Anglo-Persian, Anglo-Iranian), Mobil (Standard Oil of New York, Socony, Socony Vacuum), Standard Oil of California (SoCal, Chevron), Texaco, and Gulf. SoCal acquired Gulf in 1984, reducing the above Seven Sisters to six. In addition to the four U.S. international companies, there are several other companies counted among the U.S. majors. Included are Standard of Indiana (Amoco), Shell U.S. (owned by Royal Dutch Shell), and Arco (formed in the late 1960s through the merger of Atlantic Refining Co. with the Richfield Co. and a subsequent takeover of Sinclair Oil Company) (Blair, 1976).

intentions, *i.e.*, to maintain a relatively high price through artificial restriction of supply, justified by the desirability of stability and the need for conservation.*

From the 1930s into the 1960s the major oil companies, with varying degrees of success, undertook efforts to keep production down and prices up. This included the direct suppression of Iraq's oil production and an arranged shortage in the U.S. in the 1945-1947 period in order to justify a more than 100 percent increase in the crude oil price. These and other efforts** continued a pattern of activity stretching back to the monopolistic practices of Rockefeller's Standard Oil trust of the late 1800s. The 1970s began, however, as one of those periods of difficulty for the international companies. An abundance of oil supplies and Libya's independent dealings with some of the lesser international companies were causing the big international companies problems. On behalf of the oil companies,*** John J. McCloy went to Washington, D.C. seeking help from the Nixon administration in applying pressure on Libya, but didn't get it.[23]

What the oil companies needed were real or contrived crises that would justify higher prices. Such crises would indeed appear, and, before the 1970s ended, the major oil companies would put on a display of economic and political power that would have impressed the most prodigious monopolists of any earlier era. They did what they could in 1972 to limit or reduce supply in the U.S., cutting production in Texas and pressuring the Nixon administration to reject a Canadian offer to increase the flow of its oil to the U.S.****[24] The required crisis presented itself in the following year in the form of the 1973 Arab-Israeli war. In reaction to U.S. support for Israel, Arab nations declared an embargo against the U.S., and the price of oil rose dramatically.

Several aspects of this 1973-74 "crisis" are of interest here. Although a shortage of oil was proclaimed in the U.S., the Arab nations did not create this shortage and in fact had no capacity to do that. Second, the price increases generated by the producing nations were only one part of the increase experienced by consumers; the other part, probably about equal, was implemented by the oil companies. In addition, the oil-producing countries could not readily

---

* W.S. Farish, chairman of the executive committee of Standard Oil of New Jersey, would later tell a congressional committee that in his mind "conservation and stabilization of the industry" are "synonymous terms; they mean practically the same thing" (Sherrill, p. 533).

** Additional discussion of efforts to limit production and create shortages in the 1930 to 1960 period can be found in the following: Blair (1976, pp. 39, 84-85), Sampson (pp. 132-33), Sherrill (pp. 13-14, 35-36, 43-53, 533).

*** McCloy's extensive connections to Rockefeller interests were noted earlier. He had also spent 15 years with the Morgan-related law firm of Cravath, de Gersdorff, Swaine & Wood (Marquis *Who's Who*, 1962-63). Given the relationship between the Rockefeller-Morgan financial institutions and the oil companies, McCloy was a very logical choice as oil company representative to OPEC nations and to the U.S. government.

**** Also, a Senate subcommittee produced evidence in 1973 that the Colonial Pipeline Company, owned by the ten major oil companies in the U.S., was withholding home heating oil from the Midwest during the winter of 1972-73 (Sherrill, p. 178). As noted earlier, Robert Kennedy's Justice Department was involved in bringing a case against the Colonial Pipeline Company in 1963.

spend all the revenues generated, and most of what they could not use wound up in U.S. and British banks. The Chase Manhattan Bank would later estimate that between 1974 and 1978 OPEC (Organization of Petroleum Exporting Countries) accumulated a surplus of $185 billion, three-fourths of which passed through Western financial institutions, most of that becoming loans to Third World nations.[25]

At the time of the crisis, the Arab countries supplied only 6 percent of U.S. oil consumption. During the 1973-1974 crisis, overall production by Arab nations did not go down. In any event, the Arab producers had virtually no influence on world distribution, which was in the hands of the U.S. and British oil companies, and, therefore, they had no ability to impose an embargo on particular nations without the cooperation of those companies. Various evidence did surface showing that the shortages in the U.S. were contrived by the oil companies.[26]

John Blair, one of the leading oil industry experts in the United States, observed[27] a couple of years later:

> By now, the commonly accepted explanation for the oil price explosion of October 1973 to January 1974 has become firmly embedded in folklore. Through incessant repetition in every medium of communication, responsibility has been effectively transferred to rulers of distant and undeveloped lands whose attitude toward the United States ranges from casual indifference to belligerent hostility. Today's high prices are invariably traced back to the "Arab embargo" and the resultant "shortage."

In that context, Blair pointed out that production during the "shortage" was about the same as at the end of 1974, a time in which there was a glut. Sherrill[28] demonstrated that the oil companies cut their production in 1974 to keep prices up and in the process saved OPEC from disintegrating in a competitive struggle.

The oil companies came out of the crisis in good shape, even if the economy did not. Profits were up, and the federal government had opted not to prosecute the oil companies, a consequence of pressure brought to bear by the National Security Council.*[29]

Between 1973 and 1975 real earnings for employees in the private sector declined, on average, by 4 percent, beginning a 20-year period in which the overall trend would be downward.[30] The prices of petroleum based fertilizers rose rapidly, causing problems for farmers and consumers. Utilities experienced large increases in fuel costs and attempted to pass those costs on to customers. The auto industry in the U.S. found itself at a sudden disadvantage trying to sell

* As noted earlier, Nixon was immersed in the Watergate crisis, and this along with the earlier problems around Vice-President Spiro Agnew's resignation had undermined his capacity to act, had he wanted to do so. The National Security Council's intervention on behalf of the oil companies was not surprising, given the importance in the NSC of longtime Rockefeller associate Henry Kissinger (Burton Hersh).

cars that were larger and less fuel-efficient than those offered by foreign competitors, and it did not respond well to the new situation.[31]

Compared to 1973-74 and to what was coming in 1979, oil affairs did settle down in the 1975 to 1978 period, but not completely. Higher prices for gasoline had produced a greater decline in demand in 1974 than had been expected. The oil companies' solution was not to lower prices; instead, they succeeded in driving the price still higher, counting on there being limits to drivers' abilities to reduce auto usage. Gasoline production was cut back, leading to a 21.5 percent rise in prices at the pump between January and August of 1975. None of this had anything to do with OPEC prices, which were stable until the end of the year.[32] Anger in the U.S. at the oil companies was intense, and the companies almost lost a battle in the Senate in 1975 over a bill that threatened to break up the major companies into separate production, transportation, refining, and marketing units. That might have destroyed their capacity to manipulate supply and price.[33]

The widespread suspicions in the country that energy was being manipulated were given support in 1977 by an Interior Department study indicating that natural gas was being withheld from the market, something which OPEC, of course, had nothing to do with. In two separate instances, government officials who disagreed with industry claims about shortages of natural gas were relieved of their positions; one of those was director of the U.S. Geological Survey.[34] Meanwhile, President Carter, who came into office with strong connections to Rockefeller interests,* was asking for voluntary sacrifice and warning the nation of an impending scarcity of oil.[35]

In August of 1977 a group of top executives from the largest banks and corporations in the U.S. published an open letter to the American people in newspapers around the country. The full-page ad proclaimed in bold print: "Energy is not a political issue. It's an issue of survival." The letter commended Carter for his role in focusing attention on the energy problem and went on to say that everyone must be ready to sacrifice and conserve. It called for a national effort to reduce energy consumption. It then emphasized that the private sector, not government, should solve these problems. The chairmen of 31 banks and corporations signed this letter.[36] Among them were the leaders of banks in the Rockefeller-Morgan orbit, including David Rockefeller. Also included were chiefs of numerous corporations with connections to Rockefeller-Morgan interests,** including Exxon, the top U.S. oil company.

---

* All presidents in the second half of this century have appointed to high positions people who have past associations with Wall Street and have been members of organizations such as the Council on Foreign Relations. This was true of Kennedy. Carter was, however, a politician who only became a national figure after his association with the Rockefeller-led Trilateral Commission, at a time when he held no elected office. Carter, in spite of populist rhetoric, reacted to the actions of oil companies and banks in a way that was little different from President Ford's, whose response to the problems created in the 1973-1974 period was to admonish people to consume less (Domhoff, 1983, pp. 136-43; Shoup, 1980).

** The banks were Chase Manhattan, Citibank, and Morgan Guaranty. Among the corporations with

It is not often that corporations ask their customers to consume less of the product they sell. This only makes economic sense in a market where profit margins can be protected through influence on supply or direct control over prices. In the case of energy, such influence or control is present, and, in any event, consumers can only cut back so far on energy consumption before they freeze to death or fail to get to work. This ad, then, is best understood as political propaganda aimed at justifying energy scarcity and high prices and as a warning against government intervention. It also could be read as a forecast on energy consumption, one that would prove to be strikingly accurate. In the 1950 to 1960 period, energy consumption per person in the U.S. rose by 10 percent, with most of the increase occurring in the first half of the decade. Between 1960 and 1973 it increased by 44 percent. From the first energy crisis, 1973, through 1990, energy consumption declined by 7 percent.[37] The authors of that 1977 missive to the public have to be credited with great analytical powers, prophetic capabilities, or inside knowledge.

Contrary to the implications of that letter, the situation one year later was again too much oil, not too little. Increased oil flowing from new fields in Alaska, Mexico, and the North Sea, combined with a global economic slowdown, again made glut rather than scarcity the problem for the oil companies.[38] Once again a crisis would be useful to sustain or justify high prices and to buttress claims of shortage. This time the crisis was provided by the overthrow of the Shah of Iran, whom Allen Dulles's CIA and the oil companies had helped to regain power in the early 1950s.[39]

According to Sherrill,[40] the Shah was out of favor with the oil companies by the late 1970s, having proved himself to be entirely too independent.* His overthrow in 1979 was probably not mourned within the international oil companies, and it did present the opportunity for new claims of shortage and for new price increases. An alleged shortfall in world supplies, attributed to a cutback in Iranian production under the new government, was cited by President Carter and his Energy Secretary as evidence of a global energy crisis. Evidence that the Iranian cutback was small and had been more than offset by increases elsewhere came from numerous sources, but was ignored. There was also evidence showing that about two-thirds of the large price increase in gasoline (33¢ a gallon) that occurred in the first half of 1979 was attributable to the oil companies. Evidence also accumulated showing that the serious shortages that

---

connections to Rockefeller-Morgan interests were Chevron, Corning Glass, General Electric, IBM, National Steel, Prudential, and U.S. Steel (Blair, 1972, p. 262; Kotz, pp. 85, 196-98).
* The British and U.S. oil companies and their supporters within the respective intelligence agencies had a stormy relationship both with this Shah and with his father before him. Both Iranian leaders challenged the British-U.S. oil interests at times but also sought to accommodate them (Yergin, pp. 270-71, 449-56). One of the U.S. intelligence operatives involved in Iran in the 1940s and 1950s was Colonel H. Norman Schwarzkopf; among other things, he helped organize the SAVAK, Iran's secret police (Burton Hersh, pp. 330, 333). The colonel's son, General H. Norman Schwarzkopf, would lead the U.S. forces in the Persian Gulf War.

did occur in the U.S. were the result of oil company actions, not Iranian cutbacks or OPEC policy.[41]

This second energy crisis, accompanied by a rise in the prime interest rate to 18.9 percent in 1981, rocked the U.S. economy and produced, as we will see below, an economic disaster for the poorer nations in the world. The energy shock and the unheard of interest rates brought about a massive redistribution of wealth while producing the worst economic downturn since the Great Depression. Oil company revenues and profits rose by billions, and dividends paid to oil company stockholders jumped by 20 to 50 percent.[42] Between 1978 and 1981 real hourly earnings in the U.S. fell by about 8 percent and weekly earnings by 10 percent.[43] Even many of America's sizable companies did not do well. Within the top 500 companies, the 56 companies involved with oil and gas took 98 percent of the total increase in profits between 1978 and 1980, leaving 2 percent for the other 444 companies.[44]

The oil companies had often justified raising prices by pointing to the need for increased investments and exploration. However, in the 1980s they became leaders in what developed into an avalanche of corporate acquisitions and mergers. Oil companies engaged in a huge takeover of strategic raw materials, copper being one primary target.[45] They also began buying up each other, a process that peaked in 1984 when oil company mergers reached giant proportions. Chevron (SoCal or Standard Oil of California) acquired Gulf Oil for $13.3 billion, reducing the Seven Sisters to six. Texaco took over Getty Oil at a cost of $10 billion and Mobil acquired Superior Oil for $5.7 billion. Investment banks, led by Morgan Stanley and Goldman Sachs, were paid tens of millions of dollars to arrange these mergers.[46] The diversion of $29 billion from production-oriented investment into just these three mergers puts the runaway-shop phenomenon in perspective. For example, the listed value of all of the accumulated manufacturing investments by U.S. companies in Latin America amounted to just over half the value of these three mergers.[47] Capital running away to low-wage areas has had less impact on the overall U.S. economy than has capital running away from production in general.

The combined impact of rising energy prices, extraordinarily high interest rates, economic stagnation, and an outburst of corporate mergers and speculation of various kinds was to change fundamentally the nature of the U.S. economy. The rising interest rates and energy prices were related to each other not only in terms of their general timing and effects, but also because the leading institutions in the two areas were and are tightly interconnected.

In 1939, 28 years after Rockefeller's Standard Oil empire was supposedly broken up, the Securities and Exchange Commission concluded that Exxon, Mobil, SoCal, and Standard of Indiana were still under Rockefeller control.[48] The Federal Trade Commission's research in 1973 and 1974 led to a judgment that it was leading banks, such as the Rockefeller-controlled Chase Manhattan, that controlled the oil companies.[49] Many of the same oil companies involved in cooperative relationships involving pipelines and offshore leases also had ties to banks such as Chase, Chemical, Citibank, and Morgan Guaranty.[50] Investigations in the early and late 1970s showed a complex web of relationships among leading oil companies, banks, and insurance companies.[51] Finally, in 1980 a private study by Corporate Data Exchange, Inc., showed that top banks (Chase, J.P. Morgan, Citicorp) were among the leading stockholders in many of the oil companies (*e.g.*, Chase Manhattan and J.P. Morgan were both among the top five stockholders at Exxon and Mobil).[52] Financial interests, led by the Rockefeller-Morgan groups, and the top oil companies are, if not one entity, something close to one entity.

When the price of energy and the price of money went up dramatically in the early 1970s and again in the 1979 to 1981 period, the oil-banking network delivered a severe blow to the U.S. and world economies. The effects of this were most severe on underdeveloped nations. The economic damage done to poorer nations by rising energy prices, high interest rates, and a stagnating global economy was compounded by painful policies imposed by the banks and the International Monetary Fund.

Decades of Debt and Austerity

President Kennedy declared the 1960s the decade of development. The Alliance for Progress, development aid, low-interest loans, nation-to-nation cooperation, and some measure of government planning were some of the ingredients of that policy. Within a few years of Kennedy's death most of this had been abandoned. By the early 1970s, this type of effort and the optimism associated with it had vanished altogether.

In 1963 George S. Moore, president of First National City Bank (Citibank/Citicorp), offered a different focus for the growing U.S. role in the world economy. Moore, who was second in command at City Bank to James Stillman Rockefeller, stated his general opposition to government interference in international trade and went on to say:[53]

> With the dollar the leading international currency and the United States the world's largest exporter and importer of goods, services and capital, it is only natural that U.S. banks should gird themselves to play the same relative role in international finance that the great British financial institutions played in the nineteenth century.

What role had those British banks played? Essentially it was to create a financial relationship that operated to keep underdeveloped countries in the position of being backward exporters of raw materials.[54] This was not JFK's idea of the purpose of loans, nor was it his goal to perpetuate the backwardness of Third World nations. Getting rid of this sort of policy had been a central goal in Kennedy's foreign policy. It was the reason for the new initiatives in foreign aid, loans, and trade, and Kennedy viewed the replacement of colonialist and imperialist economic policy with a development policy as a necessary step in neutralizing the appeal of communism. Kennedy's efforts had been attacked publicly in *Fortune* and the *Wall Street Journal* and declared dead by David Rockefeller in *Foreign Affairs* in 1966.

In a book published in 1966, Thomas Balogh, economic adviser to the British Cabinet, observed:[55]

> ...neo-imperialism does not depend on open political domination. The economic relations of the U.S. to South America are not essentially different from those of Britain to her African colonies. The International Monetary Fund fulfills the role of the colonial administration of enforcing the rules of the game.

That the IMF was coming to play this role, as in the aftermath of the 1964 Brazilian coup, is apparent. What the oil and interest rate shocks and the global slowdown did was to expand that role vastly, a development that occurred with the support and participation of the major international banks.

The 1973-74 rise in oil prices and a stagnating global economy meant that for most of the underdeveloped nations the cost of imports, including oil, rose faster than did their export earnings. The cost of the money they were borrowing had also risen. In 1973 the cost of imports for developing countries was $11 billion more than their export earnings; by 1978 the difference was $31 billion, and it rose to $40 billion in 1979.[56] In Latin America, where U.S. banks have been the primary private lenders, the accumulated international debt guaranteed by Latin governments rose from $29 billion in 1972 to $110 billion in 1978.[57] Even before the next round of interest rate and energy price hikes began in 1979, many underdeveloped countries were in serious trouble.

By 1977 underdeveloped countries were using 20 percent of their export earnings just to pay the interest on debt. Two-thirds of the $75 billion owed to private banks was owed to U.S. banks, most of it to the top banks. Much of the money being borrowed was OPEC oil money recycled through banks operating in what had become known as the Eurodollar market. The private banks, backed up by the IMF and the Carter administration, were demanding austerity as the solution to debt problems. That is, the banks demanded that the indebted nations reduce the gap between their exports and imports by reducing consumption.[58]

When nations get into trade and debt difficulties, they are referred to the IMF, which dictates the conditions, called IMF conditionalities, under which the debtors can continue to borrow. These arrangements were mentioned in Chapter Three; they were the kinds of policies that Kennedy tried to circumvent with foreign aid and long-term, low-interest government loans. The IMF conditionalities are aimed at achieving three basic goals: reduce government influence in a way that makes it easier for foreign interests to operate; reduce domestic consumption to free up resources for export in order to earn the money to service or pay debt; offset inflationary pressures (caused in part in the 1970s and 1980s by high energy prices and interest rates and by IMF demands themselves) by implementing a policy of tight money, high interest rates, and cuts in government spending.[59]

For Third World governments, whatever their goals or politics, the adoption of such a program typically generates political problems. The problems range from street demonstrations to strikes to complete breakdowns in legitimacy. For those leaders who reject IMF demands, the problems can be worse. For example, in 1978 Prime Minister Michael Manley of Jamaica lost much of his popular support after accepting IMF policies that led to a 35 percent decline in real wages in one year. When he refused two years later to impose additional austerity measures, all loans from the IMF and private banks stopped.[60] Also in 1978, the Peruvian government of General Francisco Morales Bermúdez followed up one IMF austerity program that had already cost workers one-fourth of their purchasing power with a second IMF program that doubled the price of fuel, basic foods, and public transportation. This led to strikes and political unrest, to which the government responded by canceling elections and imposing martial law.[61]

By the beginning of 1979 the development efforts of dozens of nations had been seriously undermined.* Even with non-Third World nations such as Poland and Turkey,** the banks and the IMF were demanding that standards of living be lowered. The world, particularly the poorer nations, was about to be hit again with the combination of rising oil prices, rising interest rates (the U.S. prime rate going from 6.8 percent in 1977 to 18.9 percent in 1981), and falling economic demand. Soon after the new crisis erupted, the banks decided to reduce their lending to Third World nations.

With the prices of most export commodities declining in the world market, with rising interest rates adding $30 billion to Third World interest payments, and with oil prices skyrocketing, the underdeveloped nations' ability to pay for imports declined in two years, 1981-1982, by about $100 billion.[62] In some underdeveloped countries, years of progress in reducing poverty were reversed (as also happened in the U.S.), and starvation and child mortality rates began rising.

The debt crisis also directly affected the U.S. The IMF's policies led to a reduction in Latin America's imports from the U.S., resulting in a loss of 400,000 U.S. jobs in 1982 and 1983. Also, in 1982 a shortfall in payments from Latin America to U.S. banks was covered when the U.S. government gave billions of

---

* Also during the 1970s, the World Bank, under the direction of former Secretary of Defense Robert McNamara, adopted a policy of linking the adoption of population control measures to eligibility for World Bank loans. The Bank also began to shift its loans away from development projects such as dams and industry to what was called basic needs, *i.e.*, projects to partially alleviate the worst poverty. In 1977 Mexico turned down a World Bank loan rather than adopt the bank's population policy (Farnsworth, 1980). These policies were a thorough rejection of JFK's views that population policies should be left to independent nations and that rapid economic development should be a primary goal.

** By the end of 1979, Turkey's Prime Minister Bulent Ecevit was forced out of office following a crushing defeat in the October congressional elections. In a long speech Ecevit noted that the economy was already in a state of collapse when he took power in 1978 and that his government could not find a way to deal with the oil price increase of 1979, which led to oil imports using up all of Turkey's export earnings. Turkey's long-term growth had been reduced to zero, and inflation was heading toward 100 percent at the end of 1979 (*New York Times*, 1979).

dollars to Brazil and Argentina, so that they could pass it on to the banks in interest payments. This bailout of the banks was accompanied by demands that the Latin nations undergo additional belt-tightening.[63]

In June of 1979 David Rockefeller noted in a neutral, if not indifferent, manner that rapidly rising energy prices would severely limit economic growth in the Third World. In 1980, Rockefeller addressed 200 top bankers and government officials at a meeting of the International Monetary Conference in New Orleans, where he warned debt-ridden nations that the major banks would not be able to extend new loans to help borrowers cope with the recent 150 percent increase in oil prices. A couple of years later the hard line was elaborated in a report of President Reagan's commission on Central America, a group headed up by a longtime Rockefeller associate, Henry Kissinger. Although the commission acknowledged that energy prices, high interest rates, and recession in the advanced countries had caused much of the region's economic problems, it did not attack these problems. Instead, the commission recommended reductions in population growth, labor-intensive infrastructure and housing projects, and the development of new export industries.[64]

As the 1980s unfolded, the IMF continued to impose its austerity measures on countries already damaged by high interest rates, surging energy costs, and declining export prices. Between 1978 and 1982, $126 billion of the $140 billion lent to underdeveloped countries was used for interest payments. By 1983, 46 countries were operating under IMF austerity programs. Some Third World nations were experiencing depressions in 1983 as bad as the worst periods of the 1930s.[65] The 1980s had begun with Poland implementing its first meat rationing program since World War II, an action required in 1980 because Poland needed to export more of its meat to earn Western currencies to meet its debt obligations. The decade ended with George Bush's Treasury Secretary, Nicholas F. Brady, refusing to qualify Brazil for limited debt relief because it had not adhered to the latest austerity program demanded by the IMF.[66]

The Alliance for Progress and the decade of development were long gone, neither surviving much beyond President Kennedy's death. James Brooke commented in the *New York Times*[67] that for Brazil and much of Latin America, the 1980s was a "lost decade." Brazil's growth rate fell to 1 percent per year, two-thirds of its families were below the official poverty level, and between 1980 and 1987 Brazil paid out $50.6 billion more in debt payment than it received in new loans. In Brazil's 1984 presidential race, the IMF and its policies were major issues.[68] Throughout the underdeveloped nations, charges were made against the IMF and, implicitly, the same people and institutions with which Kennedy had been at odds.

Around the time that the IMF was coercing Morocco and Sudan to increase food prices drastically, President Julius Nyerere of Tanzania charged that the IMF was a "device by which powerful forces in some rich countries increase their power over poor nations."[69] The view that IMF policies represented a brand of imperialism was validated by the observations of Thomas Balogh, adviser to the British government, referred to earlier. This view was reportedly common throughout Africa, and it was voiced elsewhere.

In 1984, when new IMF demands were being made on Peru, a former labor minister said that the "IMF is the ruler of the developing world."[70] Also in 1984, the *New York Times* observed that in Argentina the IMF was widely viewed, even among businessmen, as an arm of U.S. and bank imperialism.[71] Shortly thereafter, Peru's new president, Alan García, accused the banks of usury and, along with President José Sarney of Brazil, charged that indebted nations were being forced to choose between submitting to the banks' demands and preserving democracy.[72] In the following year, 1986, the Peruvian government accused the IMF of being an instrument of economic colonialism.[73] Brazil attempted in 1987 to get the Reagan administration to engage in government-to-government talks about changing the international monetary system and was told to go see the bankers.[74]

The 1980s ended with a spokesman for the United States Catholic Conference testifying before Congress that in the 1980s the average standard of living had fallen by over 25 percent in sub-Saharan Africa and by 15 percent in Latin America.[75] What had been desperately needed, of course, was the opposite. In the United States as well, most people were also less well off.

The Post-Industrial, Deindustrialized, Service Economy

Even before the 1979 oil crisis and the next surge upward in interest rates had hit the U.S. economy, there were serious concerns being raised about the future of the American standard of living. In its 1979 Midyear Review of the Economy, the Joint Economic Committee of the Congress observed:[76]

> The average American is likely to see his standard of living decline in the 1980s unless we accelerate the rate of growth of our nation's productivity. If no new steps are taken to address the problems of structural unemployment, lagging capital formation, and a slowdown in productivity, then the American economy faces a bleak future. It is clear from analysis that productivity is the linchpin of economic progress in the 1980s. A stagnating economy will mean fewer Americans will be able to afford the necessities of life, such as a decent home.

The rising energy prices and interest rates during the next several years hardly created the conditions for a reversal of this stagnation. In fact, of course, surging energy prices and a prime rate hitting 18.9 percent for 1981 drove both overall economic activity and income downward. Real hourly earnings fell by 8 percent between 1978 and 1981.[77]

In 1981, John Wright, head of his own investment advisory firm, offered a concise critique of the tight-money and high-interest-rate policy of the Federal Reserve, then headed by Paul Volcker, a longtime Rockefeller associate. Noting that interest rates had averaged 10 percent for the preceding eight years, Wright[78] went on to say that

These rates, if continued, will destroy the American economic system because of the following effects:
- They take from the poor and add to the rich.
- They diminish the producers and expand the lenders.
- They inhibit and diminish long-term capital investment, productivity, research and development, production and development of new sources and efficient applications of energy....
- They bankrupt small businesses, increasing the concentration of economic productive power, drastically reducing effective, competitive price cutting.

Commenting on the Fed's claim that its policies were necessary to bring inflation under control, Wright went on to say that:

In my opinion, the rise in the price of energy alone more than accounts for all of the United States inflation. The inflationary result of rising energy costs cannot be measured only in terms of its magnitude as a raw material component of GNP. Energy is also part of the cost of every other component and the cost of producing every component rises with the cost of energy.
High interest rates, instead of curing inflation, have stimulated it. They add to the costs of every business, to all forms of product distribution and to all types of consumer purchases. They are themselves a significant secondary cause of inflation.

The two rounds of sharp hikes in interest rates and energy prices, the persistently high interest rates, tight money policies, and stagnating or falling income drastically changed the U.S. economy. The productive investment the congressional committee emphasized as necessary to prevent a declining standard of living was insufficient. The 1980s did become the decade of the casino economy, the hollow corporation, and deindustrialization. The terms "post-industrialism"* and "service economy" became common in academic circles. In the early 1980s, books appeared speaking of an "age of decline" and of the "deindustrialization of America."[79]

In 1979, around the time that the congressional committee issued its warning, *Business Week* observed that the country was confronting its "Last Chance for Investment Vs. Speculation." The article completely avoided criticism of the banking-oil complex, but did assert that increasing speculation had already diverted too much money away from productive investment. Six years later, *Business Week*[80] indicated that speculation had won. Describing the U.S. as a "casino society," the magazine once again noted that "financial gamesmanship"

---

* The term "post-industrialism" appeared at the beginning of the 1960s in writing circulated privately by Daniel Bell. It led to the publication by Bell in 1973 of *The Coming of Post-Industrial Society*. As used by Bell, the term did not mean a basic deterioration in economic conditions. However, it was later adopted by others who were both predicting and recommending a shift away from manufacturing. The proposed changes were justified on the basis of arguments concerning resources, population, and pollution (Bell; Dickson; Heilbroner; SRI International).

was diverting resources away from production. Pointing to huge increases in a variety of speculative activities and in debt-financed corporate mergers, the article warned that the country was "Playing With Fire." The following year, *Business Week*[81] referred to the deindustrialization of the U.S. and criticized those who accepted or promoted this trend, saying that "the idea that a post-industrial America can become increasingly prosperous as a service-based economy appears to be a dangerous myth."

Corporate mergers, although not necessarily involving more money than other speculative activity, became in the 1980s not only a major drain of capital away from investment, but also a vehicle for reorganizing the top levels of the U.S. economy. Such activity had been, on a smaller scale, a relatively constant part of business activity for a long time. Mergers had contributed to an increase in the share of the economy owned by the top 200 companies from 45 percent in 1945 to 60 percent in 1978. In the immediate aftermath of the 1973-1974 energy-interest rate crisis, merger activity began to accelerate* and was by the late 1970s a cause of concern in some parts of the U.S. government.[82] By 1981 the "flood" of merger activity was suspected of using up capital that might have been available to small business.[83] If the 1974 to 1981 merger binge was a "flood," it is hard to come up with a term that adequately describes the 1980s. Led by such gargantuan takeovers as the aforementioned oil company mergers and U.S. Steel's $6 billion buyout of Marathon Oil Company,** the 1980s featured over $1 trillion in asset shuffling.[84]

President Kennedy's goal was to use government power to steer the economy and the country in certain directions. Improvements in technology, scientific advances, productive investment, educational opportunity and achievement (particularly in areas related to science and technology), a rising standard of living, challenges to people to make the country and world both more prosperous and more just, and the excitement of space exploration were all aspects of the kind of country he thought we should have. He attempted, in the Hamiltonian tradition, to structure laws and government policy in a way that channeled the profit motive in directions that benefited the national economy and poorer nations of the world. He actively sought to inhibit economic decisions which would undermine the country's productive powers. He opposed non-productive activity, and he viewed the tendencies of large financial institutions and monopolistically organized industries as dangerous to the general welfare.

---

* Since rising interest rates and high energy prices would logically have the effect of making new investment both more costly and less likely, it makes sense that buying up existing facilities would become an attractive activity.

** U.S. Steel, which had shown little appreciation of Kennedy's efforts to both help and encourage corporations to make production-oriented investments, became a conglomerate during the 1980s. Whereas in 1978 74 percent of its profits came from steel, the figure was 33 percent in 1983. Meanwhile, the Japanese steelworker had improved his output from 75 percent of his U.S. counterpart in 1968 to 150 percent in 1982 (*The Economist*, 1987; Wayne; Williams).

With some minor exceptions,* the government of the United States and the nation's presidents, from Johnson to Clinton, have been unable or unwilling to mount any sustained effort to stop the deterioration of the economy. President Kennedy had offered his activist program at a time when the U.S. was still the world's leading economy and was, in spite of the somewhat stagnant 1950s, still in pretty good shape. No president since has come close to Kennedy in terms of proposing a coherent program or a willingness to take on powerful private interests. Whether the issue has been destructive financial policy, monopolistic practices, mergers, or speculation in real estate and futures, the policies of presidents since Kennedy have been essentially passive. This represents what is often really meant by phrases such as "free enterprise," "free market," and "laissez faire." That is, when these phrases are used as they were in *Fortune*'s and the *Wall Street Journal*'s assault on Kennedy, they are not really in defense of a decentralized, competitive economy which supposedly works through competition to produce the best products at the lowest price. Instead, those phrases were thrown at Kennedy because he was using the powers of government against an organized and powerful set of banking and corporate interests. The issue for those in the Morgan-Rockefeller network was not competition, but who was going to shape economic events, they or Kennedy. They won.

Another critical struggle during the 1970s and 1980s involved the environmental movement.

Elite Environmentalism

At the upper echelons of the environmental movement there has been a record of opposing growth in population, industrial production, and consumption. From that standpoint, the stagnation or decline of the economies of the underdeveloped nations and of the United States and some other nations can only be viewed as some sort of triumph. Some leaders within the movement have criticized growth and development in the most extreme fashion. This sort of criticism is so pervasive that we can only touch on it here; we will review some of the anti-progress rhetoric that has come from sources close to the Rockefeller-Morgan network.

In 1977 a report sponsored by the Rockefeller Brothers Fund was published in book form under the title *The Unfinished Agenda*. The report was edited and partially written by Gerald Barney, a member of the Brothers Fund staff. The Fund's board of trustees included at least six members of the Rockefeller family.[85] The board's chairman was Laurance Rockefeller, who involved himself directly in the production of this report, even contributing to the writing of one of the chapters. The task force itself included Barney and representatives of a dozen environmental and population control organizations. Still other such

---

* The effort by some in Congress to reorganize the energy industry is one example. President Nixon's half-hearted efforts to deal with economic problems in the early 1970s is another (Evans and Novak, pp. 368-70, 401, 420).

groups were represented in the writing of the report.* The presence of so many contributors did lead to some ambiguities in the report, but the overall thrust was still clear: the U.S. and the world should move in the direction of ending population growth, and protection of the environment should be given an importance equal to or greater than that of improving the standard of living. This represents a general continuation of the policies promoted by Laurance Rockefeller's ORRRC and other groups at the time Kennedy was president and is at odds with Kennedy's policies.

On population the Rockefeller report[86] proposed that the U.S. adopt a policy of either freezing population growth or reducing it, and suggested that the public be "educated" to accept this goal. It recommended that more resources be committed to the promotion of population control through contraception, abortion, and sterilization. Like Malthus a century and a half earlier, the report had some specific ideas about achieving these goals. For example, it recommended the elimination of tax benefits to families for children after the first two. It suggested that female employment be promoted in order to discourage reproduction. Sex education should be used with pre-teens and teenagers in a way that promotes population control. It also suggested that decisions not to marry or not to have children be given positive publicity. Finally, the report argued that immigration should be reduced and that the United States should link all foreign assistance to efforts by recipient nations to achieve zero population growth.

Whereas, 15 years earlier, President Kennedy had been emphatic about the need for an expanding supply of cheap energy and had recommended publicly supported investigation of various nuclear possibilities, the Rockefeller group recommended the elimination of nuclear energy. They proposed that the U.S. be transformed into a "Conserver Society" in an attempt to use fewer resources, including energy. Diametrically opposed to Kennedy's optimism about resources in general, the report predicted that the future would be plagued by resource scarcity.[87]

Economic growth and technology were portrayed as problems. The report recommended increasing controls over the introduction of new technologies and suggested national planning to protect the environment (not to promote economic progress). It proposed that the environment be made a top national priority,[88] and suggested a variety of other actions to protect "little spaceship earth," including the substitution of human labor for machines in agriculture.[89]

One of the contributors to the Rockefeller report was Amory Lovins from Friends of the Earth. The same year that the Rockefeller report was published, 1977, a book by Lovins, *Soft Energy Paths*, also came out. Material in this book

---

* The Rockefeller Brothers Fund task force was made up of representatives from the following organizations: Natural Resources Defense Council, Friends of the Earth, The Wilderness Society, Zero Population Growth, National Wildlife Federation, Massachusetts Audubon Society, The Nature Conservancy, Environmental Defense Fund, Izaak Walton League of America, National Parks and Conservation Association, National Audubon Society, and Sierra Club. Among the contributors to the book were representatives of Worldwatch Institute, Friends of the Earth, and the Club of Rome (Barney).

was discussed at the Aspen Institute earlier that year, and part of the book had appeared in *Foreign Affairs*. According to Lovins, Gerald Barney of the Rockefeller Brothers Fund suggested the basic ideas for the book and William Bundy* of the CFR played an important role in developing the part of the book that appeared in *Foreign Affairs*.[90] Lovins's Friends of the Earth was created in 1969 with financial support from the Ford Foundation affiliate, Resources for the Future, and from Robert O. Anderson, chairman of Atlantic Richfield and of the Aspen Institute.[91]

In his book, Lovins[92] declares himself to be a Jeffersonian rather than a Hamiltonian (repeating some standard distortions of Hamilton's policies). The decentralist ideas of Jefferson, aimed in Jefferson's time at protecting plantation interests and "states' rights," are given new life as a means to attack large-scale industrial production and government technocrats. In Lovins's view, it is large-scale production, bureaucrats, and experts who threaten democracy, not organized upper-class interests in finance, oil, and global corporations. The second group is never even alluded to, which, given Lovins's connections to them, is not surprising.

Lovins claimed that resources are "inherently limited," and suggested that the goal be energy shortage rather than abundance because "we understand too little the wise use of power." He said that we should reject "high energy society" in favor of "frugality." He also asserted that poor nations should not develop along industrial lines, and he said that material growth in the U.S. should be reduced.[93] Lovins[94] specifically recommended that existing nuclear energy technology be eliminated, arguing that the U.S. should abandon this technology even if it were perfectly safe and economic because it gives those connected to technology too much influence with government. Again, Lovins chose not to mention undue influence on government by bankers, oilmen, big business, or upper-class organizations.

Lovins[95] suggested that "people are more important than goods." Such platitudes, reminiscent of the Aspen Institute views discussed earlier, pervade environmental literature. Anyone expecting a careful distinction between the desire for mansions, yachts, limousines, private planes, etc., and the desire for decent housing, food, clothes, health care, and education would be disappointed. No such distinctions are made. What Lovins was in fact attacking is what most people in Europe and North American would think of as a reasonable standard of living. This attack was coming from either the super-rich or a fairly small stratum of upper-middle-class opponents of industrial production and middle-class consumption.[96]

Among those referred to as authorities in both the Rockefeller report and the Lovins book are the authors of the studies of global resources and population

* William Bundy was the editor of *Foreign Affairs* and had also served as a director of the CFR. His brother, McGeorge, had been National Security Adviser to JFK and LBJ. During the 1970s, McGeorge Bundy was president of the Ford Foundation, probably the single largest private source of funding for both population control and environmentalism (Dye; Marquis *Who's Who*, 1978-79; Simon).

growth sponsored by the Club of Rome, the originator of the "Small Is Beautiful" school E.F. Schumacher, and Willis Harman of the Stanford Research Institute. The Rockefeller report also draws on the work of Paul Ehrlich and Lynn White, Jr. All of these people have expressed a general disdain for modern industry and economic growth, and have used rhetoric that devalues human life.

Paul Ehrlich is best known for his 1968 book, *The Population Bomb* (or for his appearances on the Johnny Carson show). The book was co-published by the Sierra Club and included a foreword by David Brower, Lovins's superior at Friends of the Earth and a member of the task force producing the 1977 Rockefeller report. In a 1970 interview, Ehrlich agreed with unidentified "scientists" who said that the U.S. population should be reduced to 50 million (from just over 200 million) and the world population to half a billion. Ehrlich did not specify how he thought that 150 million Americans and several billion other people could be eliminated; he merely agreed with the desirability of such an outcome. Affirming that Malthus was "fundamentally right," Ehrlich cited the threat posed by overpopulation and limited resources and indicated that one of the few ways out of this dilemma was a "massive increase in the death rate." These are themes and views which were also part of his best-selling book, *The Population Bomb*.[97]

The title of Ehrlich's book suggests that people be thought of as a destructive force, a bomb. Two other authorities referenced by the Rockefeller report began their 1974 book, a successor to *Limits to Growth*, by saying "The World Has Cancer and the Cancer is Man."[98] While they probably excluded themselves from this diagnosis, the authors of this Club of Rome study were indicating their view of much of the world's people—they are a malignant disease to be arrested or eliminated.

Willis Harman and a Stanford Research Institute (SRI) group are referred to as sources and authorities in both the Rockefeller report and Lovins's book.[99] Willis Harman headed up an SRI group which was involved in the second half of the 1960s in generating criticisms of industrial technology, economic growth, and population growth, and was providing advice along these lines to congressmen by 1969. Harman's group called for a shift in education that would devalue population growth, independent nations, technological development, economic growth and consumption, and the belief that man is separate from nature and meant to dominate it.[100]

In 1974, SRI produced a policy study offering comprehensive recommendations on ways to transform the United States. In this study much of what had been widely thought of as the achievements of the modern world were redefined as failures. Reduced mortality was viewed as a cause of overpopulation, not an achievement in preserving life. Technology and science were associated with war and the invasion of privacy, not in a positive way with a rising standard of living. Advances in production were related to pollution, dehumanized work, resource depletion, etc. Modern industrial society was in the study's view not only untenable, but undesirable. The study looked to various counterculture and subculture groups for signs that people were moving to reject the values and worldview of scientific-industrial culture. It found hope in the anti-technology bias of the young, environmentalism, "fundamentalist" Christianity, and the growing interest in Eastern religion and spiritualism.[101]

Two years after SRI published its study, Harman[102] published his own version of that work in *An Incomplete Guide to the Future*. In the preface to this book, Harman said that he was greatly influenced by Alfred M. Hubbard, Humphry Osmond, Aldous Huxley, and Gerald Heard, all of whom were using and studying psychedelic drugs and had at least peripheral connections to the CIA's notorious drug experiments.[103] The SRI International study[104] treated the use of hallucinogens and other drugs, beyond medical uses, in a positive way. Harman's book is largely an argument against rising levels of industrial production, and it explicitly rejects improvements in material standards of living. Harman[105] specifically predicted, and supported, economic decline, and warned that unless people were convinced such decline was necessary, there would be a need for increasing authoritarianism. Much of Harman's outlook was justified by him on the basis of alleged resource scarcity, overpopulation, and environmental degradation.

Harman's warning that authoritarianism might be needed converges with the views of Lynn White, Jr., also cited as an authority in the Rockefeller report. In a 1967 essay that is widely viewed among leading environmentalists as a major work, White began by recounting a conversation with Aldous Huxley and went on to portray Judeo-Christian values and democracy itself as sources of scientific-industrial society and, therefore, as impediments to the environmental movement. White attacked the Judeo-Christian worldview, democratic values, and technology as forces which have disrupted the human connection to nature. In this essay White transformed historical changes which have been virtual definitions of progress—material advances and the rise of democratic values, and human-centered, monotheistic religion—into transgressions against nature.[106] White argued that since the source of the problem was rooted in religion, the solution must be also. White praised Zen Buddhism but figured that its Asian identity would make it difficult for Westerners to accept. He opted for St. Francis of Assisi as a nominally Christian figure whose views, like Zen, can be used to counter traditional Christianity's support for science and technology.*

---

* White (p. 29) referenced Sir Steven Runciman as an expert on the Franciscan doctrine. Runciman was cited as an apparently friendly expert on the history of anti-democratic, anti-modern, elitist movements in Europe by the authors of a best-selling occult work entitled *Holy Blood, Holy Grail*. This book and its sequel, *The Messianic Legacy* (Baigent, Leigh, and Lincoln, 1982; 1986), promote and predict the restoration to power of various aristocratic or noble families in Europe and on a global scale. The movement to restore the old order is justified to some extent by referring to the environmental crisis. The movement allegedly has a U.S. contingent which is connected by the authors to the CIA, Aspen Institute, the CFR, and certain banks and corporations (*e.g.*, Atlantic Richfield, First National Bank of Chicago). It may or may not be of significance, but the name Sir Steven Runciman was among a list of European aristocrats in the address book of Clay Shaw, the CIA-related figure indicted by District

Another "authority" referenced by the Rockefeller task force was E. F. Schumacher, known as the author of *Small Is Beautiful*[107] and the founder of the globally oriented Intermediate Technology Development Group, created in 1965. Schumacher stated many views that are fairly common in environmental literature. Nature is good, self-balancing; man, because of greed, has subjected himself to the virtually independent force of the machine and technology (technology as "Frankenstein").[108] He attempted to portray large-scale technology as something that eliminates interesting work and is at odds with the true state of humans, which is that they are small.[109] He recommended small-scale technology and production where men can be more easily supervised and controlled.[110] He blamed science and technology for its role in promoting energy use, recommending instead low-energy production, and he blamed only OPEC for monopolizing the control of energy.[111] In a rather stunning statement of what his views actually mean, Schumacher[112] explicitly and with great care recommended that the labor being performed by average people be increased "sixfold"! He specifically suggested this as a way to bring children and "even old people" back into the labor process. This would allow us to turn away from large-scale technology. Would people object to this "enormous extension of working hours"? According to Schumacher, people who "work in this way [*i.e.*, in the new small scale work place] do not know the difference between work and leisure."*

Some idea of what Schumacher's ideas mean when implemented is provided in the 1981 book, *Small Is Possible*.[113] What this program promoted was a hodgepodge of primitive technologies including rickshaws, pedal-driven machines, windmills, and woodstoves. What it added up to was backward, labor-intensive forms of production. Among those promoting this have been Friends of the Earth, Worldwatch Institute, and the British government.** Ehrlich, Harman, Schumacher, and the authors of the Rockefeller report are certainly not the only ones to make extreme arguments about population and the environment. Stewart Udall, who as Secretary of the Interior complained about Kennedy's lack of interest in conservationism, suggested in 1970 that a reduction of the U.S. population by 50 percent would be desirable to avoid destroying the environment.[114] Garrett Hardin, [115] cited in the Rockefeller report, recommended mandatory sterilization on behalf of population control. Richard Falk[116] sug-

Attorney Jim Garrison in his investigation of the assassination of President Kennedy (Garrison, p. 146). (Runciman's first name is given two different spellings in Shaw's address book.) These circumstantial relationships indicate nothing about the actions or involvements of the people referred to. They are, however, interesting coincidences that warrant additional research.

* In a remark that is almost beyond belief, Schumacher (p. 60) observed that, "Much of the economic decay of Southeast Asia...is undoubtedly due to a heedless and shameful neglect of trees." He didn't seem to think that a decade of war, carpet-bombing, napalm, etc., was any problem; they aren't mentioned.

** Yergin (p. 615) notes that the oil crisis of 1973-74 helped to make Schumacher's views influential. His politics attracted the attention of one of the world's wealthiest families, as Schumacher was given an award by the Queen of England and invited to dine, on separate occasions, with the Queen and with Prince Philip.

gested that compulsory abortion and forced sterilization might be necessary to defend the environment.* While noting a decline in the global population growth rate, Heilbroner[117] warned that the increase in the number of people is a "cancer" that will "continue to spread."

These extreme statements devaluing human life are matched by extreme criticisms of modern, industrial society. Heilbroner[118] argued that behind the problems of overpopulation and environmental deterioration are the root causes —science, technology, and industrial growth. He went on to say[119] that it was industrialism, whether in a capitalist or a socialist form, that was the problem. Heilbroner also said [120]that the abandonment of industrial society may require the abandonment of democracy, something he accepted. William Ophuls[121] has recommended the abandonment of industrialism and its high levels of consumption. In his ecologically sound future, lower levels of consumption and more work may require a "macroauthority" to regulate things. Andrew Dobson[122] argues that resource limits, overpopulation, and pollution require a new goal of minimizing production and consumption. Achieving this goal necessitates the humbling of human beings so that they know their place.

The preceding review demonstrates the deep conflict between the goals of someone like Kennedy and the direction in which the "new conservation" was about to go in the 1960s. The divergence in outlook between Kennedy and the groups involved in creating the new movement could not have been apparent to many people in the early 1960s.** By the time the Rockefeller task force report was published in 1977, such differences would be obvious to anyone familiar with the two sides. By the 1980s, environmentalism became entrenched in the educational system, and few politicians could be heard criticizing it, even if in office they did not always satisfy environmentalists. It seems safe to say that most Americans are unaware of the movement's origins and the extensive support given the movement by ruling-class institutions.*** Although the specifics have changed over the last 30 years, the general argument has remained

---

* John Fischer, the editor of *Harper's* whose interview with Kennedy was quoted at the end of Chapter Five, wrote an essay in 1969 which generally embraced the views of Falk and called for the creation of an environmentally oriented university to be called "Survival U." The essay first appeared in *Harper's* and was then reprinted in *The Environmental Handbook* (DeBell, 1970) along with the views of Lynn White, Garrett Hardin, Paul Ehrlich, and other spokespersons for the emerging environmental movement.

** The president's brother, Robert Kennedy, gave speeches in the mid-1960s that indicated some sympathy with the environmental movement, but he also showed an enthusiasm for science and technology as a means by which to improve the material conditions of life (*e.g.*, Ross, pp. 274-86, 355, 543-49). According to Douglas Ross (p. 286), Robert Kennedy said "almost nothing about conservation" during the last 18 months of his life, which included his campaign for the presidential nomination. Ross added that he could not explain the "sudden loss of interest" in conservationism.

*** For example, the Foundation Center's Grants Index indicates that in 1984 about $142 million was given by private foundations to support environmentalist activities. Even if the information is complete, and it may not be, this represents a major effort to influence public opinion, education, government policy, and national direction (Foundation Center, 1985).

quite consistent. That is, there are too many people, industrial production and mass consumption are depleting the world's resources, and technology is destroying the environment. Environmentalists might distance themselves for various reasons from oil companies and banks. They also may say that the deterioration that has occurred in so much of the world over the last 20 years was not what they had in mind. It remains, however, that the implied or stated goals of the Establishment element within the environmental movement include less consumption, less industrial production, and fewer people. Orchestrated energy crises, high interest rates, credit crunches, IMF austerity programs, mergers, and speculation have all played a role in making a part of these goals a reality. All of this has happened with little sustained opposition from either presidents or Congress. The federal government has actually elevated its own failures to protect the public from organized private power to a position of principle by embracing in many areas a laissez-faire doctrine of deregulation, with largely negative results.[123]

Early in the country's history, Alexander Hamilton worried about the destructive influence of hereditary wealth, privilege, and power. In his time he pointed to the dangers to the nation produced by financial and market manipulation. He attempted to contain those dangers with the policies he provided for President Washington. President Kennedy's efforts to combat a modern version of the same dangers were ended prematurely. At the center of his program was the attempt to make the investment process work on behalf of the general welfare. In the 1970s the investment process broke down. The oil-banking network treated the U.S. with little more regard than it showed for Third World nations. The interest rate and energy price shocks delivered to the U.S. economy between the late 1960s and early 1980s disrupted the investment process and brought economic progress in the U.S. and in the Third World to a halt. The speculation and mergers of the 1980s became the chief economic symptoms of and important contributors to U.S. economic decay, such activity both reflecting and causing a declining rate of investment in productive activity.

Carroll Quigley,[124] one of President Clinton's professors at Georgetown University, wrote in 1961 that Western civilization and the United States were at an important juncture. The coming period would involve a choice between a renewed commitment to creating and investing in new technologies or a future of stagnation and decline. As Quigley pointed out, the outcome would be substantially decided in contests for influence or control over policies. President Kennedy's death had ended one such contest, a contest between a president committed to using government powers to promote economic progress and organized private interests protecting both their private power and their ability to influence governmental policy. The virtually uncontested exercise of power by the banking-oil network from the late 1960s onward has left the United States, and much of the world, with a somewhat different choice in the 1990s—whether or not to allow an already established pattern of decline to continue.

SEVEN

The Establishment, Clinton,

and the Future

When President Kennedy came into conflict with Morgan-Rockefeller interests over domestic and foreign policy, he was up against the core of the U.S. Establishment. These two groups, descended from the titans of the late 1800s, J.P. Morgan and John D. Rockefeller, had survived changes in the U.S. economy over a whole century and remained the dominant financial forces in Kennedy's time and beyond. Neither group features today such prominent family figures as the original founders or even their successors in the early 1900s, John D. Rockefeller, Jr., and J.P. Morgan, Jr. In the case of the Rockefeller group, the family's role in the 1990s is not as apparent as in the 1960s when David Rockefeller and James Stillman Rockefeller were leaders at Chase and Citibank. With or without strong family presence, the two financial groups survived the Great Depression and the Roosevelt administration's reforms. The threat posed to them by the federal government's World War II economic planning and intervention in banking came to an end with the conclusion of the war and the defeat in Congress of efforts to continue that intervention.[1]

Based on his study of financial control of corporations in the 1967-69 period, David Kotz[2] concluded that the power of financial groups, led by Morgan and Chase Manhattan, was enormous and that it was growing.* Kotz[3] described these

---

* In Kotz's view, the core of the Chase group was comprised of two banks and two insurance companies—Chase Manhattan, Chemical Bank, Metropolitan Life Insurance, and Equitable Life Assur-

bankers as a "plutocracy" and noted several dangers they posed to the economy beyond the general problem of excessive power. These financial groups, he argued, favor monopolistic practices in production and pricing, corporate mergers, and financial practices that put short-term profits ahead of long-term production and investment. Kotz relied on existing government studies, historical evidence, and his own research. He suspected that the available evidence understated the real power of financial interests. That suspicion and his conclusion that the power of those groups was growing was supported by a government study of economic power at the beginning of the 1980s.

In December of 1980, the Senate Committee on Governmental Affairs published a study entitled "Structure of Corporate Concentration." The study was supervised by E. Winslow Turner and was based on information for 1980 compiled and analyzed by the Senate Computer Center. The analysis built on, extended, and updated earlier investigations of financial and corporate power, which included the 1913 Pujo Committee's study of the "Money Trust," the 1937 Temporary National Economic Committee investigation, the 1968 Patman Committee report, and studies done in the 1970s. The 1980 study focused on institutional ownership of stock in the top 100 banks, insurance companies, and corporations. It also examined direct and indirect connections among the boards of directors of the 100 firms. Because of gaps in reporting requirements, the study did not include individual holdings of stock, and some specific categories of institutional holdings were also missing. The staff nevertheless felt that the analysis provided a big part of the picture of economic power in the United States, and they suspected that the missing data would only reinforce their findings.[4]

This is the most thorough investigation of institutional stockholders and of connections among boards of directors that has ever been done.* The findings are immensely detailed, and the summary presentation of the data takes up hundreds of pages. The basic conclusions, however, are concise and quite straightforward: Financial institutions, part of or extensively interrelated with the Morgan-Rockefeller complex, are the dominant force in the economy. For example, J.P. Morgan was the leading stockholder in 15 major companies; it was among the top six stockholders in 43 top corporations. Citicorp was among the top six in 30 companies, and Manufacturers Hanover (merged in 1991 with Chemical Bank) was among the top six in 26 companies. TIAA/CREF, the insurance and pension program for people in higher education, was among the top six in 30 companies. Among the trustees managing TIAA/CREF funds were

ance Society. Kotz concluded that this group controlled 21 large nonfinancial corporations. The Morgan group included Morgan Guaranty Trust, Bankers Trust, Prudential Life Insurance, Morgan Stanley, and Smith, Barney. This group controlled 15 major corporations (Kotz, 1978, pp. 85, 196-98).

* The staff that prepared the report recommended that the study be maintained on an ongoing basis with annual updates. They also suggested changes in reporting requirements to close the gaps in the data. Phone calls by the author to past and present staff members of the Committee on Governmental Affairs indicated that the study was not continued or updated as proposed by the staff.

directors of Morgan, Citicorp, Chase Manhattan, Exxon, and Brown Brothers, Harriman.[5]

The board of directors of Morgan included individuals serving on the boards of 31 of the top 100 firms. Citicorp* was directly tied to 49 top companies, and Chase Manhattan, Chemical Bank, and Metropolitan Life each had 24 other top companies represented on their boards. These and a multitude of other overlaps among the top 100 firms provide a dense network of relationships reinforced by frequent ties through private clubs, educational background, marriages, and membership in organizations such as the Council on Foreign Relations and the Business Council.[6]

As examined earlier, various studies have shown extensive relationships between leading financial institutions and oil companies. The Senate Committee study adds to this. Morgan was the largest institutional stockholder in Mobil and among the top six in Exxon, Gulf, and Standard of California (Gulf and SoCal merged in 1984). Chase Manhattan was first at Exxon and among the top six at Mobil, SoCal, and Standard of Indiana. Citicorp was among the top six for Exxon, Standard of Indiana, and Atlantic Richfield. Manufacturers Hanover was among the top six at Exxon, SoCal, Texaco, and Atlantic Richfield.[7] When one adds to this the historical relationships between the banks and oil companies and the involvement of other Rockefeller family interests in these areas, there is abundant evidence for concluding, as Chris Welles[8] did earlier, that banking and oil are one financial-corporate complex.

Some of the banks were also substantial holders of each other's stock through their parent holding companies. In what would seem to be rather flagrant violations of the spirit, if not the letter, of anti-trust law, Morgan was the leading institutional owner of stock in Bank of America** and Citicorp, and the third largest stockholder for Manufacturers Hanover. Citicorp was in turn the leader for Chase Manhattan and Bankers Trust, and was fourth largest at both Bank of America and Manufacturers Hanover. TIAA/CREF, connected through directors to Chase, Morgan, and Citicorp, was among the top seven stockholders for Chase, Citicorp, Manufacturers Hanover, and Wells Fargo.[9]

Extensive interconnections existed in other sectors of the U.S. economy. For example, J.P. Morgan was the leading institutional stockholder in Eastern Airlines and Pan Am, second in United Airlines, and third in American. In retailing Morgan was first at K Mart and J.C. Penney and second for Sears Roebuck. Financial institutions in the Morgan-Rockefeller orbit were leading stockholders in most of the country's largest corporations. For example, in each of the

---

* Relationships between this Stillman-Rockefeller bank and Morgan go back to 1909 when Morgan and Company became a large stockholder in the National City Bank, now Citicorp/Citibank. J.P. Morgan, Jr., served for a time after 1912 as a director of Citibank (Kotz, 1978, p. 39).

** Kotz (1978, p. 46) briefly relates the story of a battle in the 1930s between A. P. Giannini, the founder of the Bank of America, and the Morgan group. Quoting other sources, Kotz says that Giannini almost lost control of his bank. The Senate Committee's data suggest that Morgan and other New York banks did by 1980 control, or share control of, Giannini's bank.

following at least two Morgan-Rockefeller institutions were among the top six stockholders: AT&T, General Motors, DuPont, Exxon, General Electric, IBM, United Technologies, and Union Pacific.

Commenting on the general phenomenon of intercorporate ownership and interlocking boards of directors, Michael Useem observed in his 1984 book, *The Inner Circle*,[10] that the corporate community in the U.S. (and in the United Kingdom) had achieved a level of "transcendent organization without precedent." This network, according to Useem, constituted an organization of economic power which in its scope and depth surpassed the structure dominated by the House of Morgan in the early 1900s. The high level of organization that exists at the top of the economy shows that the image of a competitive, decentralized economy, which is a staple of media discussions, is an illusion.

It is finance capital and the organized sectors of big business that Carroll Quigley, Bill Clinton's Georgetown professor, viewed around 1960 as a potential threat to the well-being of the United States as a nation and to Western civilization in general. At the heart of this concern was Quigley's conclusion, validated by events prior to and following 1960, that the groups in command of the nation's financial and corporate establishment were inclined to place their interests in protecting their own power and in extracting profits from other economic sectors ahead of the well-being of the majority of human beings. Based on his analysis of the history of periods of progress and of decline in Western and non-Western civilizations, Quigley was convinced that tendencies present in the finance-monopoly sector of the U.S. economy would, if not checked or circumvented, lead to the decline of the United States. He also thought that such a decline could involve Western civilization in general. The developments of the last 30 years are tragic testimony to the insightfulness of his analysis of the dynamics of growth and decay.

Essentially, Quigley's work is a study of processes of progress and growth and of decline and decay. He says that in its simplest terms, civilization is a society that produces, is literate, and supports urban centers ("city life"). In order for progress to occur, such societies must be organized to encourage the creation of new ways of doing things. They must generate a surplus (*e.g.*, as profits, credit, or tax revenue) and use that surplus for investment in existing and new means of production. Periods of progress are characterized by increasing production and a rising standard of living, population growth (largely from declining death rates), increased knowledge, and advances in science. Such periods also typically feature some kind of increasing democracy.[11]

In Quigley's view, the periods of progress enjoyed by Western civilization are substantially attributable to aspects of the Judeo-Christian worldview. That view includes the idea that material wellbeing is a precondition for spiritual wellbeing and that the material world is generally good. In this view the world was created in a developmental process, and its principles are comprehensible. Individuality is valued, but it is also emphasized that people need each other to develop their potentials. The idea that all individuals have value and the idea of democracy are supported by the belief that all people have souls (*i.e.*, are created in the image of and participate in the divine*). The Judeo-Christian tradition also promotes, or can promote, a commitment to understanding the world, rather than viewing it as random or chaotic. That commitment along with sense of purpose and optimism are the bases for scientific, economic, and social progress.[12] It is these dimensions of the Judeo-Christian worldview that are specific targets of the élite environmentalists and also, of course, of far-right political figures, aristocratic élitists, racists, eugenicists, Social Darwinists, and neo-colonialists.

Progress is interrupted, and decline and decay take over, usually as a result of a breakdown in investment. If the institutions or policies responsible for the breakdown are not reformed or circumvented, then the other elements of progress, invention and accumulation (profits, tax revenues, etc.), also begin to break down. Once an investment crisis is underway, there are, according to Quigley, three general possibilities. First, existing institutions and practices may be reformed to allow a renewal of progress. Second, existing institutions and practices can be circumvented and new processes of investment created (as occurred during World War II and was a part of Kennedy's efforts**). The third possibility is that reaction sets in, whereby "privileged vested-interest groups" successfully prevent reform and circumvention and perpetuate the decline. According to Quigley, the forces responsible for the crisis are often in a position to protect their own interests and therefore see no need for change in the early stages of decline, and may never see that need.[13]

The period of crisis, the time when reform or circumvention must occur to prevent deepening decay, features declining rates of investment, increased class conflict, and increasingly frequent and increasingly violent imperialist wars, and is a period of "growing irrationality, pessimism, superstitions, and other worldliness." In such circumstances, violence becomes an attractive answer for all domestic and international problems, even when it is impossible to explain its utility in solving the problems. Privileged interests find imperialist wars and irrationality to be of use to absorb the interests and energies of the non-privileged, particularly in diverting their attention away from the breakdown in investment and those responsible for it. As the élite pours more and more resources into the imperialist wars and the promotion of irrationality, the institutions carrying out these functions take on a life of their own and become

---

* What I take this to mean is not that human beings are gods, but that, like the Judeo-Christian God, humans are potentially knowers, creators, and moral actors. The process of development for individuals and for societies involves growth in understanding, increasing powers to create and produce, and higher levels of social justice.

** The book by Quigley referred to here was published in 1961 and has no discussion of Kennedy. In his 1966 book *Tragedy and Hope* there is a brief discussion of Kennedy and it is generally negative; however, there is no indication that Quigley was aware of most of the efforts by Kennedy covered in this book. It may also be that Quigley shared some of the financial Establishment's hostility toward Kennedy. In spite of Quigley's insightful and often severe criticism of the Anglo-American Establishment, he seemed to maintain loyalty toward and admiration for it.

additional impediments to any positive change, and may become forces in their own right.[14]

As of around 1960, Quigley[15] viewed the future of the United States, and perhaps Western civilization, as more or less up for grabs. The destructive influence of finance capital and monopolistic industries had been somewhat blunted by the reforms and government policies of the 1930s and 1940s. During that time the government became somewhat more responsive to the needs of labor, farmers, consumers, civil servants, and businesses outside of the core financial and monopoly sector. These developments, in Quigley's view, temporarily checked tendencies leading to economic decline, imperialist wars, and cultural irrationality. As we have seen in earlier chapters, Kennedy took office at a time when economic stagnation was again appearing (in the 1953 to 1960 period) and he set out to change that. He also attempted to inject a feeling of optimism and challenge into the political climate and to make both economic progress and social justice part of the national purpose. Since his death, the idea of progress and the emotional experience of hope and optimism have been overwhelmed by economic deterioration, wars fulfilling no obvious purposes, and increasing levels of cultural irrationality. The idea of progress has also been undermined by claims that the world is overpopulated, that resources are limited, and that industrial production inevitably destroys the environment.

As the 1990s began, real hourly earnings for workers and employees were down, on average, 11 percent from 1973, and weekly earnings were off by 18 percent.[16] These numbers do not take into account what was actually a rising tax burden on most people in the 1980s, and there is some evidence that rising prices are not being fully accounted for in government figures.[17] These numbers also do not take into account the shrinking car, longer payment periods on big items, or higher interest payments on consumer debt. For example, in 1979 it took 28 weeks of gross income for a person earning an average weekly income to buy a Buick LeSabre. By 1991 it took 50 weeks of income. (And the 1991 model was 1,200 pounds lighter than the 1979 model.) Also, government assessments of changes in real income ignore the longer payment periods and higher interest costs in the later period. Housing prices have also risen much faster than incomes.[18]

The percentage of the U.S. labor force employed in manufacturing fell from 29 in 1968 to 17 in 1991; in absolute numbers, there were fewer people in manufacturing in 1991 than in 1968. Meanwhile, service sector employment, generally at lower wages than in manufacturing, had risen from 18 million in 1968 to 61 million in 1991. Service sector employment was 40 percent of the labor force in 1960, 41 peercent in 1968, and 56 percent in 1991.[19] While the overall decline was occurring in income, wealth was being redistributed upward, partly as a result of changes in tax policy.[20] Although most politicians have been reluctant to discuss it, the number of poor people has been growing, and they, even more than the middle class, have lost real income. The number of people officially defined as poor in the United States had fallen from 39.5 million in

1959 to 24.1 million in 1969, and then to 23 million in 1973. By 1991 the number was back up to 35.7 million.[21] The common source of middle-class decline and of growing and deepening poverty is the transformation of the U.S. economy into the post-industrial or service economy.

This decline can be reversed. However, consistent with Quigley's observations, there is little indication that such a change is going to come from the financial-corporate establishment, which means that the system will have to be changed through reforms or circumvention. Indeed, anyone attempting such change can expect powerful opposition from that establishment, which takes no responsibility for the economic misery created in this and other countries by the oil-energy cartel manipulations nor finds fault in the policies of the banking system over the last 25 years, or the wasteful speculation and corporate acquisition of the 1970s and 1980s. When the Establishment publicly confronts the country's problems, it seems more comfortable—far too comfortable—blaming the government, middle- and working-class entitlement programs, or the average person's alleged proclivities to spend rather than save. Representatives of the Morgan-Rockefeller-dominated core of the Establishment have been quite open about this.

In 1987 one of the Establishment's leading figures ventured to give the readers of the *Atlantic Monthly* his assessment of what is ailing the U.S. economy and his prescription for (perhaps) restoring its health. The author of this assessment, Peter G. Peterson, was at the time chairman of the Blackstone Group (investment banking) and chairman of the Council on Foreign Relations, an office he assumed when David Rockefeller retired in 1985. Rockefeller had been the CFR's chairman for 15 years after succeeding John J. McCloy.*

Peterson's article[22] is self-contradictory in some important ways. On one hand, Peterson identifies crumbling infrastructure, declining productivity, trade and budget deficits, rising poverty, and stagnating wages as important problems. In the same context, however, he says we are the envy of the world with our burst of new businesses, jobs, and Dow-Jones records. Returning to the negative,

---

* Peterson had been the chief executive officer of Lehman Brothers and of Bell and Howell. He had served or was serving as a director of RCA, Federated Department Stores, General Foods, and Minnesota Mining and Manufacturing. Morgan-Rockefeller institutions were leading stockholders in two of those, RCA and Federated, in 1980. Peterson was also a trustee of the Committee for Economic Development and of the University of Chicago. Finally, he was, with David Rockefeller and the chairmen of CBS and IBM, a trustee of the Museum of Modern Art (Dye, pp. 37, 148, 160; U.S. Senate Committee on Governmental Affairs, 1980). When John J. McCloy died in 1989, Peterson was among the ushers at the funeral, joining such Establishment luminaries as McGeorge Bundy and former Fed Chairman Paul Volcker. At the funeral, President Bush's Secretary of State, James A. Baker III, read President Bush's letter of homage to McCloy (Bird, pp. 15-16). On the board of directors of the CFR around the time Peterson wrote this article were figures who would be prominent in the Bush administration (Secretary of Defense Dick Cheney and National Security Adviser Brent Scowcroft) and the future Secretary of State under Clinton, Warren Christopher. Christopher was also vice-chairman of the CFR. Federal Reserve Board Chairman Alan Greenspan was also among the CFR directors (Council on Foreign Relations, 1988).

he warns that the basis for future prosperity is being "insidiously" weakened and that the loss of jobs for millions of Americans is part of a self-inflicted injury related to growing imports. What is the cause of stagnating (actually falling) real wages and rising poverty and the other problems? The "root malady" according to Peterson is too much consumption. The cause, he says, of wage stagnation and rising poverty (*i.e.*, declining consumption) is too much consumption. The solution for a falling standard of living would then apparently be to drive down the standard of living still further. In reaching that conclusion, Peterson manages to wind up with the same recommendation that is promoted by his colleagues among the élite environmentalists, even though the justification is different. Peterson also provides an example of what Quigley meant when he said that dominant interests would not see the need for real changes once a crisis was under way.

Peterson correctly identifies lagging investment in real production as a basic source of the country's problems. He also mentions insufficient commitment to research and development and the country's lack of investment in the development and wellbeing of people. He points out that the aging of our population will put new demands on the economy after the second decade of the next century. Peterson notes that problems will emerge if future obligations for Social Security, Medicare, and federal pensions run up against continuing stagnation in production and income. Warning that we are in danger of emulating Britain's sad economic history, he says that we have been undergoing since 1980, or the 1970s, a process of deindustrialization. The decline of private industry is matched by insufficient investment to build and maintain public infrastructure.* He also emphasizes growing trade problems and increasing reliance on foreign money to fund government debt and investments.

Peterson outlines what he says are our two basic choices. We can allow things to continue as they have been, and this will lead to an eventual plunge in the value of the dollar, producing a "crash" and indefinite impoverishment. The alternative to this, he says, is to begin an "enormous shift" away from consumption to savings, which should be invested in a way that increases our exports. Doing this, he says, may require a "further decline in consumption."[23] What he means by "further decline" is not clear since he has charged the American people with engaging in a consumption bacchanalia and with gorging themselves.

This gets us to Peterson's explanation for the source of the crisis. His identification of the source leads logically to the solutions he proposes. He does not find any of the causes in the oil companies' abuse of economic power or in the unheard-of level of interest rates during much of the last 25 years. Similarly,

---

* Walt Rostow, an expert on economic development who served in the Kennedy administration, thought that the public investment problem was becoming so severe by the early 1980s that he wrote a book, entitled *The Barbaric Counter-Revolution* (1983), dealing with the dangers posed to the U.S. economy. According to his analysis (p. 119), public infrastructure investment boomed in the 1962-1967 period and then rapidly declined between 1968 and 1977 (the last year for his data). Unlike Peterson, Rostow (pp. 36, 61) does emphasize the damage done to the U.S. economy by high interest rates.

there is no mention of the corporate merger binge nor high-level speculation. There is no critical discussion of corporate disinvestment, downsizing, or lay-offs. There is no criticism of the International Monetary Fund's policies and no questioning of the actions and purposes of the Federal Reserve. In short, the entire financial-corporate Establishment is implicitly held to be without blame. Who is at fault? The vast majority of human beings who have or hope to have a secure, decent standard of living.

According to Peterson our current mess began in the early 1970s. It is not the interest rate and energy price surges he has in mind. Rather, he says that in the 1970s and 1980s, there has been too much growth in government spending, too much welfare for the middle class, and too little saving. Specifically, he says that the country made a mistake when it began protecting middle-class and working-class entitlement programs from inflation in the early 1970s (*i.e.*, by introducing automatic cost-of-living adjustments). He criticizes President Reagan for his failure to seek tax increases in the 1980s. He also attacks Reagan for allowing consumption to rise through government borrowing and through the shift from saving to consuming.* Peterson does find virtue in the Reagan record. He praises Reagan for breaking the air traffic controllers' union, for his contribution to the deregulation of airlines, banking, and energy, and for leadership in rejecting national economic planning, wage-price controls, and jobs programs.

Peterson's solutions follow from his choice of causes. Government spending, in real terms, must be frozen or reduced. Budget deficits should be eliminated. Overall levels of consumption and income must decline (the word "further" should have been added). Military spending should be reduced, and other nations should assume more of the foreign aid burden. He recommends that cost-of-living adjustments in entitlement programs be cut back to 60 percent of price increases. This means, of course, that any surge in prices will significantly reduce the standard of living of older people. He argues for later retirement for civil service employees, lower initial benefits for retired government employees, and reductions in their cost-of-living adjustments. We should also reduce what he calls "excessive and wasteful" use of health care services. Taxes on gasoline should be increased over time by 25 cents per gallon, and a value-added tax of 5 percent should be placed on all products. We should also consider reducing or eliminating tax breaks for interest paid on home mortgages.

None of this, says Peterson, will produce any improvements in people's lives in the near term. In fact, a declining standard of living in the next several years

---

* Peterson says that real consumption per worker rose by $3,100 between 1980 and 1987. No source for or explanation of this figure is provided. It is inconsistent with many economic figures and with other assessments of the trends of that period. It also seems to have warranted some explanation, given his remarks about rising poverty and stagnating wages. This may be based on Peterson's estimates of consumption financed through growing indebtedness. Throughout the discussions of the decline in savings, Peterson faithfully ignores the clear correlation between falling real wages and falling savings rates. Recognition of falling income as a cause would have interfered with the theme that Americans have been binging and must now face "The Morning After."

would be a sign of his program's success. Any resources saved in the short term (five years) should be used to pay off foreign debt. Maybe by the late 1990s the country could turn its attention to domestic investment. We may be by that time, however, in the midst of an indefinite 1930s-style depression, or perhaps just a British-style decline.

Quigley, as noted earlier, observed that in periods of decline, the dominant forces typically see no need for changes that would stop the decline and restore progress in investment and consumption. Peterson's recommendations are based on a perception of the last quarter of a century that totally overlooks the errors, reckless pursuit of self-interest, and abuse of power on the part of wealthy and powerful interests. There is not the slightest inclination to reform existing institutions or circumvent them with new processes or institutions. His solutions, which are morally wrong, have no connection to the real sources of the crisis, and for the vast majority of people he proposes even more of what is for them the crisis—a declining standard of living. In an economy suffering from declining purchasing power, he proposes to reduce it still further.

Peterson is both an advocate of reactionary change and a defender of the most powerful and most vested interests of the status quo. In that role, he can only propose change that further erodes the conditions of life of the majority of people. His solutions are meant to protect the wealth, profits, and freedom of action of leading upper-class interests. The program proposed by Peterson for the United States is similar to the policies demanded of Third World nations over the last 30 years. It is essentially a program of IMF conditionalities for the United States. Cuts in government spending and services, reductions in income and consumption, taxes on basic necessities, and freeing up of resources for export have all been part of the standard IMF program imposed on troubled economies around the world. As in Brazil or any other Third World nation, the financial Establishment needs a government in the U.S. that is willing to carry out the unpleasant duties.

The 1992 election eliminated a man who could be counted on to make at least a good effort to carry out those duties. The election brought into the White House a man whose true intentions often seemed to puzzle the Establishment as much as they did a large part of the voting public. William Jefferson Clinton will probably be one of the pivotal figures in U.S. history, for better or worse. He can oversee the decline, becoming a contributor to the process of reaction, or he can attempt to create the processes of reform and circumvention needed to restore progress and growth. Clinton has taken office in the midst of the longest period of general stagnation and decline in U.S. history. He is the first president to take office since Kennedy who has emphasized both economic problems and the need for federal intervention in the economy to solve those problems. If he fails to get things done, he may further discredit the idea that a president can do anything other than supervise austerity.

Bill Clinton has pointed to his early, brief encounter with President Kennedy as a significant event in his life. He has occasionally referred to Kennedy in speeches, visited his grave, and recovered JFK's desk for his use. From a distance, it is impossible to know what all of that means to the new president. Clinton has also referred to the impact on him of the man whose ideas have been cited in this chapter, Carroll Quigley.

In his acceptance speech at the Democratic Convention, Clinton[24] remarked:

> As a teen-ager I heard John Kennedy's summons to citizenship. And then, as a student at Georgetown, I heard that call clarified by a professor I had named Carroll Quigley, who said America was the greatest country in the history of the world because our people have always believed in two great ideas: first, that tomorrow can be better than today, and second that each of us has a personal, moral responsibility to make it so.

Clinton had made essentially the same remarks when he announced his candidacy in October of 1991, and others have commented on the general effect that Quigley had on Clinton.[25] In some ways, Clinton seems to view the country's economic problems through the eyes of Quigley.

In a relatively early version of his economic program, Clinton[26] said that the country needs more public and private investment. He suggested that the country had to close both the "budget deficit and the investment gap." Peterson and, as we will see below, other representatives of the financial Establishment view government, government spending, and, therefore, the budget deficit as the primary problems. As in President Kennedy's time, they do not want direct government involvement in the investment process.

In that early statement, Clinton[27] went on to criticize Washington for rewarding those who "speculate in paper" instead of investing in people. He accused the government of creating tax breaks that encouraged companies to move production and jobs overseas.* He also pointed to inadequate capital and credit for small business. Clinton said that the government had betrayed the country's basic values, values related to creating opportunity, rewarding work, and personal responsibility. He charged the Republicans with responsibility for the worst period of income, job, and general economic growth since the Great Depression. Noting, and apparently accepting, that capital, factories, and whole industries are internationally mobile, he emphasized the need to improve the education and training of people, the one major resource that stays in the country.

---

* As was noted in Chapter Two, Kennedy had attempted, unsuccessfully, to get Congress to adopt tax policies that would discourage U.S. corporate investment in Canada and Europe, and encourage investment in the U.S. and in Third World nations. He had also sought to inhibit various types of foreign financial activities by U.S. firms and investors. Total U.S. corporate investment abroad, officially valued, was $32 billion in 1960. In 1991 it was $451 billion, and most of that was still in other advanced countries, primarily Canada and Europe. Less than 10 percent of the total was manufacturing investment in Third World nations. Since the 1960s, foreign investment in the U.S., led by the United Kingdom, has also grown enormously (U.S. Bureau of the Census, 1985-1991; U.S. Department of Commerce; Wilkins).

He added that the country's transportation and communication systems had to be improved.

Bill Clinton then identified four "critical areas" in his economic program. Two of those were the improvements in the transportation and the communications systems, which, he argued, would boost the manufacturing sector. The other two were conversion of military resources to civilian use and environmental technology. Concerning the environment, he emphasized, as he had elsewhere,[28] that in his view there was no inherent conflict between economic growth and protection of the environment. Clinton did not elaborate on this. In certain ways it is obviously true. For example, without a prosperous economy, it will be difficult to create or allocate resources to deal with whatever environmental problems actually develop. Also, advances in technology can lead to much less damaging methods of production (as in the movement in energy production from wood and coal to oil, natural gas, hydroelectric, and nuclear). What Clinton's statement overlooked is that there is a conflict between economic growth and the stated goals of élite environmentalists.

To address the investment gap, Clinton proposed policies to "dramatically increase" private investment. His proposals included the following: reinstatement of the investment tax credit (in place intermittently since first initiated by President Kennedy); tax breaks for small business and for those willing to make long-term investments in new businesses; permanent extension of tax credits for research and development; and efforts to open up foreign markets. Clinton[29] had also indicated that he would try to end the diversion of billions of dollars of capital away from productive investment to mergers and speculation.

After Clinton won the nomination and selected Al Gore as his running mate, an expanded version of the economic program was published in book form with Clinton and Gore as co-authors. The first 32 pages and parts thereafter are a repetition and extension of Clinton's earlier statements. There are a few additions. One of the obvious ones is a much greater focus on environmental issues. This probably reflects Gore's involvement. The new version repeats the earlier assertion that there is no conflict between protection of the environment and economic growth and includes the statement that "sound scientific data" and not politics should be the basis for environmental decisions. Perhaps reflecting Gore's influence, however, they go on to accept the existence of widely disputed problems such as global warming.[30] The environmental issues, however, remained in the background as the presidential campaign developed around more traditional economic issues.

Beside campaigning on a promise to do something about the investment, income, and employment problems, Clinton also emphasized issues of fairness and social justice. In his convention speech Clinton[31] warned "the forces of greed" that their time was over. He said that for too long the average person had "gotten the shaft" while those "who cut corners and cut deals have been rewarded." He accused Bush of raising the taxes of people who drive pickup trucks while lowering them for those riding in limousines. As Kevin Phillips[32] has pointed out, this kind of populist rhetoric has been used by both traditional liberals and non-Establishment conservatives. As Phillips also points out, and extensively documents, that rhetoric makes sense to many people in the early 1990s after two decades of growing inequality.

To some extent, at least, Clinton did show an extensive awareness of the country's economic problems. During the campaign he seemed to imply that he would act in a serious way to change the direction of things, to, in Quigley's terms, reform or circumvent existing institutions. As noted earlier, Quigley concluded from his study of periods of decline that dominant economic forces typically do not see the need for such reforms or circumvention. Instead, they promote policies that protect their own interests and that contribute to the decline. Peterson's complete refusal to address or even to acknowledge the financial-corporate Establishment's destructive action is an example of this problem. So is Peterson's determination to end up blaming working- and middle-class Americans for the crisis. Not surprising, even if no less depressing, has been the response of those financial and corporate interests to Clinton and to his probably all too modest proposals to change the direction of the economy.

In the face of falling income, rising poverty, increasing inequality, diminished social services, deteriorating infrastructure, and a shrinking industrial base, the Establishment is primarily worried that the new president will actually try to use governmental powers to deal with these problems. In other words, certain things have remained exactly as they were when Morgan-Rockefeller interests severely attacked Kennedy as an "enforcer of progress."

About three months after the 1962 steel crisis, David Rockefeller had written his letter to Kennedy advising him about the proper role of government in a free-enterprise economy. As noted earlier, Rockefeller's letter admonished Kennedy to control government spending, pursue a balanced budget, and allow interest rates to rise. Kennedy had either rejected or ignored the advice.[33] Kennedy instead sought to use reforms and various methods of circumvention in pursuit of his growth and development goals.

Thirty years after the Rockefeller-Kennedy exchange, David Rockefeller, Jr., offered advice to Bill Clinton in an editorial published in the *New York Times*. The article, published on October 16, 1992, was titled "Why I Trust Clinton." By this time it was quite clear that Clinton was going to win the election. As in his father's public statement to Kennedy, there are polite comments and even positive assessments of the Democrat. David, Jr.'s advice to Clinton is a little less explicit than was his father's to Kennedy, but very similar. He advises Clinton to "unshackle us from the enormous weight of our accumulated deficit." He trusts that Clinton will pick the right advisers and be willing to "take the heat" for necessary decisions. It is reasonable to assume that Rockefeller is not talking about decisions that will encroach on the financial Establishment's interests. Rather, the decisions and heat likely refer to the kind of measures recommended by David, Jr.'s colleague at the Council on Foreign Relations, Pete Peterson. Rockefeller expects that Clinton will take a balanced approach in the use of government power and that he will not undermine the private sector with either public statements or tax policy. Finally, he states his confidence that Clinton will not shrink from our "global engagement."*

A stronger version of the Peterson line appeared in the CFR's official journal about the time of Clinton's inaugural. The article was by Jeffrey E. Garten, a CFR member who is also a senior adviser to the Blackstone Group, which Peterson chaired in the late 1980s. Garten's[34] article was directed at Bill Clinton and was entitled "The 100-Day Economic Agenda." The article started by criticizing Clinton, as president-elect, for not preparing the country for sacrifice. Clinton was also criticized for not paying enough attention to the desires and expectations of "powerful international financial markets." These "markets," Garten warned, are ready to "unleash their fury" at Clinton's "first fiscal misstep." A similar view was attributed elsewhere to Roger C. Altman, vice-chairman of the Blackstone Group.[35] Appointed Assistant Secretary of the Treasury, Altman can give Clinton such warnings on a regular basis. Garten went on in the *Foreign Affairs* article to say that "Wall Street and its foreign counter-parts" have the capacity to bring government "policymakers to their knees overnight." He later restated his disappointment that Clinton did not prepare the country for the "painful policies" that will be needed. There is no need to review Garten's policies; they are virtually identical to the Peterson program reviewed earlier. Similar views also came from Time, Inc.

Fortune magazine, still part of the much expanded Time empire (Time-Warner, following Time's multi-billion dollar buyout of Warner Communications), also gave its support to the Establishment call for austerity. The Time-Warner media conglomerate still displays extensive connections to Wall Street in general and to Morgan-Rockefeller interests in particular.** Just before the

---

* In an April 18, 1993, *New York Times Magazine* article entitled "Colonialism's Back—and Not a Moment Too Soon," Paul Johnson (1993) provided an indication of what global engagement might be about. The article was subtitled "Let's face it: Some countries are just not fit to govern themselves." Johnson focused on Africa, but said the same policy would apply elsewhere. His argument was that since decolonialization, about 20 African nations have shown themselves to be unable to create adequate governments. The resultant horrors both justify and require a return to a policy of trusteeship, involving intervention to establish governments, set up security networks, and/or manage economies. The United States and Britain, he said, will take the lead in this and later be joined by other countries. He suggested that the first nations to be so controlled should be chosen carefully and treated as "pilot projects." Priority candidates are Somalia, Liberia, Zaire, Angola, Mozambique, and Haiti. Responding to an argument like this is difficult, because it is so outrageous. It is like trying to react to E.F. Schumacher's statement that the problem in Southeast Asia in 1973 was a neglect of trees or to Noam Chomsky's (1993) assertion that neither Kennedy's presidency nor his death produced any change in policies. Let's just say that Johnson does not bother to mention in his discussion of difficulties in the Third World a single thing that would reflect negatively on the Anglo-American Establishment or its allies in other nations. There is then no mention of energy crises, interest rates, IMF policies, global stagnation, lack of economic assistance, or trade policies. Even the legacy of colonialism is dismissed as a problem. Johnson actually claims that there is "grass-roots" support in the Third World for the return of colonialism. What is his evidence for that? It is a comment allegedly made by one "humble" person in Liberia to a Marine guard.
** The Time-Warner board includes connections to the following: Chase Manhattan, Equitable Life

1992 presidential election, *Fortune*[36] published a special report on the economy written by its editors. They warned the American people that they will have to give up their desire to feel good and face the problems of the global labor market and the need for disinflation. They even derided Reaganesque "morning-in-America reverie." It is something like Peterson's "morning after" that they had in mind. They identified the following general economic problems: lack of investment and savings, inadequate job growth, and mounting debt. Their discussion was similar to Peterson's, and, in the end, they agreed with Peterson that the American people are going to get hurt; they should "grow up" and accept it.

As in Peterson's diagnosis of the country's economic ills, there is some ambiguity in *Fortune*'s reading of the economy. Using output in goods and services as a measure, it claimed that U.S. productivity was still the best in the world, but went on to say that the growth rate in productivity was less than one-third the U.S. rate for 1937 to 1973 and less than one-third of Japan's in the last decade. It also indicated (in an understated way) that improvements in U.S. productivity come not from investments in new technology, but from eliminating jobs and getting rid of the least efficient operations. It also noted that U.S. companies benefit from relatively little government regulation and the absence of strong unions. What *Fortune* seems to be recognizing is that U.S. companies are not in real terms producing more with better technology, but have merely improved their cost and revenue situation by eliminating jobs and downsizing. This is not rising productivity for the nation.

Fortune did point out that big corporations are eliminating jobs on a "whole-sale" basis and that there is too little private and public investment. It quoted from a government study of 5.1 million full-time workers who lost jobs between 1987 and 1992. Only 2.7 million of them got new full-time jobs and almost half of those jobs were at lower pay. The magazine noted that much of the technology in the U.S. is aging and is not as efficient as Japan's. Long-term problems in research and development were mentioned, and *Fortune* said that these problems have gotten worse since the mid-1980s.

So much for the assessment of problems; it is *Fortune*'s view that it is government and average people who will have to change. It finds no fault with those in charge of our most powerful financial and corporate institutions. Some of the discussion resembles that of a hard-nosed "expert" on alleged runaway medical costs who is seeking to justify denial of treatment to or euthanasia for costly patients. In *Fortune*'s view, our sad economic condition necessitates "hard decisions," "bitter medicine," and "short-term pain." None of this is prescribed, of course, for Wall Street banks, giant corporations, or wealthy investors.

The editors do acknowledge as a fact the problem of disinvestment. According to them, the biggest cause of disinvestment is government spending. They do

Assurance, Prudential, Bankers Trust, IBM, Rockefeller Center Properties, and TIAA/CREF. There are also board connections to the CFR, Business Council, Committee for Economic Development, Rockefeller Brothers Fund, and the University of Chicago. At least one descendent of Henry Luce sits on the board (Moody's Investors Service, 1992; Marquis *Who's Who*, 1992-93).

not choose to explain why this is the primary problem instead of corporate mergers or massive speculation; those problems are simply excluded. Similarly, they see no need to question the policies of banks, the energy cartel, the Federal Reserve, the International Monetary Fund, or anything else that might put great wealth or private power in a bad light. What the country should do is cut government spending and raise taxes on the majority of people. The spending cuts should be focused on entitlements—meaning Social Security, Medicare, Medicaid—and on student loans, unemployment benefits, and federal retirement programs. *Fortune* favors a value-added tax and higher gasoline taxes. The country, in its view, does not need to restore earlier levels of infrastructure spending, because shifting from manufacturing to services means fewer such needs.

The policy of more taxes and fewer benefits for people in general is reversed for corporations. The government should allow corporations to count dividend payments as tax-deducible expenses, actually a likely benefit for large stockholders. Capital gains tax rates should be reduced. *Fortune* also supports reductions in government regulations and supports the North American Free Trade Agreement. It did support restoration of the investment tax credit (eliminated most recently in 1986), and perhaps some of the regulations it opposed have been counterproductive. However, the package as a whole represents a continuing transfer of wealth from the majority to the privileged minority.

How the country's general problems would be solved by further reducing consumption and purchasing power is not dealt with. There is no attempt to explain why investment will increase if most Americans are going to lose government payments and services and pay higher taxes. Those policies would lead to further declines in purchasing power. In his analysis of crisis and decline, Quigley[37] argued that investment and consumption must be restored through reform or circumvention in order to stop a decline. What the chairman of the Council on Foreign Relations and *Fortune*'s editors have proposed is neither reform nor circumvention. It does not address the most direct sources of the decline, and the proposals to further reduce consumption are likely to deepen the decline. It is the kind of action, or reaction, Quigley viewed as typical of dominant classes.

Immediately after Clinton won the election, *Fortune*[38] speculated on the direction he would take. It wondered if he would follow the lead of deficit hawks such as Roger Altman of the Blackstone Group (now Assistant Secretary of the Treasury); Robert Rubin (formerly co-chairman of Goldman Sachs, a leader in merger finance, and now a senior economic advisor to Clinton); Senator David Boren of Oklahoma; and Alan Greenspan, chairman of the Federal Reserve Board. Or would Clinton seek to boost the economy with some sort of stimulus package? *Fortune* was hopeful but not yet convinced that Clinton would follow the hawks and make the "tough calls."

After Clinton's first budget was proposed, *Fortune*[39] again devoted a major article to Clinton and his policies. It liked his increasing focus on the deficit and expressed cautious hopes that he would stay committed to reducing government spending. It also argued that he should go much further and offered a list of additional cuts in spending. The part of this article that perhaps best represented *Fortune*'s outlook was the warning that something would soon have to be done about the "reckless generosity" that Washington has shown to the well-off elderly. Who are these "prosperous" old people? They are, says *Fortune*, the 25 percent of households headed by persons over 65 with annual incomes of $30,000 or more. These "well-heeled retirees" should be made to pay more; they are a threat which will eventually "bankrupt" the country. (*Fortune*'s editors do not pause here to wonder how the 75 percent of the elderly who are below $30,000 are doing.) It seems safe to assume that the owners and editors of *Fortune* would themselves find $30,000 a year to be a level of impoverishment that would send them into a panic.

Fortune's ambiguous treatment of Clinton is reminiscent of its initial views of Kennedy. As we have shown, that early uncertainty was replaced with hostility, as Kennedy moved in directions unacceptable to the Morgan-Rockefeller-Luce forces at Time, Inc. Part of *Fortune*'s concern about Clinton has to do with its editors' suspicions that he will not sufficiently reduce government spending. This was the major preoccupation of the *Wall Street Journal*.*

After Clinton won the 1992 election, the *Wall Street Journal*[40] said that, while it agreed with (unidentified) people close to Clinton that "something happened around 1973" to the world economy, things are now moving in a fairly good direction. The *Journal* asserted that the only real "emergency" is the excessive level of government spending. In its view, it is the spending and excessive government that is more the problem than the deficit in and of itself. The *Journal* advised against any stimulus package for the economy and recommended that

---

* As in Kennedy's time, connections to Morgan-Rockefeller interests through the Dow Jones board of directors were apparent in the early 1990s. The Dow Jones board was linked to Chemical Bank, Bankers Trust, Mobil Oil, ITT, J.C. Penney, and American Express. The Dow Jones board also interconnects with the full array of upper-class policy formation and lobbying groups. It is linked to the Business Council, Business Roundtable, Trilateral Commission, Conference Board, Committee for Economic Development, American Enterprise Institute, and the Council on Foreign Relations. The *Wall Street Journal*'s chairman, editor, and managing editor were also all members of the Council on Foreign Relations. Morgan-Rockefeller interests play a leading role in those organizations. The board also provided links to the following: New York Stock Exchange, New York Federal Reserve Bank, Associated Press, Amoco, Shell Oil, Eli Lilly, RJR Nabisco, Union Carbide, Corning, Continental Corporation, Ford Motors, Chubb Corporation, and Dayton-Hudson. There is also a link to the Aspen Institute (Council on Foreign Relations, 1988; Domhoff, 1983; Kotz, 1978; Marquis *Who's Who*, 1992-93; Moody's Investors Service, 1992; U.S. Senate Committee on Governmental Affairs, 1980). The Aspen link and connections to Rockefeller interests make the *Wall Street Journal*'s attack on environmentalists somewhat puzzling (*e.g.*, editorials of December 30, 1992, and April 2, 1993). Whether this represents a real dispute or not, it is important to note that the *Journal*'s editors see protection of "property rights" and the free market as the alternative to government activism on behalf of the environment. The choice offered by the two voices of the Establishment is between government protection of nature and "free enterprise." Excluded then is active government on behalf of people, development, and progress. The Establishment will give us Paul Ehrlich or Milton Friedman, but not Kennedy.

Clinton cut government spending, abandon the gospel of fairness, and give new tax breaks to either corporations or upper income people.

About a month after the inaugural, the *Journal*[41] admitted to confusion about Clinton's overall policy. It said that after Clinton's victory in November 1992, it had been convinced by certain "Democratic thinkers and financial types" to give Clinton a chance—which would be more than it gave Kennedy. By the time of this editorial, February 19, 1993, the *Journal* had concluded that the "Clintonites" were much too committed to the public sector and to increased government intervention in the economy. Three months later the *Journal*[42] attacked Clinton's spending and tax policies, advising him to withdraw the tax increase (which was aimed mostly at upper-income people) and to seek, instead, deep cuts in government spending. The *Journal* then asserted that the "strongest political consensus in the system" is for such deep reductions.

The *Journal*'s editors did not explain what "the system" is, nor did they indicate how they had detected that consensus. As one of their own articles[43] showed immediately after Clinton had defeated Bush, 51 percent of people polled on election day said that they thought the country was in a "serious long-term economic decline." Seventy-nine percent thought the economy was in "not good" or "poor" shape. The *Journal* also noted that the economy in general, and not the deficit, was most often cited by voters as the most important concern. Those views did not fit with the *Journal*'s own perception of how well the economy was doing. Also, in spite of some loose interpretations of apparent voter opposition to growing government, there was nothing in those poll results that showed a consensus in the country for deep cuts in government spending. Other polls did indicate that there was near consensus (80 percent) among Americans in 1992 that government decisions favored the rich and powerful.[44] One can only suspect that "the system" they refer to is the network of financiers and moguls represented on the Dow Jones board.

By the middle of 1993 the *Wall Street Journal* was even more pessimistic than before. The reasons for its editors' gloom had nothing to do, of course, with the policies of the rich and powerful over the last 30 years. The villain, the primary problem, was Clinton's tax and spending program. Clinton's program would provide the *Journal* with grist for future diatribes against the evils of government. Jousting with Clinton over his limited program also helps the *Journal* editors to go on denying that any of their associates bear any responsibility for the long-term decline of this country.

All of this is quite amazing. Clinton's proposals do not add up to a serious attempt at what Quigley called reform and circumvention. Even so, his program has been severely criticized. More significant, perhaps, has been the consistent rejection by the Establishment of any attempt to use government powers to redirect the economy. Embodied in this rejection are tendencies that fit all too well Quigley's observations of what happens during periods of decline, crisis, and reaction. That is, dominant economic groups see no need for constructive change, they continue to pursue the policies that have led to the crisis, and they become increasingly reactionary in their outlook. In the process, violence and/or irrationality become increasingly prominent features of both societal policy and everyday life.

It is fair to say that President Clinton has focused more attention on the deterioration of the U.S. economy than has any other mainstream political figure in recent times. Unless it turns out that this was done merely to contain growing anger and fear, he deserves some credit for this. Over the course of two years, as candidate and president, he has also laid out a somewhat coherent, if limited, program to reverse the decline. This included a stimulus package, increased infrastructure spending, restoration of the investment tax credit, other tax incentives for investment, more support for and coordination of research and development, and his community bank proposal.

During the campaign, and at other times afterward, he emphasized that inadequate public and private investment (the "investment deficit") were at least as important as the budget deficit. Clinton might also be given credit for trying to ignite some optimism about the possibility of restoring economic progress. Similarly, he deserves some appreciation for his emphasis on social justice (expressed in his proposal to use a tax credit to elevate working people above the poverty line and his proposal to shift the tax burden to those at the upper end of the income scale). Also, he rightly said or often implied that the middle class and the poor—blacks and whites—shared common interests. Finally, Bill Clinton did say emphatically that the government of the United States can play a constructive role in changing the direction of things, and he did say that the president has a responsibility to promote actively the general welfare (as the Constitution indicates).

Given the condition of the country, Bill Clinton's words have not been bold enough, and his deeds have not lived up to the words. There have long been problems in the words. Too much acceptance, even if vaguely, of the rhetoric of global free markets and the globalization of business and investment. Too much vagueness or contradiction in his statements about the industrial base of the economy and the possibility of restoring it. The focus on people as a resource, though correct, seems at times to be a substitute for a direct effort to stimulate investment in technology and production. His stimulus program was not much to begin with, and he accepted defeat on this without much of a fight. The same is true for the rejection of his investment tax credit proposal. The long-term program for spending on infrastructure is probably much too small. He has, at least in public, dropped the earlier emphasis on shifting money from mergers and speculation to productive investment.

He has rarely gone beyond sound-bite descriptions of what has gone wrong at the top of this economy. He has not, therefore, built up a base of well-informed support for reforming or circumventing existing institutions. He also failed in the early months to make a serious effort to educate people on the deficit issue. Other than occasional brief comments, he has not attempted to explain to the country that in the midst of declining production, income, and consumption, you can't solve debt and deficit problems with policies that further reduce income and consumption. That is, it is wrong and futile to make deep cuts in government programs in order to free up money for large banks and corporations that have had plenty of money to finance mergers and other forms of speculation. The only effect the cuts will have with any certainty is to further depress purchasing power.

Clinton has never made any criticism, that this author is aware of, of the Establishment's global economic policies, the International Monetary Fund's policies, or any other national or private policy concerning economic development. I could not locate a single instance in which he focused on economic backwardness, Third World poverty, or the need for development. All, or nearly all, of his concern with international affairs has been on increasing "free trade" and, to a lesser extent, supporting agreements on the environment. While in Japan promoting the idea that governments should play a smaller role in international trade (thereby increasing the role for organized private interests), Clinton seemed to be telling the Japanese to give up policies that helped to make them a successful nation. Does Clinton want Japan to imitate Wall Street?

The mainstream media have accused Clinton of backing away from promises. Television news organizations probably gave more air time to Clinton's compromise on military policy toward homosexuals than they had devoted over the preceding 20 years to high-level misuse of economic power. The media also seemed well prepared to make deficit reduction the measure of Clinton's success. The pressure on Clinton to cut and reduce rather than invest and build was coming from a variety of sources outside of the government. There were also internal sources of such pressure.

In July of 1993 the *New York Times*[45] reported that White House economic policy was increasingly influenced by Robert Rubin, former co-chairman of Goldman Sachs and the director of President Clinton's new National Economic Council. According to the report, Rubin was making his mark in a number of areas. He was fighting to protect China's preferred trading status, to protect employers' interests in health care reform, and to pursue a tougher policy in negotiations with Japan. Reportedly, Rubin had also surfaced as a Clinton administration leader on the deficit issue. Even though Rubin was being criticized by members of the Business Roundtable* for the administration's failure to make deep cuts in government spending, he was a leading deficit hawk within the administration. At Goldman Sachs, Rubin had been involved in the kind of high-level paper shuffling that Bill Clinton had said was undermining the economy. Goldman Sachs, along with Morgan Stanley; First Boston; Dillon, Read; and others, had arranged corporate mergers and acquisitions costing hundreds of billions of dollars in the 1980s. Goldman Sachs and other invest-

---

* The Business Roundtable is a lobbying organization created in 1972. It is led by the top men at major banks, insurance companies, and corporations. It has consistently favored smaller government (Domhoff, 1983, pp. 135-36; Dye, 1983, p. 155).

ment banks were paid many millions of dollars to arrange these deals. For example, Goldman Sachs earned $10 million arranging U.S. Steel's 1982 buyout of Marathon Oil. Rubin's firm was paid $18.5 million for its role in the 1984 Texaco takeover of Getty Oil, and it was paid $15 million for facilitating General Electric's 1986 acquisition of RCA/NBC.[46] In other words, Rubin would seem to have been part of the problem.

According to the *Times* story, Rubin was in mid-1993 pushing President Clinton to "remain credible with the financial markets." If President Clinton didn't have the time, or stomach, to read *Fortune*, the *Wall Street Journal*, or *Foreign Affairs*, it didn't make much difference. He had Rubin and the Blackstone Group's Roger Altman nearby. Given the extremism of Wall Street's publicized views, Rubin and Altman could even play the roles of moderate and compromiser and still steer policies away from serious change, meaning reform and circumvention.

In his inaugural address President Clinton had stated a resolve "to reform our politics so that power and privilege no longer shout down the voice of the people." He went on to say that those who serve in Washington should "resolve to make our Government a place for what Franklin Roosevelt called bold, persistent experimentation, a Government for our tomorrows, not our yesterdays. Let us give this capital back to the people to whom it belongs."

The only bold experimentation that the Establishment seems interested in is finding ways to make the majority of people bear the burden for the Establishment's destructive actions. If their fixation on government spending and the deficit becomes Clinton's focus, then "our tomorrows" will be sacrificed to "our yesterdays." With people such as Altman and Rubin in the White House, power and privilege may not need to shout down the people, whispers may be sufficient.

It may be that Establishment forces are simply expecting that Clinton will listen to those whispers. The demands put forth by *Fortune* and the rhetoric used by establishment organs are extreme. When Clinton is warned that the "financial markets" can bring government policymakers to their knees, this may be as much an attempt to intimidate Clinton as it is an accurate assessment of where economic power resides. It may be part bluff, part real threat. If President Clinton is going to stop the decline and restore progress, he will have to call that bluff and be prepared to deal with the threat. He will also have to stop hearing the whispers.

President Clinton should look again at his former mentor's analysis of growth and decline, progress and reaction. If he moves, or continues to move, in the direction of pleasing Rubin, Altman, Peterson, Rockefeller, *Fortune*, the *Wall Street Journal*, etc., he will end up being the financial community's overseer of decline. The further he moves toward being the manager of decline and the enforcer of austerity, the more he will be part of what Quigley called the reactionary process.

President Clinton should also take a fresh look at President Kennedy's effort to institute a process of reform and circumvention. Not all of it could be literally repeated, and in some ways it would have to be intensified, but it is the most relevant and recent example of a U.S. program for progress. Tax policy should encourage productive investment and discourage speculation, mergers, and other non-productive activity. Clinton should not give up on the investment tax credit. The president should take a fresh look at Kennedy's proposals to reduce the incentives for wealthy people and private firms to transfer capital out of the United States. He should review Kennedy's overall budget strategy in regard to support for technological progress, energy development, and education of mathematicians, scientists, and engineers.

President Clinton might also give new thought to what President Kennedy's purposes were, beyond competing with the Soviet Union, in promoting the space program. In September 1962, President Kennedy said:[47]

> We choose to go to the moon. We choose to go to the moon in this decade, and do the other things, not because they are easy but because they are hard; because that goal will serve to organize and measure the best of our energies and skills; because that challenge is one that we are willing to accept, one we are unwilling to postpone, and one which we intend to win—and the others too.

The country needs a new example that demonstrates what the organization of our energies can accomplish. President Clinton should identify new projects that have great potential inspirational or practical payoff, and he should push them relentlessly.

President Kennedy criticized the policies of the World Bank and the private banks. He looked for and initiated changes in lending and aid policy in an effort to circumvent those institutions. The Alliance for Progress was an instrument of reform and circumvention. Kennedy's rejection of neo-colonialism and his economic initiatives had the potential to change qualitatively the international role of the United States. Such change was consistent with both the nation's interests and with what is right. President Clinton should seek out people in other nations who are committed to progress. The need for change is at least as great today as it was in Kennedy's time.

President Clinton might take a very hard look at what President Kennedy was trying to do in his last 18 months in the areas of money supply, credit, and loans. What new government actions and policies were either under consideration or in the process of being adopted? If this review does not provide President Clinton with ideas for circumventing the existing financial processes, there are other possibilities. He might assemble a team of non-Establishment experts and direct them to provide a peacetime version of the United States government's intervention in the banking system during World War II. Since this peacetime version will not require the diversion of any resources to war production, it will have even greater potential for immediate improvements in production and standard of living. Even with the demands of war, those policies ended the Depression and improved the conditions of life. President Clinton cannot expect from the financial Establishment the compliance shown during World War II. It will be, to say the least, displeased.

As noted earlier, John Kennedy thought that only the president can defend "the public good and the public interest against all the narrow private interests which operate in our society." He also said that "only a President who recognizes the true nature of this hard challenge can fulfill this historic function." Fulfilling that function in the 1990s will not be easy. Unless the attempt is made, the decline will continue and might accelerate. President Clinton will have to decide what his life and his presidency will mean in the end. If all he wants is a few kind words from members of the Establishment, or just to be listed with Ford, Carter, Reagan, and Bush as one of the presidents who served during the decline, then he need not rouse himself. If he wants his life's work to mean more than that, he has to engage the enemy, and do it in a clear and public way.

Bibliography

Advisory Commission on Intergovernmental Relations. 1983. *Significant Features of Fiscal Federalism*. Washington, DC: Advisory Commission on Intergovernmental Relations.

Bachrach, Peter, and Elihu Bergman. 1973. *Power and Choice: The Formulation of American Population Policy*. Lexington, MA: Lexington Books/D.C. Heath.

Baigent, Michael, Richard Leigh, and Henry Lincoln. 1982. *Holy Blood, Holy Grail*. New York: Dell Publishing.

—. 1986. *The Messianic Legacy*. New York: Dell Publishing.

Bailey, Stephen Kemp. 1950. *Congress Makes a Law*. New York: Columbia University Press.

Balogh, Thomas. 1966. *The Economics of Poverty*. New York: Macmillan Company.

Barkley, Katherine, and Steve Weissman. 1970. "The Eco-Establishment." *Ramparts* (May): 48-54.

Barlett, Donald L., and James B. Steele. 1992. *America: What Went Wrong?* Kansas City, MO: Andrews and McMeel.

Barney, Gerald O. 1977. *The Unfinished Agenda*. New York: Thomas Y. Crowell Company.

Bartlett, Sarah. 1989. "A Vicious Circle Keeps Latin America in Debt." *New York Times* (January 15): E5.

Behrman, Jack N. 1970. *National Interests and the Multinational Enterprise*. Englewood Cliffs, NJ: Prentice-Hall, Inc.

Belair, Felix, Jr. 1962. "F.T.C. Is Studying Steel Advances." *New York Times* (April 12): 1, 21.

Bell, Daniel. 1973. *The Coming of Post-Industrial Society.* New York: Basic Books.

Bennett, Robert A. 1980. "The Talk of New Orleans: Agonies of World Banking." *New York Times* (June 8): Business, 1, 6-7.

—. 1982. "The Puzzling Tangle of Global Finance." *New York Times* (December 12): Business, 1, 10.

Bernstein, Irving. 1991. *Promises Kept: John F. Kennedy's New Frontier.* New York: Oxford University Press.

Bird, Kai. 1992. *The Chairman: John J. McCloy and the Making of the American Establishment.* New York: Simon & Schuster.

Blair, John M. 1972. *Economic Concentration.* New York: Harcourt Brace Jovanovich, Inc.

—. 1976. *The Control of Oil.* New York: Vintage Books/Random House.

Bluestone, Barry, and Bennett Harrison. 1982. *The Deindustrialization of America.* New York: Basic Books.

Blumberg, Paul. 1980. *Inequality in an Age of Decline.* New York: Oxford University Press.

Bowles, Chester. 1971. *Promises to Keep: My Years in Public Life, 1941-1969.* New York: Harper Row.

Brooke, James. 1985. "Peruvian Leader Issues Appeal on Debt." *New York Times* (September 24): 8.

—. 1989. "Big Latin Debtors Find That, Lacking Austerity, Relief Is Not Coming Soon." *New York Times* (July 26): 4.

Burns, James MacGregor. 1961. *John Kennedy: A Political Profile.* New York: Avon Book Division, Hearst Corporation.

Business Week. 1963. "Steel Price Increases Prompt Antitrust Probe." *Business Week* (October 26): 25.

—. 1979. "Last Chance For Investment Vs. Speculation." *Business Week* (December 31): 56-62.

—. 1985. "Playing With Fire: As Speculation Replaces Investment, Our Economic Future Is At Stake." *Business Week* (September 16): 78-90.

—. 1986. "The Hollow Corporation." *Business Week* (March 3): 57-85.

Caulfield, Henry P. 1989. "The Conservation and Environmental Movements: An Historical Analysis." In *Environmental Politics and Policy: Theories and Evidence,* James P. Lester, ed. Durham, NC: Duke University Press. 13-56.

Chernow, Ron. 1990. *The House of Morgan.* New York: Touchstone/Simon & Schuster.

Chomsky, Noam. 1993. *Rethinking Camelot: JFK, the Vietnam War, and U.S. Political Culture.* Boston: South End Press.

Clinton, William. 1992. Announcement of Candidacy for President (October 3, 1991). In Robert E. Levin, *Bill Clinton: The Inside Story.* New York: Shapolsky Publishers, Inc. 277-87.

—. 1992a. "Putting People First: A National Economic Strategy for America." In Robert E. Levin, *Bill Clinton: The Inside Story*. New York: Shapolsky Publishers, Inc. 250-76.

—. 1992b. Acceptance Speech, Democratic National Convention. *New York Times* (July 17): A12-13.

Clinton, William, and Albert Gore. 1992. *Putting People First: How We Can All Change America*. New York: Times Books/Random House.

Collier, Peter, and David Horowitz. 1976. *The Rockefellers: An American Dynasty*. New York: Signet/New American Library.

—. 1984. *The Kennedys: An American Drama*. New York: Summit Books.

Commission on Money and Credit. 1961. *Money and Credit: Their Influence on Jobs, Prices, and Growth*. Englewood Cliffs, NJ: Prentice-Hall, Inc.

Consumer Reports. 1979-1992. Annual reports on new cars. *Consumer Reports*. April issues.

Council of Economic Advisors. 1973-1993. *Economic Indicators*. Washington, DC: U.S. Government Printing Office.

—. 1983. *Economic Report of the President*. Washington, DC: U.S. Government Printing Office.

Council on Foreign Relations. 1963. *Annual Report, Council on Foreign Relations*. New York: Harold Pratt House.

—. 1988. *Annual Report*. New York: Council on Foreign Relations, Inc.

Cowan, Edward. 1961. "Kennedy Halts Business Group's Secret Briefings." *Washington Post* (March 19): A2.

Cowell, Alan. 1982. "The I.M.F.'s Imbroglio in Africa." *New York Times* (March 14): 4F.

Crittenden, Ann. 1979. "Poland, in Bid for Loan, Will Let West's Banks Monitor Economy." *New York Times* (January 26): 1.

—. 1979a. "Managing OPEC's Money" *New York Times* (June 24): Sec. 3, 1.

—. 1979b. "Economy Shaky, Jamaican Chief Has Tough Balancing Act." *New York Times* (October 1): 2.

Davenport, John. 1962. "The Priority of Politics over Economics." *Fortune* (October): 88-91, 188-200.

Davidson, Paul. 1978. *Money and the Real World*, 2nd ed. New York: John Wiley.

Davis, Deborah. 1991. *Katharine the Great: Katharine Graham and Her Washington Post Empire*. New York: Sheridan Square Press, Inc.

DeBell, Garrett, 1970. *The Environmental Handbook*. New York: Ballantine Books and Friends of the Earth.

Demerath, Nicholas J. 1976. *Birth Control and Foreign Policy: The Alternatives to Family Planning*. New York: Harper and Row.

Department of Commerce. 1965. *The Statistical History of the United States*. Stamford, CT: Fairfield Publishers.

Dickson, Paul. 1971. *Think Tanks*. New York: Atheneum.

Dobson, Andrew. 1991. "Introduction." In Andrew Dobson, ed., *The Green Reader*. San Francisco: Mercury House. 4-9.

Domhoff, G. William. 1967. *Who Rules America?* Englewood Cliffs, NJ: Prentice-Hall, Inc.

—. 1971. *Higher Circles: The Governing Class in America*. New York: Vintage Books/Random House.

—. 1983. *Who Rules America Now? A View for the '80s*. Englewood Cliffs, NJ: Prentice-Hall, Inc.

Dye, Thomas R. 1983. *Who's Running America? The Reagan Years*. Englewood Cliffs, NJ: Prentice-Hall, Inc.

Economist, The. 1987. "Japanese Mergers." *The Economist* (March 21): 94.

Ehrlich, Paul. 1968. *The Population Bomb*. New York: Ballantine Books.

—. 1973. "Playboy Interview: 1970." In Edward Pohlman, ed., *Population: A Clash of Prophets*. New York: Mentor Book/New American Library. 13-28.

Epstein, Edward Jay. 1983. "Ruling the World of Money." *Harper's* (November): 43-48.

Evening Bulletin The. 1977. "An Open Letter to the American People." Philadelphia *Evening Bulletin* (August 31): A17.

Evans, Rowland, Jr., and Robert D. Novak. 1972. *Nixon In The White House*. New York: Vintage Books/Random House.

Falk, Richard A. 1971. *This Endangered Planet*. New York: Vintage Books/Random House.

Farnsworth, Clyde H. 1979. "Debt and the Third World." *New York Times* (June 10): Sec. 3, 1.

—. 1980. "World Bank Under McNamara." *New York Times* (June 10): D1.

—. 1983. "Third World Debts Mean Fewer Jobs For Peoria." *New York Times* (December 11): E3.

—. 1984. "A Turbulent Rescue Role For the I.M.F." *New York Times* (May 4): 31-32.

—. 1986. "I.M.F. May Bar Peru From Further Credits." *New York Times* (February 7): 30.

—. 1989. "Debt Crisis For Banks Said to End." *New York Times* (January 4): 25.

Feis, Herbert. 1930. *Europe: The World's Banker, 1870-1914*. New Haven: Yale University Press.

Fortune. 1961. "Activism in the White House." *Fortune* (June): 117-18.

—. 1962. "The Quality of Foreign Aid." *Fortune* (February): 79-81.

—. 1962a. "Steel: The Ides of April." *Fortune* (May): 97-100.

—. 1963. "'What the Hell Do Those Fellows Want?'" *Fortune* (February): 81-82.

—. 1963a. "How to Save the Tax Cut." *Fortune* (March): 79-80.

—. 1963b. "The Dream Businessmen Are Losing." *Fortune* (September): 91-92.

—. 1981-1991. "Deals of the Year." *Fortune*. (Annual reports).

—. 1992. "Special Report." *Fortune* (October 19): 48-100.

—. 1992a. "His First 100 Days." *Fortune* (November 30): 41-54.

—. 1993. "Clintonomics and You." *Fortune* (March 22): 30-57.

Foundation Center. 1985. *Annual Report*. New York: Foundation Center, Foundation Grants Index.

Fox, Stephen. 1981. *The American Conservation Movement*. Madison, WI: University of Wisconsin Press.

Garrison, Jim. 1988. *On the Trail of the Assassins: My Investigation and Prosecution of the Murder of President Kennedy*. New York: Sheridan Square Press.

Garten, Jeffrey. 1992/93. "The 100-Day Economic Agenda." *Foreign Affairs* (Winter): 16-31.

Geyelin, Philip. 1963. "U.S. Support for a World Monetary Study Is Victory for Administration 'Activists.' " *Wall Street Journal* (October 3): 16.

Gibson, Donald E. 1990. "The Role of the Establishment in the Antinuclear Movement." *Sociological Spectrum* 10: 321-40.

—. 1993. "Post-Industrialism: Prosperity or Decline?" *Sociological Focus*. 26: 147-63.

Giglio, James N. 1991. *The Presidency of John F. Kennedy*. Lawrence, KS: University Press of Kansas.

Goodwin, Doris Kearns. 1991. *Lyndon Johnson and the American Dream*. New York: St. Martin's Press.

Greenhouse, Steven. 1993. "When Robert Rubin Talks..." *New York Times* (July 15): F1, 6.

Greider, William. 1987. *The Secrets of the Temple*. New York: Touchstone/Simon & Schuster.

Guthman, Edwin O., and C. Richard Allen (eds.). 1993. *RFK: Collected Speeches*. New York: Viking Penguin.

Hailey, Foster. 1962. "Hodges Warns of Inflation Danger From Steel Price Increase." *New York Times* (April 13): 20.

Hamilton, Alexander. 1850 (1790). "National Bank." In John C. Hamilton, ed. *The Works of Alexander Hamilton*, Vol. III. New York: Charles S. Francis & Co. 106-46.

—. 1850a (1791). "Manufacturers." In John C. Hamilton, ed., *The Works of Alexander Hamilton*, Vol. III. New York: Charles S. Francis & Co. 192-284.

Hardin, Garrett. 1973. "Parenthood: Right or Privilege?" In Edward Pohlman, ed., *Population: A Clash of Prophets*. New York: Mentor Book/New American Library. 351-53.

Harman, Willis W. 1976. *An Incomplete Guide to the Future*. New York: W.W. Norton & Company.

Harrison, Bennett, and Barry Bluestone. 1988. *The Great U-Turn: Corporate Restructuring and the Polarizing of America*. New York: Basic Books.

Hayek, Friedrich. 1944. *The Road to Serfdom*. Chicago: University of Chicago Press.

Hazlitt, Henry. 1962. "To Restore Confidence." *Newsweek* (May 14): 92.

—. 1963. "Sham Tax Cut." *Newsweek* (September 2): 70.

—. 1963a. "Exporting Inflation." *Newsweek*. (September 9): 78.

—. 1963b. "A Shortsighted Tariff." *Newsweek* (October 28): 84.

—. 1963c. "Tax Cut in Wonderland." *Newsweek* (November 4): 90.

—. 1963d. "Does Foreign Aid Aid?" *Newsweek* (November 25): 97.

Heath, Jim F. 1969. *John F. Kennedy and the Business Community*. Chicago: University of Chicago Press.

Heilbroner, Robert L. 1980. *An Inquiry Into the Human Prospect*. New York: W.W. Norton & Company.

Heller, Walter W. 1966. *New Dimensions of Political Economy*. Cambridge, MA: Harvard University Press.

Heller, Walter W., Kermit Gordon, and James Tobin. 1988 (1961). "The American Economy in 1961: Problems and Policies." Statement of the Council of Economic Advisers before the Joint Economic Committee, Monday, March 6, 1961. In James Tobin and Murray Weidenbaum, eds., *Two Revolutions in Economic Policy*. Cambridge, MA: The MIT Press. 17-72.

Hersh, Burton. 1992. *The Old Boys: The American Elite and the Origins of the CIA*. New York: Charles Scribner & Sons.

Hersh, Seymour M. 1983. *The Price of Power: Kissinger in the Nixon White House*. New York: Summit Books.

Hilsman, Roger. 1964. *To Move a Nation*. New York: A Delta Book/Dell Publishing Co.

Hoffman, William. 1971. *David*. New York: Lyle Stuart.

Holusha, John. 1978. "Will Booming Mergers Stifle Economic Growth?" *Wilmington Evening Journal* (September 11): 12.

Hoopes, Roy. 1963. *The Steel Crisis*. New York: J. Day Co.

Hyman, Sidney. 1975. *The Aspen Idea*. Norman, OK: University of Oklahoma Press.

Inter-American Development Bank. 1980. (July) "External Public Debt of the Latin American Countries." Washington, DC: Inter-American Development Bank.

Isaacson, Walter, and Evan Thomas. 1986. *The Wise Men*. New York: Touchstone Books/Simon & Schuster.

Jedel, Michael Jay, and John Stamm. 1973. "The Battle Over Jobs: An Appraisal of Recent Publications on the Employment Effects of U.S. Multinational Corporations." In Duane Kujawa, ed., *American Labor and the Multinational Corporation*. New York: Praeger Publishers. 144-91.

Johnson, Donald Bruce, ed. 1978. *National Party Platforms*, Vol. II, Chicago: University of Illinois Press.

Johnson, Lyndon. 1965. "Natural Beauty of our Country." *House Documents, 89th Congress, 1st Session*. Washington, DC: Government Printing Office.

—. 1965a. "National Wilderness Preservation System." *House Documents, 89th Congress, 1st Session*. Washington, DC: Government Printing Office.

—. 1966. "State of the Union Message." *House Documents. 89th Congress, 2nd Session*. Washington, DC: Government Printing Office.

—. 1967 (1964). "The Goals." In Marvin E. Gettleman and David Mermelstein, eds. *The Great Society Reader*. New York: Vintage Books/Random House. 15-19.

Johnson, Paul. 1993. "Colonialism's Back—and Not a Moment Too Soon." *New York Times Magazine* (April 18): 22, 43-44.

Kendrick, John W. 1973. *Postwar Productivity Trends in the United States, 1948-1969*. New York: National Bureau of Economic Research/Columbia University Press.

Kennedy, John F. 1940 (1962). *Why England Slept*. Garden City, NY: Dolphin Books/Doubleday & Co.

—. 1961. *The Strategy of Peace*. Edited and introduction by Allan Nevins. New York: Popular Library.

—. 1961a. "Program to Restore Momentum to the American Economy." *House Documents, 87th Congress, 1st Session, Doc. No. 81*. Washington, DC: Government Printing Office.

—. 1961b. "Natural Resources." *House Documents, 87th Congress, 1st Session, Doc. No. 94*. Washington, DC: Government Printing Office.

—. 1961c. "Foreign Aid." *House Documents, 87th Congress, 1st Session, Doc. No. 117*. Washington, DC: Government Printing Office.

—. 1961d. "Our Federal Tax System." *House Documents, 87th Congress, 1st Session, Doc. No. 140*. Washington, DC: Government Printing Office.

—. 1962 (1988). "Economic Report of the President." In James Tobin and Murray Weidenbaum, eds., *Two Revolutions in Economic Policy*. Cambridge, MA: The MIT Press. 87-113.

—. 1962a. "Our Conservation Program." *House Documents, 87th Congress, 2nd Session, Doc. No. 348*. Washington, DC: Government Printing Office.

—. 1962b. News Conference, April 11. *New York Times* (April 12): 20.

—. 1962c. News Conference, April 18. *New York Times* (April 19): 16.

—. 1963a. "State of the Union Address." *House Documents, 88th Congress, 1st Session, Doc. No. 2*. Washington, DC: Government Printing Office.

—. 1963b. "Revision of Our Tax Structure." *House Documents, 88th Congress, 1st Session, Doc. No. 43*. Washington, DC: Government Printing Office.

—. 1963c. "Program for Education." *House Documents, 88th Congress, 1st Session, Doc. No. 54*. Washington, DC: Government Printing Office.

—. 1963d. "Our Foreign Assistance Act." *House Documents, 88th Congress, 1st Session, Doc. No. 94*. Washington, DC: Government Printing Office.

—. 1964. *The Burden and the Glory*. Allen Nevins, ed. New York: Harper &

Row.

—. 1964a (1955). *Profiles In Courage.* New York: Harper & Row.

Kihss, Peter. 1965. "Man-in-the-Street in Rebel Area Insists that Movement Isn't Red." *New York Times* (May 4): 14.

Koenig, Louis W. 1964. "Kennedy and Steel: The Great Price Dispute." In Alan F. Westin, ed., *The Centers of Power: 3 Cases in American National Government.* New York: Harcourt, Brace & World. 1-52.

Kolko, Joyce. 1974. *America and the Crisis of World Capitalism.* Boston: Beacon Press.

Kotz, David. 1978. *Bank Control of Large Corporations in the United States.* Los Angeles: University of California Press.

Krock, Arthur. 1963. "Mr. Kennedy's Management of the News." *Fortune* (March): 82, 199-202.

Langer, Gary. 1992. "What Voters Really Want From Clinton." *Wall Street Journal* (November 16): A12.

Leacock, Ruth. 1979. "JFK, Business, and Brazil." *Hispanic American Historical Review* 59: 636-73.

—. 1981 " 'Promoting Democracy': The United States and Brazil, 1964-68." *Prologue* 13: 77-99.

Lee, Martin A., and Bruce Shlain. 1985. *Acid Dreams: The CIA, LSD, and the Sixties Rebellion.* New York: Grove Press, Inc.

Lekachman, Robert. 1966. *The Age of Keynes.* New York: McGraw-Hill Book Company.

Levin, Robert E. 1992. *Bill Clinton: The Inside Story.* New York: Shapolsky Publishers, Inc.

Life. 1961. "Kennedy Economics, Short-Term." *Life* (February 10): 26.

—. 1962. "For a Year's Foreign Policy: 'A' for J.F.K." *Life* (April 13): 4.

—. 1962a. "How to Put More Zing into the Economy." *Life* (June 8): 4.

—. 1962b. "A Businessman's Letter to J.F.K. and His Reply." *Life* (July 6): 30-34.

—. 1963. "How to Rescue the Tax Cut." *Life* (March 1): 4.

—. 1963a. "Why Kennedy's Tax Cut Trouble Gets Deeper." *Life* (March 29): 4.

—. 1963b. "Unblock That Merger Track!" *Life* (April 5): 4.

—. 1963c. "Misery with the Dollar or Happiness?" *Life* (August 2): 4.

—. 1963d. "Press the War in Vietnam." *Life* (November 22): 4.

Loftus, Joseph A. 1962. "Steel Rise Investigation by Grand Jury Ordered; Blough Defends Pricing." *New York Times* (April 13): 1, 19.

—. 1962a. "Kennedy, by Subduing Steel, Bids for a Place in the Roster of 'Strong' Presidents." *New York Times* (April 15): 54.

Lovins, Amory B. 1977. *Soft Energy Paths: Toward A Durable Peace.* New York: Harper Colophon/Harper & Row.

Lowenthal, Abraham F. 1972. *The Dominican Intervention.* Cambridge, MA: Harvard University Press.

Lundberg, Ferdinand. 1937. *America's 60 Families*. New York: The Vanguard Press.
—. 1975. *The Rockefeller Syndrome*. Secaucus, NJ: Lyle Stuart Inc.

Magdoff, Harry. 1969. *The Age of Imperialism*. New York: Monthly Review Press.
Malthus, Thomas Robert. 1960. *On Population*. New York: Modern Library.
Markmann, Charles Lam, and Mark Sherwin. 1961. *John F. Kennedy: A Sense of Purpose*. New York: St. Martin's Press.
Marks, John. 1980. *The Search for the "Manchurian Candidate": The CIA and Mind Control*. New York: McGraw-Hill Book Company.
Marquis Who's Who. 1962-63. *Who's Who in America*. Chicago: Marquis Who's Who.
—. 1978-79. *Who's Who in America*. Chicago: Marquis Who's Who.
—. 1992-93. *Who's Who in America*. New Providence, NJ: Marquis Who's Who.
Marrs, Jim. 1989. *Crossfire: The Plot That Killed Kennedy*. New York: Carroll & Graf Publishers, Inc.
Mathewson, Joseph D. 1963. "U.S. Seeks High Court Rulings to Upset Some Business Combinations." *Wall Street Journal* (July 22): 1, 10.
Mayer, Martin. 1990. *The Greatest-Ever Bank Robbery*. New York: Collier Books/Macmillan.
McConnell, Grant. 1963. *Steel and the Presidency, 1962*. New York: W.W. Norton & Co.
—. 1967. *The Modern Presidency*. New York: St. Martin's Press.
McDonald, Forrest. 1982. *Alexander Hamilton, A Biography*. New York: W.W. Norton & Company.
McRobie, George. 1981. *Small Is Possible*. New York: Harper & Row.
Medvin, Norman. 1974. *The Energy Cartel: Who Runs the American Oil Industry*. New York: Vintage Books/Random House.
Mesarovic, Mihajlo, and Edward Pestel. 1974. *Mankind At The Turning Point*. New York: Signet/New American Library.
Metz, Robert. 1981. "Oil Companies' Mineral Offers." *New York Times* (March 16).
Miller, Judith. 1977. "Sounding Alarms on Foreign Debt." *New York Times* (September 18): F1, F4.
Miroff, Bruce. 1976. *Pragmatic Illusions*. New York: David McKay Company, Inc.
Mitchell, Daniel J.B. 1976. *Labor Issues of American International Trade and Investment*. Baltimore, MD: John Hopkins University Press.
Moody's Investors Service. 1963. *Moody's Bank & Finance Manual*. New York: Moody's Investors Service, Inc.
—. 1964. *Moody's Industrial Manual*. New York: Moody's Investors Service, Inc.
—. 1992. *Moody's Industrial Manual*. New York: Moody's Investors Service,

Inc.

Moore, George S. 1963. "International Growth: Challenge to U.S. Banks." *The National Banking Review* (September): 1-14.

Mosley, Leonard. 1978. *Dulles: A Biography of Eleanor, Allen and John Foster Dulles and Their Family Network.* New York:Dell Publishing Company.

Murphy, Charles J.V. 1963. "Foreign Aid: Billions in Search of a Good Reason." *Fortune* (March): 126-30, 205-12.

Myers, Gustavus. 1917. *History of the Great American Fortunes*, Vol. III. Chicago: Charles H. Kerr & Company.

Neuhaus, Richard. 1971. *In Defense of People.* New York: Macmillan.

New York Times. 1962. "Spokesman for Steel: Roger Miles Blough." *New York Times* (April 13): 18.

—. 1962a. "Victory On Steel Expected to Spur Kennedy Policies." *New York Times* (April 15): 1, 55.

—. 1963. "Military Seizes Dominican Rule; Bosch Is Deposed." *New York Times* (September 26): 1, 3.

—. 1963a. "U.S. Orders Missions Home." *New York Times* (October 6): 33.

—. 1965. "Sukarno Threatens U.N. Bolt if Council Takes In Malaysia." *New York Times* (January 1): 1, 2.

—. 1965a. "Malaysia Asks Aid of U.N. for Defense." *New York Times* (January 7): 1, 4.

—. 1965b. "U.S. Sending Bunker on Jakarta Mission." *New York Times* (March 23): 1, 5.

—. 1965c. "Foe of Revolution: Elias Wessin y Wessin." *New York Times* (April 30): 14.

—. 1965d. "Bosch Assails Landings." *New York Times* (May 2): 5.

—. 1979. "Ousted Turk Is Backed by Party." *New York Times* (November 6): A4.

—. 1980. "Poland Is Rationing Meat for Christmas." *New York Times* (December 19): A3.

—. 1981. "Warning on Credits." *New York Times* (July 16): D4.

—. 1984. "Key Sections From Study of Latin Region by Reagan Panel." *New York Times* (January 12): 6-7.

—. 1984a. "Debt and Politics." *New York Times* (March 11): 8F.

—. 1992. "Old Hands for Clinton's New Economic Team." *New York Times* (December 11): A16.

Newman, John M. 1991. *JFK and Vietnam: Deception, Intrigue, and the Struggle for Power.* New York: Warner Books.

Newsweek. 1980. "Worried Banks For the Poor." *Newsweek* (October 6): 78-79.

Nossiter, Bernard D. 1961. "Kennedy and Fed Clash Again." *Washington Post* (March 24): A4.

—. 1964. *The Mythmakers.* Boston: Beacon Press.

Nuñez, Julio E. 1963. "The Importance of Latin America's Elite." *Fortune* (January): 70, 210.

O'Donnell, Kenneth P., and David F. Powers. 1973. *Johnny, We Hardly Knew Ye.* New York: Pocket Books.

Outdoor Recreation Resources Review Commission. 1962. *Report of the Outdoor Recreation Resources Review Commission.*

Paper, Lewis J. 1975. *The Promise and the Performance: The Leadership of John F. Kennedy.* New York: Crown Publishers, Inc.

Parmet, Herbert S. 1983. *JFK, The Presidency of John F. Kennedy.* New York: The Dial Press.

Payer, Cheryl. 1974. *The Debt Trap: The International Monetary Fund and the Third World.* New York: Monthly Review Press.

Pear, Robert. 1992. "Ranks of U.S. Poor Reach 35.7 Million, The Most Since '64." *New York Times* (September 4): 1, 12.

Peterson, Peter G. 1987. "The Morning After." *Atlantic Monthly* (October): 43-69.

Phillips, Kevin. 1993. *Boiling Point.* New York: Random House.

Pine, Art. 1984. "Unpopular Plan: IMF Program to Aid Peru Causes Turmoil Over Austerity Steps." *Wall Street Journal* (April 20): 1, 11.

Pohlman, Edward. 1973. *Population: A Clash of Prophets.* New York: Mentor Book/New American Library.

Pomfret, John D. 1962. "Competition Is Held Key Factor In Steel Industry's Price Rise." *New York Times* (April 13): 19.

Prouty, L. Fletcher. 1973. *The Secret Team.* Englewood Cliffs, NJ: Prentice-Hall, Inc.

—. 1989 "Kennedy and the Vietnam Commitment." In Robert J. Groden and Harrison Edward Livingstone, *High Treason.* New York: The Conservatory Press. 403-7.

—. 1992. *JFK, The CIA, Vietnam and the Plot to Assassinate John F. Kennedy.* New York: Birch Lane Press/Carol Publishing.

Quigley, Carroll. 1979 (1961). *The Evolution of Civilizations.* Indianapolis, IN: Liberty Press.

—. 1966. *Tragedy and Hope: A History of the World in Our Time.* New York: Macmillan Co.

—. 1981. *The Anglo-American Establishment.* New York: Books in Focus.

Raymont, Henry. 1963. "Dominicans Form 6-Party Cabinet." *New York Times* (September 28): 1, 5.

—. 1963a. "Irate Dominican Junta Reports 'Interference' by U.S. Diplomat." *New York Times* (October 16): 1, 14.

Riding, Alan. 1988. "For Latin America, It's the Decade of Unsupportable Debt." *New York Times* (March 6): Week in Review, 2.

Rockefeller, David, Jr. 1992. "Why I Trust Clinton." *New York Times* (October 16): A17.

Rockefeller, David, Sr. 1966. "What Private Enterprise Means to Latin America." *Foreign Affairs* 44 (April): 403-416.

Rosenman, Samuel I. 1952. *Working with Roosevelt*. New York: Harper & Brothers, Publishers.

Ross, Douglas. 1968. *Robert F. Kennedy: Apostle of Change*. New York: Pocket Books/Simon & Schuster.

Rostow, W. W. 1983. *The Barbaric Counter-Revolution*. Austin, TX: University of Texas Press.

Rowen, Hobart. 1964. *The Free Enterprisers: Kennedy, Johnson and the Business Establishment*. New York: G.P. Putnam's Sons.

Rust, William J. 1985. *Kennedy in Vietnam*. New York: DaCapo Press.

Sampson, Anthony. 1975. *The Seven Sisters and the World They Shared*. New York: Bantam Books.

Schlesinger, Arthur M., Jr. 1965. *A Thousand Days: John F. Kennedy in the White House*. Boston: Houghton Mifflin Company.

Schumacher, E.F. 1973. *Small Is Beautiful*. New York: Perennial Library/Harper & Row.

Schumacher, Edward. 1984. "View From Argentina: Righteous Debt Battle." *New York Times* (June 13): 29, 34.

Sherrill, Robert, 1983. *The Oil Follies of 1970-1980*. Garden City, NY: Anchor Press/Doubleday.

Shoup, Laurence H. 1980. "Jimmy Carter and the Trilateralists: Presidential Roots." In Holly Sklar, ed. *Trilateralism*. Boston: South End Press. 199-211.

Shoup, Laurence H., and William Minter. 1977. *Imperial Brain Trust: The Council on Foreign Relations and United States Foreign Policy*. New York: Monthly Review Press.

Sidey, Hugh. 1964. *John F. Kennedy, President*. New York: Crest Books/Fawcett.

Simon, Julian L. 1981. *The Ultimate Resource*. Princeton, NJ: Princeton University Press.

Solow, Robert M., and James Tobin. 1988. "Introduction." In James Tobin and Murray Weidenbaum, eds. *Two Revolutions in Economic Policy*. Cambridge, MA: The MIT Press. 3-16.

Sorensen, Theodore C. 1965. *Kennedy*. New York: Bantam Books.

SRI International. 1974. *Changing Images of Man*. Menlo Park, CA: Center for the Study of Social Policy, SRI International.

Strauss, Simon D. 1981. "Oil and Copper Don't Mix." *New York Times* (April 12): F3.

Swanberg, W. A. 1972. *Luce and His Empire*. New York: Dell Publishing Co.

Szulc, Tad. 1963. "U.S. Suspends Ties to Santo Domingo." *New York Times* (September 26): 1, 3.

—. 1963a. "U.S. Withdrawing Aides After Coups." *New York Times* (October 5): 1, 5.

—. 1965. "U.S. Sends Airborne Units Into Dominican Republic; O.A.S. Summons Ministers." *New York Times* (April 30): 1, 14.

—. 1965a "U.S. Risk in Caribbean." *New York Times* (May 2): 1, 4.

—. 1965b. "Crisis in Santo Domingo: Anti-U.S. Feeling Surges." *New York Times* (May 15): 1, 10.

Taft Foundation Reporter. 1978. *Taft Foundation Reporter*. Washington, DC: Taft Corporation.

Taus, Esther R. 1981. *The Role of the Treasury in Stabilizing the Economy, 1941-1946*. Washington, DC: University Press of America.

Tax Foundation. 1979. *Facts and Figures on Government Finance*. Washington, DC: Tax Foundation.

Thomas, Jo. 1980. "After Bullets and Ballots, Jamaican Hopes Rise." *New York Times* (November 2): 6E.

Tucker, William. 1982. *Progress and Privilege*. Garden City, NY: Anchor Press/ Doubleday.

U.S. Bureau of the Census. 1985-1991. *Statistical Abstract of the United States*. Washington, DC: U.S. Department of Commerce.

U.S. Congress. 1979. "Midyear Review of the Economy: The Outlook for 1979." *Report of the Joint Economic Committee*. Washington, DC: U.S. Government Printing Office.

U.S. Department of Commerce. 1992. *Survey of Current Business* (June and August).

U.S. Senate Committee on Governmental Affairs. 1980. *Structure of Corporate Concentration*. Washington, D.C.: U.S. Government Printing Office.

Useem, Michael. 1984. *The Inner Circle*. New York: Oxford University Press.

Vatter, Harold G. 1963. *The U.S. Economy in the 1950's*. New York: W.W. Norton & Co.

Vernon, Raymond. 1971. *Sovereignty At Bay: The Multinational Spread of U.S. Enterprises*. New York: Basic Books, Inc.

Wall Street Journal. 1961. "Depression Baby." *Wall Street Journal* (January 4): 10.

—. 1961a. "Foreign Aid-Fact and Fancy." *Wall Street Journal* (January 4): 10.

—. 1961b. "Fading Dreams." *Wall Street Journal* (January 4): 10.

—. 1962. "Those Cantankerous Congressman." *Wall Street Journal* (July 2): 10.

—. 1962a. "A Self-Defeating Strategy." *Wall Street Journal* (July 3): 10.

—. 1962b. "Flunking an Economic Test." *Wall Street Journal* (July 17): 14.

—. 1962c. "An Impractical Pragmatism." *Wall Street Journal* (July 30): 8.

—. 1962d. "No Cause for Celebration." *Wall Street Journal* (August 6): 6.

—. 1962e. "A Short-Sighted Long View." *Wall Street Journal* (September 4): 12.

—. 1962f. "The President and the Planners." *Wall Street Journal* (October 3): 18.

—. 1962g. "The World Bank's Way." *Wall Street Journal* (October 23): 16.

—. 1962h. "The Uses of Presidential Power." *Wall Street Journal* (November 6): 14.

—. 1962i. "A Compliment from Russia." *Wall Street Journal* (November 20): 18.

—. 1962j. "The Professor's Tough Course." *Wall Street Journal* (December 7): 14.

—. 1963. "Passing Debate and Abiding Questions." *Wall Street Journal* (January 14): 16.

—. 1963a. "Message From the Land of Dreams." *Wall Street Journal* (January 18): 16.

—. 1963b. "Too Much Money, Too Little Thought." *Wall Street Journal* (March 26): 18.

—. 1963c. "Enforcer of Progress." *Wall Street Journal* (May 10): 12.

—. 1963d. "Too Much for Keynes." *Wall Street Journal* (July 10): 10.

—. 1963e. "Umbrellas for the Dollar." *Wall Street Journal* (July 18): 12.

—. 1963f. "Kennedy Asks Tax on Foreign-Stock Buying And on Long-Term Lending to Foreigners." *Wall Street Journal* (July 19): 3.

—. 1963g. "Dramatizing the Dollar's Distress." *Wall Street Journal* (July 22): 6.

—. 1963h. "The New Dogmatists." *Wall Street Journal* (August 2): 6.

—. 1963i. "Trapped in a Maze." *Wall Street Journal* (August 6): 14.

—. 1963j. "When Friends Become Foes." *Wall Street Journal* (August 15): 8.

—. 1963k. "Non-Answers to Non-Critics." *Wall Street Journal* (August 27): 12.

—. 1963l. "Those Foolish Businessmen." *Wall Street Journal* (September 19): 12.

—. 1963m. "Government by Rationalization." *Wall Street Journal* (October 3): 16.

—. 1963n. "Search for a Purpose." *Wall Street Journal* (October 15): 16.

—. 1963o. "Wavelets Into Waves." *Wall Street Journal* (October 21): 12.

—. 1963p. "Mercantilists in Liberal Clothing." *Wall Street Journal* (October 31): 16.

—. 1963q. "The Anti-Business Image." *Wall Street Journal* (November 19): 18.

—. 1963r. "Blunt Talk on a Blunt Tool." *Wall Street Journal* (November 19): 18.

—. 1963s. "President Kennedy." *Wall Street Journal* (November 25): 8.

—. 1963t. "A Time for Stock-Taking." *Wall Street Journal* (November 26): 16.

—. 1963u. "Standards of Responsibility." *Wall Street Journal* (December 4): 18.

—. 1992. "Tower of Babble." *Wall Street Journal* (December 15): A18.

—. 1993. "The Clintonites Have Landed." *Wall Street Journal* (February, 19): A14.

—. 1993a. "Clinton Looks Bushed." *Wall Street Journal* (May 21): A10.

—. 1993b. "Turn Back." *Wall Street Journal* (July 12): A12.

Washington Post. 1979. "Big Oil Profits." *Washington Post* (July 26): C1.

Wayne, Leslie. 1983. "Big Steel's Puzzling Strategy." *New York Times* (July 10): 1, 26F.

Ways, Max. 1963. "The Real Case for a Tax Cut." *Fortune* (January): 72-75, 188-198.

Welles, Chris. 1975. *The Last Days of the Club*. New York: E.P. Dutton & Co.

Wendt, Lloyd. 1982. *The Wall Street Journal*. New York: Rand McNally & Co.

Westlake, Melvyn. 1983. "Third World May Hold Key to End Global Recession." *New York Times* (March 8): 34.

Whalen, Richard J. 1964. *The Founding Father: The Story of Joseph P. Kennedy*. New York: Signet Books/The New American Library.

White, Lynn, Jr. 1974. "The Historical Roots of Our Ecological Crisis." In David Spring and Eileen Spring, eds., *Ecology and Religion in History*. New York: Harper & Row. 15-31.

Wilkins, Myra. 1974. *The Maturing of Multinational Enterprise: American Business Abroad from 1914 to 1970*. Cambridge, MA: Harvard University Press.

Williams, Winston. 1984. "The Shrinking of the Steel Industry." *New York Times* (September 23): 4F.

Wofford, Harris. 1980. *Of Kennedy and Kings: Making Sense of the Sixties*. New York: Farrar Straus Giroux.

Wolman, William. 1983. "The IMF's Perilous Plan For Growth." *New York Times* (October 2): Business Sec., 1, 8-9.

Wright, John Winthrop. 1981. "Memo to the Fed: It Ain't Necessarily So About High Rates." *New York Times* (June 21): 2F.

Wyden, Peter. 1979. *Bay of Pigs: The Untold Story*. New York: Simon & Schuster.

Yergin, Daniel. 1991. *The Prize, The Epic Quest For Oil, Money & Power*. New York: Touchstone/Simon & Schuster.

Zlotnick, Jack. 1961. "Population Pressure and Political Indecision." *Foreign Affairs* 39: 683-94.

Endnotes

The citations that follow are to the works listed in the Bibliography; when an author has more than one work listed, the year of the work cited is given.

Introduction

1. Paper, p. 366.
2. *Ibid.*, pp. 68-72, 87, 154.
3. Whalen, p. 426.
4. Bowles, pp. 343, 443.
5. Solow and Tobin, p. 6.
6. Rowen, pp. 37-46, 160, 247, 294.
7. Parmet, pp. 91-99.
8. Sidey, pp. 335-36.
9. Paper, pp. 362, 365.
10. Miroff, pp. 194, 202, 220.
11. *Ibid.*, p. 272.
12. Heath, pp. 127, 129.
13. Giglio, pp. 133, 270.
14. *E.g.*, Heath, pp. 33, 81, 128; Markmann and Sherwin, p. 242; Miroff, pp. 219-22.
15. Schlesinger, pp. 621-23, 630, 1013.
16. *Ibid.*, pp. 646-47, 1012.
17. *Ibid.*, pp. 128-29.
18. *Ibid.*, p. 83.
19. *Ibid.*, p. 623.
20. Sorensen, p. 444.

21. Bernstein, p. 119.
22. Sorensen, p. 201.
23. Bernstein, 121.
24. O'Donnell and Powers, p. 476.
25. Sorensen, pp. 13, 28.
26. *Ibid.*, pp. 522-23.
27. Heller, 1966, pp. 12, 25, 74-81.
28. Paper, p. 354.
29. Schlesinger, pp. 749-56.

Chapter One: Kennedy and U.S. Steel

1. Blair, 1972, p. 635.
2. *E.g.*, McConnell, 1963, p. 4.
3. Sorensen, p. 499.
4. Hailey; Hoopes, p. 36.
5. Hoopes, p. 36.
6. Hailey, p. 20; McConnell, 1963, p. 75; Sorensen, pp. 501-2.
7. Hailey, p. 20; Sorensen, pp. 501-2.
8. McConnell, 1963, p. 77; Sorensen, p. 503.
9. Belair; Sorensen, p. 508.
10. Loftus, 1962.
11. McConnell, 1963, p. 105; Sorensen, pp. 513-15.
12. McConnell, 1963, p. 94.
13. Kennedy, 1962b.
14. McConnell, 1963, pp. 79-80.
15. Kennedy, 1962c.
16. Sorensen, p. 505.
17. *Ibid.*, p. 516.
18. *Ibid.*, pp. 513-14.
19. Schlesinger, pp. 634-40.
20. *New York Times*, 1962a.
21. *Ibid.*
22. *Fortune*, 1962a.
23. McConnell, 1963, pp. 107-9.
24. *Ibid.*, pp. 6-7.
25. *Ibid.*, p. 83.
26. Hoopes, p. 17.
27. Loftus, 1962a.

Chapter Two: The National Program

1. Burns, p. 254.
2. *Ibid.*, p. 255.
3. Kennedy, 1961a, p. 1; Heller, Gordon, and Tobin, p. 59.
4. Kennedy, 1961a, p. 2.

5. Kennedy, 1961, pp. xiv-xv.
6. Heller, Gordon, and Tobin, pp. 19, 20, 50-54.
7. Kennedy, 1961d, p. 3.
8. Kennedy, 1962/1988, p. 103.
9. Rowen, p. 122.
10. Kennedy, 1963a, p. 2.
11. Kennedy, 1963b, pp. 2, 4.
12. Kennedy, 1961b, p. 2.
13. Heller, 1966, pp. 74-76.
14. *Ibid.*, pp. 80-81.
15. *E.g.*, Rowen, pp. 238-246.
16. Kennedy, 1961a, pp. 11, 13; 1961d, pp. 2-3; 1963b, p. 1.
17. *Ibid.*, 1961d, p. 4.
18. *Ibid.*, 1962/1988, pp. 112-13.
19. *E.g.*, Behrman, p. 23; Jedel and Stamm, pp. 186-88; Kolko, pp. 45-46, 59; Mitchell, pp. 78-82; Vernon, p. 190.
20. Kennedy 1961d, pp. 6-7.
21. *Ibid.*, p. 6.
22. *Ibid.*, p. 8.
23. *Ibid.*, 1962/1988, p. 100.
24. *Ibid.*, 1963a, pp. 2-3; 1963b, pp. 4-5.
25. *Ibid.*, 1963b, pp. 17-18.
26. *Ibid.*, 1961d, p. 9.
27. *Ibid.*, 1962/1988, pp. 112-13; 1963b, pp. 16-21.
28. Rowen, p. 246; Solow and Tobin, p. 10.
29. Kennedy, 1961b, p. 6.
30. *Ibid.*, 1962a, p. 8.
31. *Ibid.*, pp. 8-9.
32. *Ibid.*, 1961a, pp. 11-13.
33. *Ibid.*, 1961b, pp. 2-5; 1962a, pp. 9-10.
34. *Ibid.*, 1961a, p. 12.
35. *Ibid.*, 1962a, p. 8.
36. *Ibid.*, 1963b, p. 14.
37. *Ibid.*, 1961d, p. 3.
38. *Ibid.*, 1963c, pp. 2-5.
39. *Ibid.*, 1963, p. 6.
40. *Ibid.*, pp. 6-7.
41. Bernstein, p. 242.
42. Kennedy, 1961a, pp. 6-7; 1962/1988, pp. 91-92.
43. *Ibid.*, 1964, p. 203.
44. *Ibid.*, 1963, p. 6.
45. Heller, pp. 30-31.
46. Schlesinger, pp. 1002-3.
47. Kennedy, 1962/1988, p. 94.

48. *Ibid.*, 1961d, p. 3.
49. *Ibid.*, 1962/1988, p. 92.
50. *Ibid.*, p. 92.
51. *Ibid.*, p. 90.
52. *Ibid.*, pp. 104-5.
53. *Ibid.*, p. 105.
54. *Ibid.*, pp. 106-7.
55. *Ibid.*, 1961a, p. 4.
56. Commission on Money and Credit, pp. 82, 87; Kennedy, 1962/1988, pp. 108-9.
57. Parmet, pp. 91-99.
58. Rowen, p. 294.
59. Paper, pp. 68-72, 154-366.
60. Giglio, pp. 135, 270.
61. *Ibid.*, p. 97.
62. Rosenman, pp. 425-26.
63. Bernstein, pp. 18, 286.
64. Donald Johnson, p. 582.
65. *Ibid.*, pp. 582-83, 586.
66. *Ibid.*, pp. 591-92, 594.
67. *Ibid.*, p. 598.
68. *Ibid.*, pp. 581, 598.
69. Heller, Gordon, and Tobin, p. 19.
70. Bailey, pp. 56-59; 243-48.
71. *Ibid.*, pp. 17-18; Davidson, p. 4; Lekachman, pp. 88, 177, 188-96, 242-43.

Chapter Three: The International Policy

1. Sorensen, pp. 277-88.
2. Kennedy, 1961c, p. 3.
3. *Ibid.*, 1961, pp. 150-51.
4. *Ibid.*, pp. 170-71.
5. *Ibid.*, pp. 185-86.
6. *Ibid.*, p. 81.
7. *Ibid.*, p. 82.
8. *Ibid.*, pp. x-xi.
9. *Ibid.*, 1961c, pp. 4-5.
10. *Ibid.*, pp. 7-8.
11. *Ibid.*, p. 8.
12. Giglio, pp. 223-24; Heath, p. 106.
13. Sorensen, pp. 275, 599.
14. Kennedy, 1964, p. 153.
15. *Ibid.*, 1963d, p. 2.
16. O'Donnell and Powers, pp. 43-44, 408-29.
17. Guthman and Allen, pp. 104-10.
18. Kennedy, 1960, p. 260.

19. Bowles, p. 383; Kennedy, 1964, p. 162.
20. Hilsman, pp. 159-229.
21. Newman, pp. 115, 138; Sorensen, pp. 668-78.
22. *E.g.*, Paper, pp. 62-63, 66, 295.
23. Sorensen, p. 277.
24. Kennedy, 1964, p. 72.
25. Bowles, p. 453; Giglio, p. 221; Hilsman, pp. 246-47, 362-67; Paper, pp. 52-62, 335; Sorensen, p. 586.
26. Sorensen, pp. 606-7.
27. Schlesinger, pp. 775-76; Sorensen, p. 604.
28. Bowles, pp. 439, 450.
29. Wofford, p. 365.
30. Hilsman, pp. 125-55.
31. Newman, pp. 9-10; O'Donnell and Powers, pp. 281-82.
32. Newman, p. 9.
33. Bowles, pp. 334-41.
34. *Ibid.*, pp. 296-97; Wyden, pp. 67-69.
35. Chernow, p. 542; Mosley, p. 17; Wyden, pp. 10-18.
36. Sorensen, p. 330; Wyden, pp. 67-69.
37. O'Donnell and Powers, p. 316.
38. Wyden, p. 319.
39. *Ibid.*, p. 305.
40. *Ibid.*
41. Sorensen, p. 332.
42. Wyden, p. 309.
43. Sorensen, p. 332.
44. Wofford, p. 363; Wyden, pp. 90-92.
45. Wyden, pp. 139-40.
46. *Ibid.*, p. 169.
47. Sorensen, p. 334; Wyden, pp. 136, 161-68, 198-200, 206, 270.
48. Sorensen, p. 333.
49. Chernow, p. 542.
50. Wyden, pp. 10-11.
51. *Ibid.*, p. 278.
52. Wofford, p. 407; Wyden, pp. 101-2.
53. Hilsman, p. 80; Mosley, pp. 17, 509; Wyden, p. 268.
54. Kennedy, 1964, p. 160.
55. Sorensen, p. 717.
56. Bowles, pp. 419-29.
57. Hilsman, pp. 249-59
58. Bowles, p. 419.
59. *Ibid.*, pp. 421, 424.
60. *Ibid.*, p. 427.
61. Hilsman, pp. 252, 258.

62. Mosley, pp. 497-99.
63. Sorensen, p. 720.
64. Hilsman, pp. 368-71.
65. *Ibid.*, pp. 363-64, 369.
66. Mosley, pp. 470-72.
67. Hilsman, p. 377.
68. *Ibid.*, pp. 379-80.
69. *Ibid.*, p. 380.
70. Kennedy, 1961, p. 86.
71. *Ibid.*, pp. 88-89.
72. *Ibid.*, pp. 91-93.
73. Bowles, pp. 452-53; Hilsman, pp. 423, 536, 578; Newman, p. 129.
74. *E.g.*, Bowles, pp. 452-53; Newman, pp. 138, 158, 236-37, 320-25, 360, 403, 441-42; O'Donnell and Powers, pp. 13, 16, 18; Rust, pp. ix-xii; Sorensen, p. 737.
75. Newman, pp. 137, 380-81, 404.
76. *Ibid., passim*; Prouty, *passim*.
77. Quigley, 1979, pp. 333-48.

Chapter Four: Kennedy's Opponents

1. Sorensen, p. 523.
2. *Ibid.*, p. 564.
3. Cowan, p. A2; Domhoff, 1967, p. 75.
4. Bernstein, p. 131.
5. Sorensen, p. 458.
6. Kennedy, 1964 pp. 226-27.
7. Sidey, p. 215; Sorensen, pp. 354-55; Wendt, p. 371.
8. Swanberg, pp. 85-87.
9. *Ibid.*, p. 45.
10. Lundberg, 1937, pp. 10-11, 36, 103, 262-64; 1975, p. 44.
11. Swanberg, p. 1.
12. *Ibid.*, pp. 105-14, 186, 230.
13. *Ibid.*, pp. 248, 303, 446-48, 483, 583, 592, 670-72.
14. Lee and Shlain, p. 71; Swanberg, p. 648.
15. Lee and Shlain, p. 72; Swanberg, p. 648.
16. *Fortune*, 1963, pp. 81-82.
17. *Ibid.*, 1961, p. 117.
18. *Ibid.*, pp. 117-18.
19. *Ibid.*
20. Davenport, p. 88.
21. *Ibid.*, p. 90.
22. *Ibid.*, pp. 89-90.
23. *Ibid.*, pp. 188, 194.
24. Ways, p. 198.
25. *Ibid.*, pp. 73-74.

26. *Ibid.*, p. 188.
27. *Fortune*, 1963a, pp. 79-80.
28. *Ibid.*, 1962, pp. 79-80.
29. Krock, p. 83.
30. *Ibid.*, pp. 82, 201.
31. Nuñez, p. 70.
32. Swanberg, pp. 581, 653.
33. Murphy, p. 206.
34. *Ibid.*, p. 210.
35. *Ibid.*, p. 212.
36. *Ibid.*, pp. 211-12.
37. *Ibid.*, p. 212.
38. *Ibid.*, p. 126.
39. Moody's Investors Service, 1964.
40. *Life*, 1961, p. 26.
41. *Ibid.*, 1962, p. 4.
42. *Ibid.*, 1962a, p. 4.
43. *Ibid.*, 1963 p. 4; 1963a, p. 4.
44. *Ibid.*, 1963b, p. 4.
45. *Ibid.*, l963c, p. 4.
46. *Ibid.*, 1963d, p. 4.
47. Wendt, pp. 13-99, 179, 213.
48. *Ibid.*, pp. 299, 362.
49. *Ibid.*, pp. 360-64.
50. *Wall Street Journal*, 1961, p. 10; 1961a, p. 10; 1961b, p. 10.
51. *Ibid.*, 1963n, p. 16.
52. *Ibid.*, 1963p, p. 16.
53. *Ibid.*, 1963q, p. 18; 1963r, p. 18.
54. *Ibid.*, 1963s, p. 8; 1963t, p. 16; 1963u, p. 18.
55. *Ibid.*, 1962d, p. 6; 1963b, p. 18; 1963j, p. 8.
56. *Ibid.*, 1962g, p. 16.
57. *Ibid.*, 1962e, p. 12.
58. *Ibid.*, 1962b, p. 14; 1963a, p. 16; 1963d, p. 10; 1963e, p. 12; 1963h, p. 6; 1963l, p. 12; 1963m, p. 16.
59. *Ibid.*, 1963c, p. 12.
60. *Ibid.*, 1962, p. 10; 1962a, p. 10; 1962c, p. 8; 1962f, p. 18; 1962h, p. 14; 1962i, p. 18; 1962j, p. 14; 1963, p. 16; 1963c, p. 12; 1963f, p. 3; 1963g, p. 6.
61. *Ibid.*, 1963i, p. 14.
62. Mathewson, pp. 1, 10.
63. Geyelin, p. 16.
64. Rowen, p. 179.
65. Epstein.
66. Davis, p. 134; Quigley, 1966, p. 956.
67. Hazlitt, 1962, p. 92; 1963, p. 70; 1963a, p. 78; 1963b, p. 84; 1963c, p. 90; 1963d,

p. 97.
68. Lundberg, 1937, pp. 257-59, 308.
69. Moody's Investors Service, 1964.
70. Chernow, pp. 312-13, 480-85; Isaacson and Thomas, pp. 120-22; Kotz; Marquis *Who's Who*, 1962-63; Moody's Investors Service, 1963.
71. Chernow, pp. 417, 534; Lundberg, 1937, p. 37; Marquis *Who's Who*, 1962-63.
72. Bird, 1992.
73. Lundberg, 1937, p. 289.
74. Collier and Horowitz, 1976, p. 91.
75. Chernow, pp. 420-21; Marquis *Who's Who*, 1962-63.
76. Kotz, p. 163.
77. Marquis *Who's Who*, 1962-63.
78. Davis, p. 173.
79. *Ibid.*, pp. 132-34.
80. Domhoff, 1971, pp. 112-23; Quigley, 1966, pp. 950-56.
81. Blair, 1976; Kotz; Lundberg, 1975; Medvin; Welles.
82. Chernow, p. 211.
83. Collier and Horowitz, 1976, p. 412; Quigley, 1966, p. 952.
84. *Life*, 1962b, pp. 30-34.
85. Commission on Money and Credit, pp. viii-x, 64-67, 126-30, 255-58.
86. *Ibid.*, pp. 227-28, 236-41.
87. Collier and Horowitz, 1976, pp. 413-14.
88. Rockefeller, David, Sr., p. 408.
89. *Ibid.*, p. 416.
90. Chernow; Collier and Horowitz, 1976; Greider; Hoffman.
91. Collier and Horowitz, 1976, p. 412.
92. Sorensen, p. 726.
93. O'Donnell and Powers, p. 316; Sorensen, pp. 330-31.
94. Kennedy, 1961, pp. 96-100.
95. Burns, pp. 186-87.
96. Kennedy, 1961, pp. 252, 260-61.
97. Kennedy, 1955, p. 216.

Chapter Five: Short-Term Changes

1. Bernstein, pp. 254-58, 297.
2. Collier and Horowitz, 1976, p. 414; Lowenthal; Szulc, 1965b.
3. *New York Times*, 1965c; Szulc, 1965b.
4. *New York Times*, 1963; 1963a; Raymont, 1963; 1963a; Szulc, 1963; 1963a.
5. Kihss; Lowenthal; *New York Times*, 1965c; 1965d; Szulc, 1965; 1965a; 1965b.
6. Murphy.
7. Bird, pp. 550-53; Payer, pp. 153-54.
8. Bird, pp. 550-53.
9. Collier and Horowitz, 1976, p. 414.
10. Payer, pp. 155-65.

11. Leacock, 1979, pp. 653-55; 1981, pp. 77, 82, 87-88.
12. Hilsman, pp. 399-409.
13. *New York Times*, 1965; 1965a; 1965b; Payer, pp. 78-79.
14. Payer, pp. 78-86.
15. *Life*, 1963d, p. 4.
16. Newman.
17. Goodwin, pp. 195-96; 253-66; Isaacson and Thomas, pp. 644-46.
18. Shoup and Minter, pp. 225-31.
19. Quigley, 1966, pp. 132, 952; 1981, pp. 182-94; Shoup and Minter, pp. 226-36.
20. Shoup and Minter, pp. 237-47.
21. Newman, pp. 225-29, 442-49.
22. *Ibid.*, pp. 387, 458.
23. O'Donnell and Powers, pp. 16-18.
24. Rockefeller, David, Sr., pp. 408, 416.
25. Kendrick, p. 51; Sorensen, pp. 444-45; Vatter.
26. Kendrick, pp. 51, 68, 94, 100.
27. Advisory Commission on Intergovernmental Relations; Council of Economic Advisors, p. 248.
28. Blumberg, pp. 254-55; Heath, pp. 117-22; Kendrick, p. 51; Sorensen, p. 522.
29. Greider, p. 329.
30. Harrison and Bluestone, pp. 23-24.
31. Kendrick, pp. 36, 51.
32. *Ibid.*, p. 2.
33. Malthus.
34. *Ibid.*, 1960, pp. 151-65, 335-38, 356, 454, 470-76.
35. *Ibid.*, pp. 51-52.
36. *Ibid.*, pp. 34-35, 368, 530-31, 549, 580-81.
37. *Ibid.*, pp. 29-33, 149, 366-67, 507.
38. *Ibid.*, p. 537.
39. *Ibid.*, p. 370.
40. *Ibid.*, p. 591.
41. *Ibid.*
42. *Ibid.*, pp. 14, 128-31, 136-38, 538-43.
43. Outdoor Recreation Resources Review Commission, pp. iii, 1, 6, 8, 13-14, 23-24, 86, 113, 183.
44. *Ibid.*, pp. 8, 113, 121, 152.
45. Collier and Horowitz, 1976, pp. 381-83.
46. Kennedy, 1961b.
47. Kennedy, 1962a.
48. Fox, pp. 289-90; Tucker.
49. Collier and Horowitz, 1976, pp. 302-7.
50. Bachrach and Bergman, pp. 43-48; Demerath, pp. 38-44.
51. Hyman, p. 98.
52. *Ibid.*, p. 26.

53. *Ibid.*, pp. 125, 128, 151-62, 172.
54. *Ibid.*, pp. 231-41, 272.
55. *Ibid.*, pp. 237-69.
56. *Ibid.*, p. 161.
57. *Ibid.*, pp. 249-50.
58. Bachrach and Bergman, p. 50; Demerath, p. 43.
59. Kennedy, 1961, pp. 265-67.
60. Zlotnick, p. 686.
61. Johnson, Lyndon, 1967 (1964), pp. 15-19.
62. *Ibid.*, 1965a, p. 13.
63. *Ibid.*, 1965.
64. *Ibid.*, 1966.
65. Bachrach and Bergman, p. 50.
66. Demerath, pp. 26-38; Bachrach and Bergman, p. 51.
67. Caulfield.

Chapter Six: Long-Term Changes

1. Kennedy, 1961.
2. McDonald, p. 3.
3. *Ibid.*, pp. 4, 18-20, 55, 103, 109, 117, 157, 212-13.
4. *Ibid.*, pp. 98, 111, 123, 234-35.
5. *Ibid.*, pp. 227, 331.
6. Hamilton, 1850, pp. 108, 129-31, 134; McDonald, pp. 193-95, 216.
7. McDonald, pp. 201-9, 217, 237.
8. Hamilton, 1850, pp. 120, 128-29.
9. Hamilton, 1850a, p. 250.
10. *Ibid.*, pp. 235-57.
11. *Ibid.*, pp. 231-32, 243, 281.
12. Medvin, p. 106.
13. Welles, pp. 412-15.
14. Greider, pp. 340-41.
15. Yergin, p. 619.
16. Kennedy, 1961a; 1961b; 1962a.
17. Sherrill, pp. 4, 103.
18. Sampson, p. 29.
19. Sherrill, p. 529.
20. *Ibid.*, p. 530.
21. Blair, 1976, pp. 31-33.
22. *Ibid.*, pp. 55, 156-57; Sampson, pp. 86-89; Sherrill, pp. 531-32.
23. Blair, 1976, pp. 81-87, 113-16; Sherrill, pp. 98-100.
24. Sherrill, pp. 145, 150.
25. Crittenden, 1979a.
26. Sherrill, pp. 167, 175, 198-99.
27. Blair, 1976, p. 275.

28. Sherrill, pp. 226-27.
29. Blair, 1976, p. 75.
30. Council of Economic Advisors, 1973-1993.
31. Sherrill, pp. 229-30.
32. Blair, 1976, p. 310.
33. Sherrill, p. 273.
34. *Ibid.*, pp. 353-55.
35. *Ibid.*, pp. 344, 352.
36. *Evening Bulletin*, 1977.
37. U.S. Bureau of the Census, 1985-1991.
38. Sherrill, p. 413.
39. Blair, 1976, pp. 78-80; Burton Hersh, pp. 332-35.
40. Sherrill, p. 410.
41. *Ibid.*, pp. 422-40.
42. *Washington Post*, 1979.
43. Council of Economic Advisors, 1973-1993.
44. Sherrill, p. 501.
45. Metz; Strauss.
46. *Fortune*, 1981-1993.
47. U.S. Bureau of the Census, 1985-1991.
48. Blair, 1976, pp. 39, 127, 149.
49. Sherrill, p. 243.
50. Blair, 1976, pp. 131-56.
51. *Ibid.*, p. 145; Medvin, p. 106; Sherrill, pp. 416-18.
52. Sherrill, p. 492.
53. Moore, p. 6.
54. Feis, pp. ix, 3-4, 88.
55. Balogh, p. 29 or Magdoff, pp. 146-47.
56. Farnsworth, 1979.
57. Inter-American Development Bank, 1980.
58. Miller; Sherrill, pp. 374-75.
59. Payer.
60. Crittenden, 1979b; Thomas.
61. *Newsweek*, 1980, pp. 78-79.
62. Bartlett; Crittenden, 1979; Farnsworth, 1979; Westlake.
63. Bennett, 1982; Farnsworth, 1983; Westlake.
64. Bennett, 1980; Crittenden, 1979a; *New York Times*, 1984.
65. Farnsworth, 1984; Wolman.
66. Brooke, 1989; *New York Times*, 1980.
67. Brooke, 1989.
68. *New York Times*, 1984a.
69. Cowell.
70. Pine.
71. Schumacher, Edward, 1984.

72. Brooke, 1985.
73. Farnsworth, 1986.
74. Riding.
75. Farnsworth, 1989.
76. U.S. Congress, 1979.
77. Council of Economic Advisors, 1973-1993.
78. Wright.
79. Bluestone and Harrison; Blumberg.
80. *Business Week*, 1985.
81. *Business Week*, 1986.
82. *Business Week*, 1985; Holusha.
83. *New York Times*, 1981.
84. *Fortune*, 1981-1991; U.S. Bureau of the Census, 1985-1991.
85. Gibson, 1990; Taft Foundation Reporter.
86. Barney, pp. 12-13, 29-33.
87. *Ibid.*, pp. 15-16, 66, 70-71.
88. *Ibid.*, pp. 20-22, 135-38.
89. *Ibid.*, pp. 18-19, 44-45.
90. Lovins, pp. xx, 220.
91. Fox, p. 322; Hyman; Barkley and Weissman.
92. Lovins, pp. 14, 148.
93. *Ibid.*, pp. 12-14, 57.
94. *Ibid.*, pp. 13, 56.
95. *Ibid.*, p. 12.
96. Tucker.
97. Ehrlich, 1968; 1973.
98. Mesarovic and Pestel, p. 1.
99. Barney, p. 177; Lovins, p. 58.
100. Dickson, pp. 335-38.
101. SRI International, pp. 7, 78.
102. Harman.
103. Lee and Shlain; Marks.
104. SRI, pp. 118-19.
105. Harman, p. 143.
106. White.
107. Schumacher, E.F., 1973.
108. *Ibid.*, pp. 31, 37, 146-47.
109. *Ibid.*, pp. 149, 159.
110. *Ibid.*, p. 181.
111. *Ibid.*, pp. 131, 142-43.
112. *Ibid.*, pp. 151-52.
113. McRobie.
114. Pohlman, p. 169.
115. Hardin.

116. Falk, p. 303.
117. Heilbroner, p. 63.
118. *Ibid.*, pp. 54, 56, 74-75.
119. *Ibid.*, pp. 89-92.
120. *Ibid.*, pp. 106, 130.
121. Ophuls, pp. 109-10.
122. Dobson, pp. 5-9.
123. Barlett and Steel; Harrison and Bluestone; Mayer.
124. Quigley, 1979 (1961), pp. 137-39; 150-54.

Chapter Seven: The Establishment, Clinton, and the Future

1. Bailey; Kotz.
2. Kotz, p. 146.
3. *Ibid.*, pp. 134-48.
4. U.S. Senate Committee on Governmental Affairs, pp. 1, 6, 9.
5. *Ibid.*, pp. 12-13.
6. Domhoff, 1983.
7. U.S. Senate Committee on Governmental Affairs, p. 13.
8. Welles, pp. 412-15.
9. U.S. Senate Committee on Governmental Affairs, pp. 13-14.
10. Useem, p. 148.
11. Quigley, 1979 (1961), pp. 76, 132, 137, 149.
12. *Ibid.*, pp. 336-39.
13. *Ibid.*, pp. 116-17, 138, 144-45, 368.
14. *Ibid.*, pp. 150, 152, 405.
15. *Ibid.*, pp. 404-14.
16. Council of Economic Advisors, 1973-1993.
17. Phillips, pp. 102-128.
18. *Consumer Reports*; Council of Economic Advisors, 1973-1993, Gibson, 1993; U.S. Bureau of the Census.
19. Council of Economic Advisors, 1973-1993; Gibson, 1993.
20. Harrison and Bluestone, pp. 117-38; Phillips, pp. 95-105.
21. Pear; U.S. Bureau of the Census.
22. Peterson, pp. 43-69.
23. *Ibid.*, p. 52.
24. Clinton, 1992b.
25. Clinton, 1992; Levin, pp. 48-49.
26. Clinton, 1992a, pp. 250-59.
27. *Ibid.*
28. *E.g.*, Levin, pp. 300-13.
29. Clinton, 1992.
30. Clinton and Gore, pp. 34, 93-94.
31. Clinton, 1992b.
32. Phillips.

33. *Life,* 1962, pp. 30-34.
34. Garten.
35. *New York Times*, 1992.
36. *Fortune*, 1992.
37. Quigley, 1979 (1961), pp. 138-40.
38. *Fortune*, 1992a.
39. *Fortune*, 1993.
40. *Wall Street Journal*, 1992.
41. *Wall Street Journal*, 1993.
42. *Wall Street Journal*, 1993a.
43. Langer.
44. Phillips, pp. xvii-xviii.
45. Greenhouse.
46. *Fortune*, 1981-1991.
47. Kennedy, 1964, p. 244.

Index